God's Commissioned People

God's Commissioned People

M. THOMAS STARKES

BROADMAN PRESS
Nashville, Tennessee

© Copyright 1984 ● Broadman Press
All rights reserved
4263-38
ISBN: 0-8054-6338-0
Dewey Decimal Classification: 266.09
Subject Heading: MISSIONS-HISTORY
Library of Congress Catalog Card Number:84-4968
Printed in the United States of America

Library of Congress Cataloging in Publication Data

Starkes, M. Thomas.
  God's commissioned people.

  Bibliography: p.
  Includes index.
  1. Missions—History. I. Title.
BV2100.S83 1984   266'.009   84-4968
ISBN 0-8054-6338-0 (pbk.)

**To Elizabeth Lawler
for faithful love
and caring witness**

Acknowledgments

Paul Gericke is director of Library Services at the New Orleans Baptist Theological Seminary. He has been most helpful in the provision of resources and the room for writing. Dr. Gericke's untiring patience and encouragement have proven helpful in this project.

Landrum P. Leavell serves as president of the New Orleans Baptist Theological Seminary. He is already known as a warmhearted evangelist and excellent administrator. I have also found him to be a source of constant inspiration in academic research. Dr. Leavell has worked tirelessly in the establishment of the Chester L. Quarles Chair of Missions at this seminary. This has allowed me the luxury of a full-time secretary and the additional time necessary to pursue such a time-consuming writing project. He continues to be a source of personal inspiration.

Jennifer Smith and Donna Charlton have worked long and tedious hours rendering typing and editorial assistance. This work would have proven impossible without them.

It is to Elizabeth Lawler that this book is dedicated. She is a dedicated lay teacher and witness from Fayetteville, Georgia. For more than a score of years she has been more loving and giving to me than I have deserved. She ranks as one of the world's greatest mothers-in-law.

All of these people and more have been of great personal motivational help in the writing of this volume. I am also immensely grateful to other writers whose classic efforts have been helpful in providing basic guidelines for this new history of missions. I have profited from each work and hope to have combined the best qualities of each in a creative and readable updating of missions history.

I am grateful also and ultimately to the God of missions for all gifts flowing through him, especially that of salvation.

M. THOMAS STARKES
Chester L. Quarles Professor of
Christian Missions and World Religions
New Orleans Baptist Theological Seminary

Contents

Introduction

Why a New Work Is Needed Now

Oh, no! Here comes another work on the history of missions. But, why now? What makes the mid-1980s the time for a reconsideration of missions history? The answer lies in the obvious truth that this is the beginning of a new age. The last sixth of the twentieth century promises to be a period of turmoil and triumph in at least four major areas.

First, the Falklands (or Malvinas) Islands dispute signaled clearly that the era of colonialism is dead. The year 1983 marked the centennial celebration of the Berlin Congress in which the dominant European powers divided up the continent of Africa, without much reference given to the natural and ethnic boundaries already existent there. Such terms as the Belgian Congo and French West Africa are now anachronisms from the past. A century ago such bases in Europe as Great Britain served as launching pads for Christian missions into "uncivilized" portions of the world. Today, Great Britain's days of glory are past. Argentina can stand defiantly against what laughingly passes itself off as the British fleet. Even the United States is losing some ground as the center and sender of Christian missionaries.

Second, there is the emergence of the Third-World church with the accompanying awareness of that fact in the

13

Western world. Such bright spots as Korea and Indonesia have pumped new life and hope into missions. "House church" movements and emphasis on the Holy Spirit and spontaneous worship forms now affect the established churches even "back on the home front" of missions.

The continent of Africa can be seen as a type of the challenge facing the churches of the entire world in 1984. Future church growth in Africa will be largely dependent on the degree of interchange between North America and African Christians. This healthy interchange can come only when American Christians stop viewing the 350 million persons in Africa as being on the "Dark Continent." Today Africa is a continent of more than a thousand large ethnic groups, each reflecting its own distinctives. Semites, Ashanti, Fons, Wolofs, Zulus, Yorubas, Ibo, and Fulanis all combine with thousands of others to make Africa a place of rainbow-rich diversity.

It is also important to note that the population of Africa is expected to grow from 280 million in 1960 to 350 million in 1984 and to almost 800 million by the year 2000. Today the birth rate in Africa is higher than in most regions of the world. However, the death rate is also higher than elsewhere, with an average of 23 per 1,000 annually compared with 16 per 1,000 in the rest of the world. The result is that about half of the growing population of Africa in 1984 is less than sixteen years old. Africa is also a continent filled with poor people. Seventeen nations in Africa, with 55 percent of the continent's population, have only an $80.00 per capita annual income. So, it is evident that Africa is not as most North Americans perceive it. This is especially true when church growth is considered. In 1984, church growth in Africa is three times faster than in North America. It is not beyond reason that a Roman Catholic pope from Africa will preside over his worldwide flock by the time the twenty-first century arrives. Missionaries from Christian churches in Africa will be commonplace in North America by that time, sent on mission to stagnating churches and nonbelievers in "Christian" America. The healthy emergence of the Third-World churches in the 1980s signals the dead end of the one-way thoroughfare on which missionaries traveled previously. The two-way street is open and traffic is beginning to move, a trickle in comparison to the flow by the twenty-first century.

Third, the churches of 1984 are being propelled toward the unfinished task of reaching previously hidden peoples. Whole tribes and other cultural groupings have gone unnoticed by traditional-minded missionaries heretofore. In 1984, mission strategists speak often of the "unreached peoples" and "hidden peoples" of the world. This awareness is opening up two major realizations: there is much that has not been done in previous mission efforts (that is, whole peoples have gone untouched and there is much to be done). Second, 1984 stands as a turning point. These "hidden peoples" are now being identified with suggestions of how they may be reached. Two examples will suffice.

There are about 27 thousand bachelors in Lagos, Nigeria, with the majority being under twenty-five years of age. They may feel vulnerable emotionally in a culture which has traditionally honored polygamy and fertility. Further, there are in 1984 some 150 thousand homosexuals in San Francisco. Many of the gay people feel lonely and rejected. Thus the suicide rate is high. Some Evangelicals engaged in the arts have found success in witnessing to the gays on a one-to-one basis. Yet, a coherent and overall effective strategy for seeing the conversion and assimilation of homosexual persons into churches has not been developed. They are part of the "hidden peoples" now being seen for the first time, forcing a reevaluation of mission strategy in 1984.

Fourth, 1984 marks the time when there is a widespread awareness that the battle is on for the allegiance of persons in the world. Religious pluralism is such a fact that one can no longer afford to speak of "Christian" America or "Moslem" Turkey. Each of the major world religions is to be found almost everywhere in the world trying to prove its respective claim to be universal. For example, 1984 is the year in which the number of Moslems in the United States exceeded five million for the first time, approaching 2 percent of the total population. Perhaps one in eight American adults is now involved in one of the new cults, from The Way, International, to Nichiren Shoshu. It is now clear that Christian mission strategists cannot rely on methods and literature of the past. Almost every literate person in today's world is exposed to a choice in faith among Islam, Christianity, Communism, Buddhism, and/or Hinduism. In such a context and contest, Christian missions cannot merely repeat the errors and frustrations of the past. Therefore, a critically written book is in order as never before.

These four reasons, among others, make the writing of Christian missions history a must in 1984.

A Time Line

God's people have been on the move with his word since the Nazarene Carpenter sent them forth with the Great Commission. These faithful ministers have, singly and collectively, been a part of the most consistent and productive social movement in world history.

Jesus said, "Before Abraham was, I am." He was reflecting his eternal being and stressing the time-honored truth that God has been in the missions business since the first moment of creation. This unfolding reality has had some high moments in terms of dates, places, ideas, and movements. *God's Commissioned People* is an attempt to highlight those moments and to provide connecting links and motifs as the history of missions unfolds. (The time line found at the end of each chapter will help the reader to put some of these moments into temporal focus.)

Chapter 1 is a brief but basic summary of the biblical basis of missions. The starting point for missions is in the dim untimed past in the early mists of God's creation. Creation itself is presented as the first of God's saving acts. About 1900 BC, the scene shifted to the individual Abraham as a sign that God calls individuals to do his ministry in the mission task. Abraham was chosen to be the first of the people called "Jews." Their collective missionary faith laid the groundwork for subsequent Christian missions. The active missionary faith of the Jews produced the eighth-century prophet Amos and those who prophesied later in his footsteps. These strong men paved the way for John the Baptist and his cousin by preaching with conviction and compassion.

About 5 BC Jesus was born to make this the "Visited Planet" and to initiate the Christian mission era by his life, death, and teachings. Near his death (about AD 28) he spoke the Great Commission, the marching orders for God's commissioned people. That commission was followed first by those called apostles, outstandingly Peter, Paul, and John. The end of the apostolic era came in AD 125. The original apostles were dead, but the cause continued. There were sufficient unifying trends to give the missions movement impetus into the next era.

Chapter 2 deals with the mission era from AD 125-500. Rome replaced Jerusalem as the center of mission activity. The first envoys for Christ went out in anonymity as far as subsequent historians are concerned. Yet, these "Nameless Ones" bridged the gap between the apostolic era and the coming into prominence of Christianity in the later Roman Empire. The first named missionary in the post-apostolic era was Pantaenus of Alexandria. He was followed by such early pioneers as Ulfilas and Martin of Tours. In the early fourth century, the emperor Constantine and the council he called at Nicea gave the missionary movement a level of unity and tolerance never before enjoyed. A negative by-product of Constantine's rule was to be harmful to the spread of Christianity. Many were only nominal believers. This nominalism gave rise to the monastic movement which had a lasting impact on Christian missions in the ages to follow. By AD 500 the Roman Empire was dying. The glory that was Rome had provided Christian envoys a strong unified base. The march of the commissioned people had begun in earnest.

Chapter 3 is designed to highlight the events in the difficult seven centuries following AD 500. One major barrier to Christian missions during this period was the founding and early growth of Islam. There were, however, some encouraging signs. The baptism of Clovis did for the Franks what the baptism of Constantine had done for the Romans in an earlier era. Columba took the gospel to Scotland and surrounding territory. He and Augustine helped to eradicate the ancient and stubborn Old Religion in northern Europe, as converts to Christ were made. Monasticism came to full strength with the work of Benedict of Nursia. This impact on missions was refined and reformed even further by Charlemagne. This led to Christian growth in such remote regions as Scandinavia.

Meanwhile, the Eastern church was being reformed and experiencing positive growth under Justinian and Theodora. This renewed strength of the Eastern churches was to lead eventually to the East/West schism, a lasting negative influence on Christian missions. Thus, the seven hundred years between AD 500-1200 were years of darkness caused by Islam and disunity. There were tiny rays of light for the discerning eye, however, including Columba, Boniface, and the Benedictines.

Chapter 3 is also designed to illuminate mission effort through the twelfth century. The era began with Viking intrusion into the British Isles. But such brave and heroic men as Anskar began to evangelize the Vikings with great numerical success. Converted Vikings such as Olaf Tryggveson began to Christianize his peers.

A mixed blessing to missions were the Crusades. While these efforts to regain Muslim-held lands were tragic in the loss of human life, they did result in the founding of military orders and gave rise to the dreams of European Christians for territorial expansion of their faith.

The church in Eastern Europe was given dynamic leadership in the eleventh century by such men as Vladimir, Knut, and Adalbert. They built on the tenth-century work done by Boleslav of Poland.

By the end of the Dark Ages, the churches, particularly in the East, were at least partially controlled by the kings. Christianity was, therefore, defined by politics and some of the missionary movement's impetus blunted. Nonetheless, good days lay ahead, with the monastics about ready to go about missions in earnest and such creative individuals as Ramón Lull ready to live sacrificially in new territory.

Chapter 4 presents the period just prior to the Protestant Reformation. During the three centuries following AD 1200, a bright spot was the founding of such powerful new monastic orders as the Franciscans, Dominicans, and Carmelites. Another force for subsequent mission effort was the emergence of the "heretics" and their accompanying movements during the thirteenth century. The influence of such men as Peter Waldo and others caused the popes to initiate the Inquisition. Marco Polo's visit to and sojourn in China opened the way for such mission pioneers as John of Monte Corvino to go there. Meanwhile, Ramón Lull was initiating productive mission work among the Muslims. Vincent Ferrer was launching similar pioneer work among the Jews.

The fourteenth century was the scene for the obvious breakdown of the "Medieval synthesis" (that is, a conglomeration of cultural and religious beliefs and practices which gave coherence to the life-style of most Europeans). The Avignon papacy and the Great Schism gave force to the breakdown of that synthesis. Other disintegrating forces included the spread of mysticism and the Renaissance.

The churches in the East, meanwhile, were flourishing, especially in Russia as the seedbed of what was to be known as Russian Orthodoxy. This led to the final rift between

Eastern and Western Christianity in the middle of the fifteenth century. This rift, however, did not deter the valiant mission efforts of such Roman Catholic individuals as Bartholome de las Casas and the hundreds of unnamed priests who accompanied the conquistadores to the New World. The stage was set for the Protestant Reformation.

Chapter 5 deals with the Reformation and its lingering impact on missions until the time of William Carey. This movement within the European churches was aptly called "the turning upside down of the whole world" and had its lasting impact on missions. In this chapter, the reader will meet such giant reformers as Erasmus of Rotterdam, Martin Luther, John Calvin, and John Knox. Each is analyzed as to his impact on subsequent mission effort. Anabaptists and Apocalyptists are also analyzed and given their proper place among God's commissioned people.

The Jesuits are spotlighted, with emphasis on the mission work of Ignatius Loyola, Matteo Ricci, Roberto de Nobili, and others of that order. The total mission effort of the Roman Catholics during the post-Reformation period is analyzed with attention given to the Sacred Congregation for the Propagation of the Faith.

Early Protestant mission work is highlighted with a look at the work of John Eliot and David Brainerd. Pietism and its lasting impact on evangelical mission effort is examined through a look at such individuals as Jacob Spener and August Francke. The pietistic spillover into early Methodism is accented through a brief biography of John Wesley. The chapter concludes with an analysis of the contributions of the Reformation to Christian missions.

Chapter 6 is a summary of the era between the missionary career of William Carey and beginning of World War I. In this section, the beginning of the modern missionary movement is scanned. One of the significant developments of the modern era is that of missionary societies. These sending agencies gave rise to effective missionary planning and gathering of funds.

After a brief look at the beginning of Home Mission Board and Woman's Missionary Union of the Southern Baptist Convention is provided, giants among nineteenth-century missionary pioneers are reviewed. These include David Livingstone, Hudson Taylor, and Lottie Moon.

Roman Catholic missions in the century past are reviewed next and placed into the context of longer developments within the Church.

The chapter concludes with a broad geographical sweep across the political world of nineteenth-century Christian missions. These were exciting times for such brave pioneers as Adoniram Judson and John Mason Peck. The British Isles were the scene for the development of such strong parachurch movements as the Young Men's Christian Association (YMCA). Chapter 6 thus brings the reader almost breathlessly to the challenging times inclusive of the great wars.

Chapter 7 begins with a summary of the social situation in the Western world at the time of World War I. Against this backdrop, a geographical summary follows with specific data given on missions in Asia, Africa, Latin America, Europe, and the United States of America. The emerging ecumenical vision of the twentieth century is summarized by capsuling the efforts of John R. Mott and Charles Brent. The great ecumenical councils of the first half of the twentieth century are surveyed. The chapter concludes with a brief evaluative essay of the state of world Christianity at the end of World War II.

Chapter 8 brings the reader to the present and beyond. The period covered is that era from the end of World War II to the present (1946-1984). Interfaith collisions, such as that going on between Christians and Muslims, are summarized with special attention given to the nature of those religions opposing the growth of Christianity.

Evangelical efforts in the present tense are surveyed by a brief look at such major bodies as the Wycliffe Bible Translators and the Salvation Army.

Significant sectarian missionary effort is then analyzed with some attention given to why that effort is so large and successful today. This is done with the suggestion that there are strong points within sectarian mission endeavor worthy of evaluation by Evangelicals and others.

Billy Graham and Oral Roberts are spotlighted in connection with the National Association of Evangelicals. The World Council of Churches is then compared with the World Evangelical Fellowship. That comparison is followed by a chart indicating Christianity's numerical strength in comparison to other major religion systems.

Chapter 8 continues with a geographical overview of current Christian mission effort. Africa, Latin America, and Asia are given particular attention. This section is followed by a look at current social issues in relation to missions. The book concludes with chapter 9, an essay on the immediate future of missions as God's commissioned people continue their work.

God's people on the march for his cause have always lived exciting adventures. That makes good reading. Let the reader beware. One may become involved on more than a cognitive level.

Brief Rationale for Missions

The mid-1980s are witnessing a raging debate that threatens the future of Christian missions. One can hear often the phrase, "moratorium on missions," which implies that the mission task has ended. Critics of the mission task of past and present threaten the Christian efforts of the future by pointing to the manifold mistakes of past missionaries. They scream that to continue taking the world for Christ speaks of colonialism, triumphalism, and parochialism. These critics are appalled at the bungled administration of relief projects, the problems posed by vested denominational and economic interests. They point to the inexcusable self-indulgence of Christians, especially in affluent North America. They point accusing fingers at what they see as intolerant evangelists who dare to make judgments about penultimate revelation in the non-Christian world religions. In short, they doubt openly the priority and place of the future mission task.

In the face of this challenge, no current history of missions would be complete without a brief pause for a validation of the Christian mission cause—past, present, and future. That validation is built on six major theological and contemporary points.

First, missions is deeply embedded in the heart of God and his plan for the universe. It clearly makes a difference to the God of Christians what happens to his dear children in the world. There is no point in time or aspect of creation in which he is not interested. God is the God of the UN and NATO as well as the YMCA. That is the clear biblical witness.

Second, God in every place and time clearly chooses specific persons and peoples to do his will among others. He brought a poor people out of Egypt to keep his covenant and show his love to all nations. Therefore, it is far from embarrassing to be chosen of God to be a light to the nations. It is an honor of blessing to the called and the people to be affected.

Third, there is the Christ event, continuing testimony of the universality, historicity, and specificity of the Christian message. The life, teaching, death, and resurrection of Jesus of Nazareth were and are witnesses to God's love for all. They are also signs that God's love always leads beyond himself. Christ was involved constantly in the lives of others. He expected no less from his early disciples and no less from those who follow him today. His life was and is one of service.

Fourth, there is the universal dimension of the gospel found in Christ. Alec Vidler, in *Christian Belief,* has made this point clear, "Either it is true for all men, whether they know it or not, or it is true for no one, not even for those people who are under the illusion it is true."[1]

Fifth, there is the inherent ability to penetrate any culture with its accompanying judgment upon that culture coupled with the Christ-centered message of grace and forgiveness. Thus, the missionary is not in the business of defending or spreading Western democracy or the merits of technology. On the contrary, the missionary simply brings persons to Christ and leaves them there. It is up to the new converts to determine how their new faith relates to their culture. This penetrating and creative power of the gospel is one of the pillars of missions.

Finally, there is the biblical witness to the power of God in Christ. Chapter 1 in this work is given to that reality. The objective presence of Holy Scripture there for the touching and feeling is tangible evidence that God has a purpose for humanity through missions. Although the Bible is far more than paper and leather or paper cover, its very physical existence is proof that God still cares. Unofficial and even underground missionaries smuggle Bibles daily behind the iron and bamboo curtains, convinced that the biblical witness can do its work once made available to unbelievers. That God is and cares and wants to communicate to every person is evidenced by his Holy Word.

These are at least six elements of the living reality called missions. God is in the missions business. That much is clear.

Explanation of the Basic Approach

There are nine chapters in this work, each given to a combination of the study of individuals and movements. Some of the classic histories of missions written previously have emphasized one or the other of these elements. Great quantities of ink have been consumed in the process of making social analyses with little attention given to the contributions of individuals in some works. Others have painted missions history as a long line of heroes unaffected by social movements. This work seeks a balance.

Further, there is to be found here a running commentary

on the interaction between mission agencies. This is especially true of the modern era (chs. 6, 7, and 8). Often agencies and individuals are presented as operating in isolation from others. It is rarely stressed, for example, that William Carey called for an international ecumenical consultation on missions to be held in 1810. That dream came to pass a century later. Today missionaries, no matter the agency under which they operate, discover on the mission field a camaraderie for those with similar calling. Interaction and its effects are analyzed here.

Finally, as to basic approach, the work concludes with a pointing to the future. The history of missions will not end with the publication of this work. A decade later, this work will have some value because it is issue oriented. Attention is given to the continuing saga of God's champions and cowards on the field called planet Earth.

Special Features

This history of missions is made unique because of several special features, not the least of which is the case study at the end of each chapter. Some of these case studies highlight and analyze failures at the mission task. An example of this is the feature on the Middle Ages, Bishop Bernard at the end of chapter 4. Some of the features case studies involve figures well known to Southern Baptists, such as Bill Wallace of China. Some are concerned with little-known but important figures in missionary history. Some of these case studies feature emerging Third World leaders, such as Osad Imasogie of Nigeria. Each is followed by a series of questions for use by individuals and/or groups.

This book is designed to highlight some lesser-known but important persons in mission history. One example is Ulfilas. This is because understanding missions is aided by seeing links. The modern evangelical missionary owes as much to Roberto de Nobili as to any of his peers. We are a product of our past.

Evangelicals who read this work may come away with a new or renewed appreciation for Roman Catholics, past and present, who spread their concept of grace. There were, after all, only a few significant missionaries prior to the Reformation who were not Roman Catholics. Today, the sheer number of Catholic missionaries, including one as well known as Mother Teresa of Calcutta, make it imperative that Evangelicals cope with Catholic presence among them. This book seeks to increase awareness and appreciation of that Catholic presence.

Great attention is given to a definition and examination of the sectarian religions and their missionary activity. As this work is published in 1984, the Church of Jesus Christ of Latter-Day Saints now has a missionary force approaching forty thousand. Why is this so? Why must they make eleven hundred visits before making a convert? Jehovah's Witnesses and others are also scrutinized here.

This work has sufficient special features to make interesting, alarming, and motivating reading.

What Is Missions?

The subject matter of a history of missions should be clear. Today a debate rages over the definition of missions, however, which makes this somewhat difficult. Missions is today defined by most American Evangelicals in terms of the ministry and witness of a church beyond its own field and/or to persons who will never likely become members of that church without some effort toward them.

European scholars of the past century have almost unanimously insisted that Christians should use the singular *mission* in order to emphasize that there is only one mission of the whole church. This term, it is argued, would avoid fragmentation into various tasks and outposts of the church's universal mission.

However, *missions* as used among most American Evangelicals implies no plurality. Rather, the plural term *missions* has come to mean the functions and activities of the church as a whole. There is, therefore, a preference for the use of the plural term. Therefore, *missions* will be used in this work to mean *the whole work of the whole church with specific attention given to ministry and witness among the otherwise unreachable.*

Mission History: Important to All Christians

There are several timeless and vital reasons why a study of the history of missions is important today to Christians at every level of service and understanding. One of the most outstanding is that missions is more and more an interaction between senders and receivers. Too often mission history has been written from the perspective of the sender who sees the receivers as mere targets or prospects. Today sensitive mission leaders are becoming more convinced that a study of the home base is equally as important. Either consciously or subconsciously, the gospel is redefined by the senders. This impacts the receivers with a peculiar brand of Christianity which may not relate well to the targeted culture. For example, modern Nigerians mix European hymn tunes with tonal languages to produce obscene sayings in their worship services, often at the insistence of naive American-based missionaries. A study of mission history can help to correct this problem area.

Second, mission history should be studied because it reflects the triumph of the gospel. In mission effort, the conversion of unbelievers is paramount. The gospel is preached and Scriptures are distributed. This positive emphasis is sometimes in other forms of church history, which often stress church feuds, the suppression of heresy, and religious wars. Mission history stresses the positive. Properly written, it is a critical coverage of the victories of the church and supplies inspiration for those still struggling to make missions history.

Third, a study of mission history will hopefully help to prevent the repetition of past mistakes. Clichés abound when people speak of history. Not the least is, "Those who refuse to learn from the past are destined to repeat its mistakes." The sensitive reader of mission history will note trends in the success and failure of mission efforts of the past. For example, almost everyone who has legislated faith from the top has been doomed to failure in winning the hearts of the people. This has been true from Theodosius and Constantine to Jim Jones in Guyana. Future missionaries can profit from such mistakes of the past.

Finally, mission history deserves to be studied because it is in the discernment of patterns that modern pilgrims can see God at work in the postbiblical era. This source of inspiration can serve as a stimulus to renewal in the late twentieth century. God has not been asleep since the times of Jesus and Paul, and this truth helps the modern missionary. The God of Abraham is the same as the God of William Carey and Mother Teresa. Thus, mission history provides inspiration for the one about to give up.

Christianity: A World Faith

When the Anglican bishop in Iran was expelled from that land in 1953, he made a confession. It was, in part,

> What the church has to do, and has largely failed to do, is to convince the world that Christianity is a universal religion with a message for all mankind at every level. It has to clear people's minds of the idea that it is inherently connected with inherent western civilization.[2]

This parochialism may be partly true, but any limitations or cultural captivity of the gospel is not inherent within the gospel itself. The gospel is, by definition, applicable to every person within any cultural context. The missionary message begins with creation itself. In Genesis, it is apparent that God's action in beginning this planet is the ultimate backdrop to the whole of human life.

This universal theme was evident again at Pentecost, when persons from throughout the known world came and heard the new gospel preached. From that day forward, it was clear that every Christian is to be a witness. The new church, as the body of Christ, was set ablaze with the conviction that its message was for all who would heed. Church membership has, from the beginning, been an invitation to join the missionary effort. The committed Christian, in the first or twentieth century, can see that one is to be a missionary wherever one happens to be. This universal task is but another aspect of the universal gospel.

But, alas, the universality of the gospel is being challenged by some who say that many peoples already have a culture and religion intact and should not be disturbed. Mission history rings with the loud footsteps of these who refused such argument, heeding rather the words of their Master, who commanded followers to go and teach and make disciples. These missionaries know the gospel is for all or none. Their example has emblazoned a trail of sacrifice and solitude for the Savior. It was because they knew such love that they willed it for all.

Let the reader embark on the reading of mission history, knowing that exposure to the story may be contagious and that Christian action may result, even in the present.

1
Missions:
The Biblical Basis

Christians worldwide agree that the Bible is the Word of God, a record of God's dealings with humans in history. The Bible today reveals the principles and foundations of missions for those who would do the bidding of its Author. This is because the doing of missions is God's favorite work. There is in that Holy Book a continuous and sustained account of God's revelations through a series of prophets and their inspired sayings.

The Bible's authority for world missions rests not merely upon a group of isolated favorite passages but upon the design and spirit of the Bible itself as it reveals God's search for persons. Therefore, the Bible is clearly God's search for people. This is in sharp contrast to other would-be holy books, which are collectively the story of people's search for God.

The efforts of Christian missionaries are rooted in the reality of history. The Bible is not concerned with fables and fairy tales but with all-too-human persons who bled when cut and cried when hurt. God called and still calls "just plain folk" to become extraordinary by attempting the unusual feat of bringing Christ to all nations.

The Bible is essential to the mission task also because it is eternal. It speaks to every person in every culture precisely because it is the eternal and transcultural Word of God. The Bible is always modern because it is a word about life from the Creator himself. God's Word cuts with pierc-

31

ing power across all ethnic groups, to all nations, and to all persons in spite of income, age, or social standing.

The human family is addressed directly and with quiet dignity by the Lord. The Bible pleads for the helpless and the hungry and against the haughty. The Word of God empowers the missionaries in the Christian community to minister to those whose lives are plagued by intense need.

People everywhere ask such questions as Who am I? and If there is a God, where is he now? The missionary, with Bible in hand, is the point of contact to those seeking answers to universal questions. Further, because Jesus is the living Word, the Bible speaks through the missionary to provide more than answers. It gives life and hope because it records that all of human history is moving toward Christ.

The Bible is a record in three tenses. As past tense, it is the record of the saving acts of God in history. It is a testimony of the power of God among chosen peoples of the past. The Bible also gives guidance to mission efforts in the present. In the future tense, the Bible reminds missionaries that they are on the winning side. It is the lordship of Christ to which all efforts are moving. In three tenses, the Bible is the source as well as the result of inspiration.

The Bible makes clear that the doing of missions is God's favorite work. Missions began in the heart of God. The whole arena of missions is all of human life and history. It is the scene for God's struggle to bring his most precious creation back to himself. He has made us to find ourselves in him, and he yearns for the close of history when those responding to him in faith will dwell with him. He desires this so much that he has spared no price to provide us with a way to find our identity in him. To make that trek back to him possible, God calls missionaries to point the way. Prophetic modern missionaries thus continue in the tradition of bringing persons back to God because they have heard the call of universal love from the

God who is love. The Bible makes this call clear in several ways.

Creation and Call

The most striking passage in the whole Old Testament is Genesis 1:1. The deep concepts contained therein are still a challenge to the modern scientific mind. Yet, in its universal sense, the Genesis account is designed to remind modern believers that God made us and we are his.

The missionary message of the Genesis account is that creation is the starting point of history. That is, the same God who will draw all human events to a close by having all bow at the feet of Jesus is the one true God who started the whole historical and natural process. Missionaries stand in the middle of that process, proclaiming both the beginning and the end because of the meaning they have found in the middle. In Hebrew and Christian theology, creation and current events are directly related. Creation is seen as the first of God's saving acts. Genesis 1 and 2 convey that there is a harmony and inherent goodness in God's creation. So, when God speaks anything or any being into existence, it is for a specific task.

Part of the message of missions is that God is continuing to work with his creation. Thus, the call to missions is a call to live out one's submission to the creator of all on a continuing basis.

Modern missionaries determine their priorities on another message in the Genesis account. That message is that the crown of God's creation is humanity. The earth is primarily present to be the human dwelling place. The missionaries are sent to the highest of God's creation. They spend their time with nothing less than the best.

Man and woman are presented in Genesis as made in God's image. (Cf. 1:26-27.) As made in God's image, they are to relate back to the Creator. They are to be God's representatives on earth. They are to function as the administrators of God's works. Men and women are able to respond and are held responsible before God for all other created beings. It is in that context that called persons go forth as missionaries. They are God's emissaries with the accompanying power and authority to get the job done. The assignment is to bring all persons to the realization that the God who made them is the one who wants to recreate them in faith. Therefore, the modern ambassadors for Christ are not bringing a nice little commentary on how to have a better life. The message is, "He who made you in the first place now has shown his love again by dying for you."

Genesis 1:1 should be properly translated, "In beginning God," emphasizing that God has no beginning. He has always been. The one true God whom we represent is not in need of any other gods. He is not dependent on time or space or any other being for his existence. The God of the Bible has not room for other would-be claimants to his throne. While people reach out to him through other religions, he seeks to bring his creation back to himself.

Even the word for "created" in Genesis 1:1 is unique to the one true God. This term (bara) is never applied to anyone except God. Only God can bara (Hebrew for create). This word is never used to mean being reliant on any kind of materials; God creates directly without any need for any substance whatsoever. He is not dependent on anything or any other god for his creative powers.

The creation materials in Genesis contain at least four major truths applicable to the modern missionary effort. They are:

1. God is without equal as Creator or Redeemer. He is dependent on nothing and no one else for any of his activities. There is no room for any other gods.
2. Humanity is the highest of all creation, being barely below the angels and infinitely above the animals. As existing in God's image, man and woman are more responsible for what goes on in planet Earth than any other creatures.

3. There is a God-desired and God-ordained order and beauty to the universe. People and other beings are created to fill a certain spot in the universe. That order is restored through Christ.

4. Human beings, as the target of missionary effort, are never to be viewed as partial beings. They are not to be seen as "souls" to be saved but humans to be redeemed.

The second central motif in Genesis is that of God's call to the disciple-missionary. The scene shifts in chapter 12 from humankind in general to the man Abraham. Abraham's call marks the beginning of God's method of dealing with the human race ever since.

A beautiful portrait of the faithful Abraham is painted in Genesis 22 when he is called upon to sacrifice Isaac. If Isaac had perished, there would have been no physical sign of the Lord's presence and blessings on future generations. The faithful Abraham was not expected to understand fully, merely to obey. That is the essence of faith. Abraham stood the test in spite of the fact that he was being asked to give up his future. Even today God asks his ambassadors to be totally faithful.

The two clear missionary themes in the Bible's first book are creation and call. Adam and Abraham share with us a common humanity and a common reminder that in being human instruments of good news today's missionary shares in the responsibility of turning the world right side up again.

Judaism: A Missionary Faith

The Judaism which formed the bedrock out of which Christianity was built was the world's first missionary religion. The Jews were the recipients of the universal missionary covenant in which all the nations of the earth were to be blessed. Israel was to be the mediator of God's universal love and justice until the Messiah came. The worship of the one true God was held to be central by the Jews. The prophets insistence on that fidelity culminated in the coming of the Messiah. When Jesus cried, "It is finished" from the cross, Judaism gave way to the modern spiritual Israel. But, Israel had been a good preparation for the universal Christian gospel.

The Old Testament itself shows the Jewish inclination to record and preserve the life-giving will of God. The Jews, even vacillating between sin and submission, preserved the background for the Messiah.

The Prophets: Prototypes of Discipleship

The Old Testament prophets had great resolve in spite of the odds created by the unfaithfulness around them. As faithful servants, they are deserving of being called prototypes of Christian discipleship in the modern era.

Hosea was just such a man. His main purpose was to call the Israelites to repentance from the growing corruption of morals, religion, and politics which marred his day. Hosea realized that Israel was behaving as an unfaithful wife to a faithful and loving God. Israel's unfaithfulness was breaking God's heart. The Israelites were trying to mix godly worship with paganism. Hosea was heartbroken, as he knew God must have been. Yet, Hosea remained faithful even with personal heartbreak, a reminder to all who follow the Christ prophesied to be "acquainted with grief."

Amos was another such prophet faithful to God. He was called to be a prophet without any previous preparation. He was just a poor boy who grew up to resent the wide gap between the income of the poor and that of the rich in nearby Jerusalem. His virtues were simple and honest. For Amos, the change from rural Judah to urban Israel was a drastic one. His eyes were seared by the sight of the dancing girls. His moral sense was offended by the sale of poor people for the mere amusement of the rich. Amos could not stay quiet.

For Amos, a holy God could only be served through a pure and holy life. Amos cried out against the dishonesty of the courts, the mistreatment of the poor, and the moral sickness within Israel's upper classes. The heart of Amos's simple theology was the deep conviction that only a nation with daily social fairness and compassion can find real favor with God. As the proclaimer of simple truths calling for simple honesty, Amos laid the groundwork for the modern missionary-disciple.

Jeremiah was called the "weeping prophet." He was a sensitive man, responsive to life as he saw it. He was never what could be called a socially adjusted person. Jeremiah was never accepted by his countrymen. Yet, he was helped by an awareness of God's call and presence. There were four major concerns reflected in Jeremiah's sayings to the people:

1. The corruption of true religion;
2. The lure of the nature cults;
3. Judah's insensitivity to the will of God; and
4. The impending invasion of a foe from the North.

Jeremiah is remembered as the "weeping prophet" because he was unafraid to reveal his deep inner thoughts. He gave his people a new covenant with feeling. That new covenant was to be marked by heartfelt love for God, a precursor of the covenant today under Christ.

Another prophet who led the way for the coming of Christ was Isaiah. His name meant, "The Lord is Salvation." His prophecies spanned forty years. For Isaiah, holiness was a picture of his own sinfulness. Sin for him was a reliance on religious ritual rather than on God's power and love. This led to Isaiah's faithfulness to God's call that made him a worthy prototype of Christian discipleship today. In that, he joined other Old Testament giants who serve as a source of inspiration today for those also called by the same God.

Christ in History

Jesus came in the fullness of time. It was 1989 years ago, or five years before the currently used chronology introduced by Dionysius Exiguus in the sixth century. It was in the year 749 of the empire of Rome. Although locked into a specific period of time, Jesus soon clarified the universal nature of his being, claims, and gospel. Jewish shepherds burst forth in missionary song when they heard of his coming. Even the unbelieving world was represented at his birth by the Wise Men from the East. Thus, Jesus came to the chosen people and the whole world alike, to Jewish pride and Gentile culture. Later, a Roman procurator would have set Jesus free but for the Jewish leaders and the ruler's own cowardice. After the ascension, the reigning King Jesus called the Pharisee Saul to be the apostle to the Gentiles.

Thus, Jesus lived and worked in the context of history. Today he demands no less from his disciples. His was and is a mission to the whole world, always in the midst of specific culture and religions. Jesus introduced a new and fresh faith, one demanding radical repentance from pride and prejudice. His is not a fable but an earthly call for specific service.

Jesus' Gospel

The first three Gospels present the teachings of Jesus from the messianic view. His teachings are memorable and useful today because they were and are direct and intensely practical.

Jesus is called a teacher more than fifty times in the Synoptics. No other title is applied to him in these three Gospels. Jesus has often been called the world's greatest teacher. But, he did not have the attitude or training of the professional teacher. He grew up in a carpenter shop. He was a practical man with simple themes—the nature of the kingdom and the kind of righteousness it demanded. However, Jesus' skills in teaching were extraordinary.

The ethical teachings of Jesus are based on the idea that this life is a state of preparation for the one to come. For Jesus, pain and injustice were made bearable by knowing that they were a part of a cleansing discipline by which God prepares his children for eternity.

The repetitive theme in all of Jesus' teaching is the kingdom of God. Followers of Jesus simply live in another frame of reference when it comes to attitudes and actions. Their rules are laid down by the Lord. They live in a state of meaningfulness built on the realization that the kingdom is not a renovated social order produced by human effort. The kingdom is God's rule becoming effective anywhere in the world of human experience. That kingdom is the foundation of the gospel today, a call to forgiveness through repentance and changed actions and values.

Jesus' Missionary Methods and Mandates

Jesus set the example for the modern missionary through his life and words. No person ever achieved so much in such a short time as Jesus. This was due partly to his sinlessness in spite of the fact that he was tempted with power and pride more than any other person in history. He fought his way through all temptation to follow through on his clear vision of messiahship. Yet, there was nothing partial or artificial about the humanity of Jesus. When he hurt, he hurt intensely. He bled real blood. His death was real.

The missionary mandate of the Lord Jesus can be found in parallel form as follows from the *Good News Bible*.

In all four accounts can be found the ascending King on his way to the City of God, using all his power and authority to teach and evangelize the world. This he chose to do through eleven poor and puzzled disciples. On them he breathed the Holy Spirit. Then he gave them the tasks of baptizing, instructing, and inspiring the new believers. The promise of his eternal presence was to comfort them as they went.

The Gospels present the Christ who taught by example through the Spirit. That same Holy Spirit today empowers

Matthew 28:18-20	*Mark 16:15*	*Luke 24:46-49*	*John 20:21-22*	*Acts 1:8*
I have been given all authority in heaven and on earth. Go, then, to all peoples everywhere and make them my disciples: baptize them in the name of the Father, the Son, and the Holy Spirit, and teach them to obey everything I have commanded you. And I will be with you always, to the end of the age.	Go throughout the world and preach the gospel to all mankind.	The Messiah must suffer and rise from death three days later, and in his name the message about repentance and the forgiveness of sins must be preached to all nations beginning in Jerusalem. You are witnesses of these things. And I myself will send upon you what my Father has promised. But you must wait in the city until the power from above comes down upon you.	Peace be with you. As the Father sent me, so I send you. Then he breathed on them and said, "Receive the Holy Spirit."	But when the Holy Spirit comes up-you, you will be filled with power, and you will be witnesses for me in Jerusalem, in all of Judea and Samaria. and to the ends of the earth.

Jesus' followers who preach and live out the kingdom ethic in the footsteps of the Master Teacher and Doer.

The Apostolic Era: Peter and Paul

The Acts of the Apostles was Luke's attempt to review the missions history of the early church. It is an excellent handbook for missions in every age. The book only covers three short decades, from Jesus' ascension to shortly before the death of Paul. Yet it is filled with missionary heroes and heroism. Its unmistakable emphasis is on witnessing and church growth.

A subtheme of Acts is the necessary dependence of the new disciples on the power of the Holy Spirit. For Luke, the gospel of the Spirit completed the gospel of the Son, with the help of faithful missionaries. Luke clearly stressed in Acts that the most important ministry of the Holy Spirit is in the fitting of Christians for service. For Luke, the Holy Spirit, as the executor of Christ's will, determined the course of missions. At least ten times in Acts, the Holy Spirit thrust disciples into new fields.

The greatest single event in church history after Christ's ascension is described in Acts 2. It happened fifty days after Passover when the 120 were gathered to pray in a large room. Peter started to preach. The Spirit then came with two symbols (that is, sound and sight).

Peter's sermon in Acts 2 is an excellent example of the early church's apologetic method. Peter wanted his hearers to know that the death of Jesus was no accident but the result of a divine and designed plan. Then Peter emphasized the risen Lord. Peter argued that because Jesus arose the Holy Spirit was upon him and upon anyone who wished to follow Jesus. Peter's argument was quickly understood, and it gave rise to a searching for missionary guidelines. What were the disciples to do now? Peter instantly demanded repentance and baptism. The sermon was highly successful. Three thousand people were baptized and came into the fellowship of the early church. It is quite important to note that these new believers were instructed in doctrine before they were allowed to go away to witness.

Acts 10 is a turning point in the book and in early mission history. The future of the church depended on its acceptance of Gentiles into the previously all-Jewish fellowship. For Luke, the gospel had to be proclaimed without regard to the Jewish rules which would have restricted its spread.

Peter's vision signals a breakthrough for the early church. In his day, the devout Jew would not even buy oil, bread, milk, or meat from a Gentile. The irony was that Peter was already being inconsistent by staying in the house of a tanner. Peter's eyes were fully opened because they were already partially exposed to the light.

The next day Peter set out for Cornelius's town of Caeserea. Peter was still so upset about his new venture into the Gentile community that he took six witnesses with him, three times the required number. In spite of the risk involved, Peter started to preach. The point of the sermon was that God's grace is for all who believe. Verses 44-48 reminds the reader that the Holy Spirit comes to Gentiles as well as Jews. The issue was settled in spite of Peter's early reluctance.

Paul's successful transcultural witness in Acts 17 is an outstanding model for similar work on the modern scene. The synagogue and public markets were Paul's pulpits as he took the risen Lord to the people. The philosophers called him names. Their favorite was "seed picker." That is to say, Paul was accused of being an intellectual scavenger who merely picked up bits of information and spread them without discernment. Paul withstood the attacks. He was successful that day. A city council member was redeemed along with others. Paul was a sign that an informed Christian with the help of the Holy Spirit can be very effective when proclaiming the risen Lord.

Acts ends with Paul in Rome. The apostle's lifelong

dream had finally come true. He was a Roman citizen. As soon as he arrived there, he consulted with the Jewish leaders. There was never a dampening of Paul's desire to spread the gospel, even as a prisoner. Even when the majority of the Jews in Rome refused to believe, Paul still took refuge in the fact that the church of the future would have Gentiles in it.

Acts 28:30-31 is Luke's summary statement: Paul had full freedom in preaching the gospel. Thus ends the greatest missionary manual in the history of the church. Luke showed the modern reader what a small group of bold believers can do when turned loose with the Spirit in the world. This small group, led by Peter and Paul, saw the Spirit leap over social, religious, and political barriers. The gospel would not be bound. It was for the Jewish and Gentile worlds.

There are clear and obvious themes in the Bible which continue to relate to the doing of missions. These include:

1. The clear call to missions. From the time of Abraham through the apostolic age, it is evident in Christian Scripture that God calls specific individuals with particular gifts to do his work. These individuals are expected to lead the people of God to a life-style of ministry to persons and reverence to God. This is done best through a servant stance.

2. The example of the Savior. The Bible is Christocentric with regard to all matters, especially in relation to the doing of missions. The modern missionary operates best in proportion to the emulation of Jesus of Nazareth. This is true especially in the areas of ethical teaching and personal-caring ministry.

3. The future hope. Peter, Paul, and John remind the serving missionary that the life of Christlikeness has its reward. The trials and setbacks are but temporary and always to be viewed in light of eternal glory. The missionary is but a pilgrim asking others to join the journey.

Christianity About AD 125: Doctrine and Discipline

By AD 125, as the result of Paul's labors, the gospel was planted in the key areas of Syria, Macedonia, Greece, and Italy. The entire Mediterranean world was evangelized by that time. Christians probably numbered about one-quarter million. These new believers were known widely for their "true believer" commitment, their childlike but not childish faith, and their readiness to suffer persecution. Yet, these early Christians were not without flaws. They were given to divisions, theological instability, and a tendency to go back to their old gods. By AD 125, the church was badly divided. This led to an incredible variety in form and function. Further, there was no central administration existing as the instrument for tying together local church units. Not even the church in Jerusalem could demand support in a unified manner.

But by AD 125, the church was displaying some organizational features which were developing almost universally. There were deacons, elders, and bishops by then. There was developing an accepted pattern. There were bishops governing most local churches with a few regional bishops.

An early Christian document, *The Teaching of the Twelve Apostles,* called for resident prophets and teachers. But not all followed that advice, and there was far from unity in polity and discipline by AD 125.

There was emerging, however, some unity in the field of early Christian doctrine. This was partly caused by the continuing debate over Christianity and its relation to Judaism. The question was whether Christianity was to exist as a Jewish sect or become a movement unique within itself. By AD 125, the radical newness of the gospel of Pauline antilegalism won out over the legalizing tendencies. The question of law versus gospel was won by the gospelizers.

Another cause of the movement toward doctrinal unity was the Greek influence on the gospel message. In this sense, the most potent danger was the threat of gnosticism. The Gnostics believed in a secret and mysterious *gnosis,* or knowledge, which was revealed only to those initiated into it. It was presented as a gift only to the lucky and secret few. Salvation for the Gnostics was defined as escape from evil matter. They saw Christ as the one making this escape possible by being the example of one who had been cleared of matter's influence. This view separated the Christ principle from Jesus. The Gnostic heresy, as it was seen by most Christians circa AD 125, tended to minimize the historical element in Christianity and to divorce the Christian faith from the life, death, and resurrection of Jesus. The Gnostic Jesus was quite different from the Jesus reported in the Gospels. Christians escaped narrowly from the temptation to be taken over by Gnostic heretics. In so doing, the Christian theologians of the early part of the second century stressed the historicity of Jesus of Nazareth.

By AD 125, Christianity was set for its missionary impact on the world. Two factors made this so. One was the embryonic church polity system newly dependent on the regional bishop. Another was the clarification of the gospel as dependent on the life-giving historicity of Jesus to free believers from legalistic Judaism. The stage was set for advance.

Case Study: Stephen, the Martyr

From the Hellenistic Jews in Jerusalem came the complaint that their widows were not being properly cared for by the Galilean disciples. Stephen was chosen as one of a new set of deacons to care for practical matters. The name Stephen means "the crown." Stephen was probably a freed slave from Rome and a goldsmith who was converted to Christ on the day of Pentecost. Stephen was chosen for his openness to the Gentile world while seeing also the importance of Jewish converts to Christ. Luke, in Acts 6:10, portrays Stephen as full of the Holy Spirit and wisdom.

This implies that Stephen was full of faith and the power of God and of an irresistible spirit.

Stephen was the first Jew to understand and apply Christ's treatment of the woman of Samaria on the matter of worship (Acts 7:48) and also of Christ's rebuking of the "scribes, Pharisees and hypocrites." He was tuned into the coming glory of Christ. He beheld the important missionary teaching of the universal church. Even while being martyred, he "looked up steadfastly unto heaven, and saw the glory of God, and Jesus standing at the right hand of God" (v. 55). He died as his Master had done, praying for his murderers. He was living proof that people would not have had the courage to die for God if God had not become man to die for them.

Questions

1. How was Stephen like Jesus?
2. What is a deacon?
3. What kind of impetus did Stephen's death give to the early church?
4. How was Stephen typical of other heroes for God in the Bible?
5. What qualities are seen in Stephen which must also be true of the modern missionary?

Time Line: ?BC-AD 125

	BC
?	Creation
1900?	Abraham
1800	
1700	
1600	
1500	
1400	
1300	
1200	
1100	
1000	
900	
800	
750?	Amos
700	
600	
500	
400	
300	
200	
100	
5	Jesus
0	
	AD
10	
20	
28	Great Commission
30	
40	
50	
60	
63	Death of Paul
70	
80	
90	
96	John's Revelation
100	
125	The end of the apostolic era

2
After the Apostles:
AD 125-500

By far the most important place for the implantation of the gospel between AD 125 and 500 was Rome. The church at Rome had the respect of the rest of Christendom, partly due to its connection with the martyrs, Peter and Paul. The church there drew its followers from both the rich and poor. It was both a Greek- and Latin-speaking church. The church at Rome grew by a few conversions but mainly by Christians moving there from the outlying provinces. By about 200, the number of followers of Christ was greater than the number of Jews.

With Rome at the center, with an ever increasingly strong church, by the end of the third century, there was no area of the Roman Empire not exposed to the gospel. There were some good reasons for this. One was the total commitment of the early Christians to their Master. Eusebius of Caesarea (about 260-340) wrote: "Leaving their homes, they set out to fulfill the work of an evangelist, making it their ambition to preach the word of the faith to those who as yet had heard nothing of it."

The early Christians were also known for the purity of their lives. For example, they were known as those who saw their bodies as temples of the Holy Spirit. They stood clearly on moral issues, mixing purity with social action.

All of this was in spite of persecution, particularly in the early part of this period. Christians were sometimes forced to meet in secret. Because this was so, they were victims of vicious rumors about what went on behind those doors. Every believer lived with the horrible thought that he might have to die a martyr as Stephen had done. When this was necessary, those early Christians were known as capable of dying with dignity. This was so true that some nonbelievers were converted while watching Christians die.

The Nameless Ones

The period of the second century AD has been called "the Age of the Nameless Ones." Unnumbered Christians were members of the young churches throughout the Roman Empire. From this era few, if any, names of Christian pioneers have survived.

The impact of "the nameless ones" was such, however, that a governor ruling in northern Asia Minor wrote about 112 to his Emperor Trajan about the Christians: "The contagion of this superstition has spread not only in the cities but in the villages and rural districts." Some of "the nameless ones" even carried the gospel to such places as Edessa. From there the word spread to Baghdad. Later, the word arrived in Persia where it encountered Zoroastrianism. Armenia also received the gospel during the second century. Even the king there became a believer in Christ.

"The nameless ones" now draw their notoriety only from God himself. They are not nameless to him, although the chroniclers of mission history today search in vain for their surnames. God knows and he knows how effective was their ministry amid both persecution and anonymity.

Survival Amid Persecution

At least ten times before the year 400, the Roman emperors tried to crush the Christian churches out of existence. Their plan was to declare the emperor to be divine and to force all subjects to bow down before his image. The Roman armies spread terror throughout the empire. Diocletian used them to enforce his decrees that all Christian places of worship should be torn down, all Christian writings burned, all Christians to be without defense in law courts, and all who persisted in professing Christianity to be subject to persecution. Diocletian in 303, also issued edicts that all Christian leaders must be captured and imprisoned. For Diocletian, anyone who believed and confessed that "Jesus is Lord" could not consistently worship the emperor. Since the emperor, for him, was god, the Christians were declared to be "atheists."

After Diocletian was finished with his reign of terror, the new emperor, Galerius, threw tens of thousands of Christians into the copper mines and chopped off the hands, feet, and ears of others. For hundreds of Christians, to remain faithful meant the loss of sight or other physical atrocities.

In spite of this intense persecution, the struggling Christian churches survived because of several indelible qualities. One was that the eternal Christ made good his promise to be with his followers even in times of trial. Secular historians may play down this reality, but it was real to the believers.

There were other reasons that the early Christians survived amid persecutions. One was the quality and depth of their shared community life. They not only shared possessions but also a high view of women and orphans and their deserving of dignity. They took care of the poor and sick, as they did all members of the churches. Another reason for survival was the quiet assurance of the Christians that their cause would outlive that of the Romans. This seemed absurd at the time but was to prove true.

Pantaenus in Alexandria's Seminary

In Alexandria, Egypt, the main focus of Christian life was a training school for both new and more mature Christians. It was in existence by 180 and had as its main purpose the instruction of new converts who were preparing for church membership. The first head of the catechetical school whom we know by name was one Pantaenus, a Stoic philosopher who knew the value of disciplined intellectual thought. When he was converted to Christ, he brought that emphasis with him. Among his most famous pupils was Clement of Alexandria, author of *The Instructor.*

Pantaenus started that early seminary in Alexandria to combat the Gnostic heretic Basilides. That school, in the process, became a great missionary school. From there Christian teacher-missionaries went to Africa, Arabia, India, and Ceylon. The school had four main subjects: evangelism, apologetics, theology, and missionary method. It was an amazing development in that early era of missions history. Pantaenus went to India about 200 to check on the missionary activity there. He found that mission work was highly advanced and going well.

Clement of Alexandria and Origen, two important church fathers, succeeded Pantaenus at Alexandria. There they carried on his tradition of Christian scholarship which was manifest in missionary enterprise. This interest culminated in Augustine.

Ulfilas on the Danube

Just beyond the northern territory of the Roman Empire in the fourth century was an active man named Ulfilas (311-381). He was sent as a lad to Constantinople to study theology and linguistics under the Eastern patriarch of the church. There he mastered Latin and Greek, was ordained as a bishop, and was sent back to the banks of the Danube as a missionary to his own people. Ulfilas gave the Gothic language its first written alphabet. For forty years, Ulfilas worked among his people with patience and success, even among the uncivilized peoples who lived there. His contribution is considered a significant early chapter in the history of missions because of his courage and perseverance. His primary contribution was the reduction of the Gothic language to an alphabet so he could translate the Christian Scriptures into that language. That act was to set the tone for future successful missionary effort. Missionaries have continued to prove the value of communicating in the language of the people.

Martin of Tours

In 316 in what we now know as Yugoslavia, a son was born to an unbelieving soldier in the Roman army. As a teenager, after becoming a Christian convert, Martin was forced to become a soldier himself. While on military duty in northern Gaul on a cold winter day, he came across a cold and shivering beggar. Quickly the young Martin slashed his cloak in two with his sword and gave one half to the beggar. The next night Martin had a vision in which he saw Jesus clothed in the half of the cloak which he had given away. Then he decided it was time to be baptized and make public his faith in Christ. Soon thereafter Martin resigned from the army and entered a monastery where he spent less than a year. A man of action, Martin left the monastery and gathered a group of disciple-missionaries about him. They traveled extensively among the unbelieving rural folk in Tours. Martin was known as a fiery apologist, convincing anyone who would listen of the truths of the Christian faith. He died about 400. By that time, dozens of altars to nature gods had been torn down and replaced by Christian worship centers. Almost half of the people in the Tours area were Christian, with some surrounding tribes won to the faith as well. Martin of Tours goes down in mission history as a wise, gentle, and courageous forerunner of other great missionaries of Europe. A younger contemporary who wrote Martin's biography, said, "He judged none and condemned none and never returned evil for evil . . . nothing was in his mouth except Christ and nothing in his heart but piety, peace and pity."

Constantine: The Power and the Glory

A major turning point in church and mission history came with the emperor Constantine. He was proclaimed emperor in 306. However, he did not overcome all rivals and become sole emperor until 323. Between these two dates, in 312, Constantine became a believer in Christ. He was commanding an army which was in northern Italy on its way to Rome. There he met a very worthy opponent named Macentius. Constantine had a vision of a cross of light in the heavens with the inscription, "Conquer by the sign." Constantine won the ensuing battle at the Milvian Bridge, near Rome, and marched into the major city as victor.

In 313, Constantine issued an edict in Milan that was to change Christian history. That edict ensured toleration for all Christians throughout the Roman Empire. The key word, it must be remembered, is *toleration.* This was not the same as complete liberty or support. Wills in favor of the church were permitted. The Christian observance of Sunday was given legal status. The bishop's court was given prestige on an equal par with the civil courts. Constantine forbade Jews from stoning Jewish converts to Christianity. The Edict of Milan read in part, "Liberty of worship shall not be denied to any, but the mind and will of every individual shall be free to manage divine affairs according to his own choice." The new breath of freedom for the Christian believers was welcomed by those who were heirs to generations of persecution.

However, the reviews by subsequent historians of Constantine's reforms have proven less than favorable. Some even assert that the churches were damaged in depth of commitment by the mere substitution of the cross for the nature god's symbols. Constantine's goodwill brought about the unifying of church and state. Some critics, including Adolf Harnack, have charged that Constantine's edict brought about a great compromise with error. Nationalism took over individualism in Christian conversion. This may have led to the easy conquest of the city of Constantinople and surrounding territories only three centuries later. Constantine's conversion to Christ was at best partial. While he commanded the Roman legions to attend church on Sunday for the hearing of public prayers, Constantine also allowed prayers to be addressed to him as emperor.

The die was cast. The church and the state were inexorably tied together in European Christianity. The repercussions into mission strategy are still alive today. In 1984, it takes a wise Christian missionary to escape the cultural captivity of the gospel. Constantine set these forces into motion.

The Council of Nicea

Constantine summoned a "great and holy synod" to meet at Nicea in 325. There was written a creed that remains the standard for Christian doctrine by most believers. Of the 318 persons who gathered for the meeting, only 8 were from the West. The conferees sat around an open copy of the four Gospels. Constantine sat on his throne and moderated the proceedings. What was to be known as The Nicene Creed was sent forth to all churches in the East and West. Christ, in that creed, was declared to be essentially divine. The date for the keeping of Easter was also set. However, the central affirmation of Nicea was that Jesus Christ was "truly God" who had become "truly man." Constantine declared at the close of the Council of Nicea that anyone who disobeyed the decrees thereof should be put to death. He also banished the heretic Arius and his closest supporters and deposed two bishops.

This council gave to future missionaries a solidification of their Christology. They were now able to know for a certainty the balance between the full deity and the full humanity of their Lord. The churches of both the East and West were forcefully unified on the core of the gospel message. A missionary to Gaul could know that his synopsis was essentially the same as one sent to India. That unification was essential to the eventual spread of the Christian message.

Monasticism: Monks, Missions, and Mystery

Constantine gave recognition and toleration to the minority Christian population in their day. Due to their efforts, by 438 the majority of the people in the Roman Empire were professing Christians. But, church discipline was greatly relaxed, and to many the nominal acceptance of Christianity was merely that. There was now a large gap between the Christian ideal and public allegiance to it. Reform and renewal were needed and almost inevitable. Out of this nominalism came the monastic movement.

In the fourth and fifth centuries, numerous monasteries were established in Egypt, Palestine, and Syria. Communities with strict rules were established. Basil of Caesarea was the author of the first widely accepted set of rules for monks. He wrote *The Longer Rules* and and *The Shorter Rules* late in the fourth century. He called for a balance between work and prayer. The obedience of the monk to his superior was to be absolute, and his commitment was to be binding for life. The monasteries were to give aid to the poor outside their walls.

The missions of these early monks continue in the tradition of modern Christian missions. Discipline, aid to the poor, the value of education, and the necessity of prayer are but a few of the attributes and actions of the modern missionary which are exercised today in light of the earlier flame of monks who lived the deeper and broader life.

Christianity About AD 500: An Assessment

By 500 the Roman Empire was a dying regime. Valentinian III (425-455) reigned over a decaying empire. Despite the fall of the empire, however, about 500 the churches could look back with some degree of satisfaction over the progress made. One achievement was its very survival after the fall of the Roman Empire. By then it had grown beyond the empire by ventures into such faraway places as India.

The church was also undergoing an inward renewal by the year 500. The Bible was settled within its canonical limits and the person of Christ was clearly defined. A system of worship was established throughout Christendom with emphasis on Sundays and such special holidays as Easter. These unifying forces made the message and the commitment to that life-style of Christianity effective agents of the mission task.

Christianity was riding high in its royal favor when the Roman Empire fell. The nature cults had almost disappeared. There was, however, one major problem to face—the relationship between the church and its surrounding culture. This was especially difficult following Constantine because the state and the church were almost interchangable. There was, to say the least, an insufficient line of separation between the church and the world. If the identification between the two was almost complete, where was the distinct role and message of the church? That was a burning question in 500.

Christians did distinguish themselves in the last days of the Roman Empire as being persons of charity and social concern. Each Christian was taught to contribute according to individual ability for the sake of the common good, both within and outside the church. This benevolence was to be done in loving response to the love of God in Christ.

About 500, the church was struggling for its identity. The struggle was for an identity in relation to the state. The early followers of Jesus were just learning to be salt and light. The good news is that the twin sources of authority, Jesus' nature and the Bible, were agreed upon virtually throughout Christendom. The church could look forward to a time of great triumph. But, alas, it did not come that quickly or easily.

Case Study: Cosmas, the Merchant Missionary

Cosmas was a merchant-missionary who retired to a monastery in 535 and issued his *Topographia Christiana*. He wrote with the conviction that the world was flat and that Christianity was to be spread soon across that level plane. Out of ignorance, he proclaimed that there were no Christians in China, although there is other evidence to the contrary. Based on his travels about 500 to most of the known world, he wrote: "Among the Huns and others Indians, and indeed throughout the known world, there were numberless churches, bishops and multitudes of Christians, with many martyrs, monks and hermits."

Cosmas was representative of a large class of Christian merchants who took Christ with them as they traveled about 500. He may have been wrong about some geographical and geological facts, but Cosmas was unrelenting in his desire that all in the known world have access to the gospel.

Questions

1. Can God use partial knowledge on the part of a follower?
2. Does God consider ignorance a virtue?
3. What do you think about the presence of Christianity in China today?
4. How and why should Cosmas's travels be emulated today?
5. Do people like Cosmas (that is, unordained lay people), still have a place in missions? What?
6. Does God honor the mistakes of zeal mixed with misinformation?
7. How does a traveler expand the horizons of others?

Time Line: AD 125-500

125	"The Nameless Ones"
150	
180	Pantaenus of Alexandria
200	
250	
300	
303	Diocletian's persecution
323	Constantine made Roman emperor
250	Basil of Caesarea
380	Ulfilas died
400	Martin of Tours died
428	Nestorius, bishop of Constantinople
450	
455	Emperor Valentinian III died
500?	The travels of Cosmas

3
The Light Shines in Darkness:
AD 500-1200

When the Roman Empire fell about 500, the church was in peril also. The verdict was out as to whether the church could survive with any force. The church was an integral part of the Roman Empire from the time of Constantine. Now the time had come to see whether Christianity could survive without direct state support.

Looking back, we are able to see several signs that the era of light shining in darkness for the churches started about 500. One was the baptism of Clovis, king of the Franks. The seat of power for the church in the West was soon to shift northward from Rome to the Germanic peoples. This was coupled with the close of the ancient schools of the Greek philosophers in Athens in 529. This was a sign that, even in Greece, the Christian thought forms were victorious. The shift away from Rome was in full swing.

The period of the seven centuries from 500 to 1200 is generally interpreted as one of decline and darkness for the churches. This is in spite of the fact that there were a few rays of missionary light that shone during the period. One such beam was the spread of the gospel further into Egypt and eventually into the Sudan. The gospel also took hold in China during this time. The British Isles were missionized under Pope Gregory the Great, and by 800 the whole British Isle system was at least nominally Christian. The eighth century witnessed the conversion of much of Germany through the efforts of the Carolingians.

Papal primacy was emerging in the wake of the Roman Empire's disintegration as a unifying force for the churches of the West. Pope Leo I (440-461) had set the stage by insisting on the sublime authority of the bishop of Rome. He was led by the deep conviction that God had given to him the watchcare of the entire Church. This he sought to prove by insisting that his reign was directly in line with that of Peter. Leo argued that anyone who did not submit to him was not being faithful to Peter or Jesus as Lord of the Church. Leo I was followed, although not directly, by Pope Gelasius I (492-496). He also furthered belief in the authority of the pope. He declared that even the emperor was to submit to the pope in matters involving the Church. The Church was set for the viewing of the papacy as a unifying factor.

Another ray of light for the Church from 500-1200 was the establishment of the Benedictine order. Benedict of Nursia (480?-547) formed many self-sustained units of disciplined life-style called monasteries. The Benedictine monasteries became centers of hospitality, learning, and worship. Thus they served as stabilizing factors in an age of fragmentation.

Near the end of the seven centuries from 500-1200, the Vikings became a major deterrent to missions. Their plundering was destructive to existing mission effort. However, the Vikings' capture and relocation of Saint Patrick actually aided mission effort. Similarly, the Crusades were a mixture of triumph and tragedy. While thousands of lives were lost needlessly, those who survived had their world view widened, and some started the syndrome of "missions by proxy." Meanwhile, such individuals as Knut of Denmark and Boleslav of Poland left their mark on the future of missions.

Islam's Spread

There were at least two factors which held the Church back in the period following 500. One was the birth and spread of Islam. The religion called Islam was founded by Muhammad (570-632). He was born in Arabia, the son of poor parents. He was orphaned by the time he was six and adopted by some uncles of the Quraish tribe. That adoption was significant because that tribe had charge of the Kaaba stone in Mecca. In that charge, they profited from the food and trinket concessions from the thousands of pilgrims who visited there annually. It was believed by the Arabians to be the place where Abraham, not Isaac as in the Old Testament, had barely escaped death by fire. It was also thought to be the spot where Hagar left Ishmael to search for water.

The boy Muhammad was sickened by the polytheism of his day in Arabia. For him, even the Kaaba stone was being polluted by the worship of fairies and desert demons called jinns. He witnessed people gambling within the shadow of the Kaaba. This feeling of hatred toward false gods intensified when Muhammad went as part of camel caravans as a teenager. At age twenty-five, Muhammad married the wealthy widow Khadija. This afforded him some leisure for contemplation of spiritual values. He often went into the wilderness near Mecca to brood over the loss of his sons born to Khadija and over the sick polytheism of his day. A bright vision came to him one day near Mount Hira through the angel Gabriel. Gabriel told him that he was to be the prophet for Allah, the god, incidentally, who was the favored one of the Quraish tribe. From that day, Muhammad began to produce portions of the Islamic holy book, the Koran.

Muhammad went to the marketplace around the Kaaba stone and began to proclaim his message that there is no god but Allah. The people were mostly unconvinced and a few were even hostile. During the first four years of his proclamations, he had only forty converts, most of them from his own clan. During this time, Khadija died. Muhammad was anything but a success as a prophet of Allah at this time. Then a turning point came in his life. A small delegation came from Medina, a city three hundred miles north of Mecca. In 622, he went with a few dozen followers to Medina where he was welcomed as one who might unify that fragmented city. That trek is called the Hegira by modern Muslims and is the dividing point for the Islamic calendar.

Muhammad returned in military and religious triumph to Mecca in 630, entering the city with ten thousand marching men. He died two years later. Muhammad's life was a unifying force for the Arabians. He codified ethical behavior for them by outlawing child exposure, adultery, and gambling. He also had the Arabians focusing on the worship of the one true god, Allah. Muhammad convinced the people that he was the greatest prophet who had ever lived, surpassing Jesus, Moses, and all others. He also convinced his warriors that to die for him and Allah in a holy war, or jihad, would guarantee direct and immediate entrance into paradise.

By 635, the Muslim armies had conquered Damascus. The Holy City of Jerusalem fell in 638. All of Palestine and Syria was in Muslim hands by 640. By the next year all of Egypt was under the rule of Muhammad's followers. Iraq was under Islamic rule by 637 and by 649 all of Persia was theirs. By twenty years after the death of Muhammad, Muslims controlled almost all of Asia Minor.

In 732, the Franks under Charles Martel stopped the Muslim hordes at the Battle of Tours. Most historians see this as the most important battle in European history. All of Europe could now be under the control of Islam if that battle had turned out differently.

By far the largest negative factor in the growth of Christianity in the seventh century was the growth of its major religious competitor, Islam. Never again until the post-World War II growth of Communism was Christianity to lose so much territory so rapidly.

Saint Patrick's Legacy in Ireland

While Alaric was preparing his soldiers to enter Italy early in the fifth century, a teenage boy, Patrick, was captured by Irish raiders and carried off as a slave to Ireland to tend their flocks. Patrick (b. 389) was the grandson of British Christian landowners. He yearned to be back with family. After serving for six years as a slave in Ireland, Patrick escaped and entered a monastery off the southern coast of France. In 432, he was ordained a missionary bishop, and he went throughout Ireland preaching. Until his death in 461, he was tireless in his efforts to make Christians of the Irish. He was named Bishop of Ireland and, in turn, ordained monks and nuns from Irish stock. He was faithful, even though occasionally attacked by thieves and other armed enemies. Further, he was undaunted in spite of attacks from English raiders who kidnapped some of his new young converts. Indeed, the captives became missionaries to their captors.

Patrick was known for his outstanding energy and tact, two qualities still important in missionary service. He established so many monasteries with their presiding bishops that Ireland became known as the Isle of Saints. Ireland was never the same after the work of its adopted son and favorite saint. One lingering contribution was Patrick's emphasis on sending missionaries from Ireland to other fields. Under his influence, the converts became the converters.

Columba's Work in Scotland

The great sixth-century missionary to Scotland was Columba (521-597). In his middle years, he was a monk and founder of monasteries in Ireland, much in the pattern of Patrick. In 563 he moved to the island of Iona, off the coast of Scotland. There he took twelve disciples and set about to evangelize Scotland from the safety of his island hideaway, under the protection of the king of Dalriada.

Most of their work was among the Picts, who occupied the northern half of Scotland. Most of the Picts were won over to the gospel by the time of Columba's death. The island of Iona was as strong and powerful a missionary training center as had been set up by Christians anywhere up to that time. Hundreds of monks and thousands of pilgrims were given inspiration and trained in techniques to make them effective missionaries. This was particularly important because the Picts were a warlike people who practiced witchcraft and some human sacrifice. The Old Religion, or witchcraft, soon wilted before the advance of the gospel.

Columba's influence lived on far beyond the date of his death. A prince named Oswald was won to the faith by a disciple trained in Columba's center. Oswald then returned to triumph to Northumbria where he sent for a missionary from Iona to come and be a bishop. The new bishop trained the people of Northumbria in the Christian faith. That bishop's name was Aidan, who found an island off the coast of Northumbria and set up an Iona-like monastery.

Columba even had a namesake. He was Columbanus, or Columba the Younger (543-615). Columbanus was a monk of a monastery in Bangor. In 585 Columbanus set forth with twelve disciple-missionaries. They settled in Burgundy where he started a monastery and missionary training center similar to Iona. Later in life, Columbanus worked for a short time in northern Switzerland where he trained Gallus as an abbot. Columbanus died in northern Italy in 615, after having founded the Monastery of Bobbio a year earlier. Thus did Columba's influence live on after him.

Augustine in England

There was an Augustine important in mission history not to be confused with Augustine of Hippo. This Augustine was sent by Pope Gregory the Great to England in 596. Augustine was told to take along a group of monks. They became discouraged on their way to England and asked to be relieved of their commission. Persuaded by the pope to continue their journey, the monks were received with gladness and allowed to settle in Canterbury. There they lived a life of virtue and proclaimed the love of Christ. The king was converted, and Augustine presided over the baptism of ten thousand Saxons before his death.

Augustine is remembered today as the Jonah of sixth-century Christian missions. Although reluctant at first, he was eventually successful. He was named Archbishop of Canterbury with jurisdiction over Rochester and London. The pope also gave Augustine rule over York.

The pope in Rome gave Augustine instruction which was to prove important in subsequent mission strategy for the Church in England. Augustine was instructed to use the nature temples of the Old Religions as Christian worship centers after purifying them with holy water. The pope also told Augustine to convert to Christian festivals those dates being used as special by the followers of the Old Religion. This led to later charges that the Christian faith was only a veneer over the Old Religion in England.

The Old Religion

The early Christian missionaries in Ireland and England found a strong opponent for human allegiance in the Old Religion. It was a form of nature worship which the soldiers in the Roman legions wrongly labeled Druidism. Later they learned the truth that the Druids were simply the priests for the Old Religion.

The belief patterns of the Old Religion encountered by Patrick, Columba, and Augustine were ancient. They included these seven:

1. The physical world is only part of reality.
2. Each person has innate capacities through which he can contact the realms beyond the visible.
3. The masculine, patriarchal concept of God is bal-

anced with the idea of personified gods and god-desses.

4. The high God is the impersonal life force of the universe.
5. Morality is highly individualistic and is based mainly on the following of one's own natural desires.
6. Thought is powerful for potential in both good and evil. The mind holds the power of magic.
7. True practice of religion is wisdom, not simply the rationalization of it.

An ancient prayer to call up "great mother goddess" in the Old Religion is as follows:

> Listen to the words of the Great Mother. Once in a month and better let it be when in a full moon, meet in some secret place and adore me, who am the queen of all magics . . . . All in my praise, for I am a gracious goddess, who gives both joy upon earth, certainly, not faith, while in life, and upon death place unutterable, rest and the ecstasy of the goddess. Nor do I demand aught in sacrifice, for behold, I am the mother of all living, and my love is poured out upon the earth!

A lesser god in witchcraft was the "lord of the shadows." In the Old Religion, he was the chief male god due to return annually at the start of winter. This was marked by a celebration which has become modern Halloween. This prayer to the "lord of the shadows" is an ancient one:

> Dread Lord of the Shadows,
>   God of Life, and the Giver of Life
> Yet it is the knowledge of thee,
>   the knowledge of death.
> Open wide, I pray thee, the gates
>   through which all must pass.
> Let our dear ones who have gone before
> Return this night to make
>   merry with us.
> And when our time comes,
>   as it must,

O thou the Comforter, the Consoler,
  the Giver of Peace and rest,
We will enter the realms
  gladly and unafraid;
For we know that when rested and
Refreshed among our dear ones
We will be reborn again by thy grace,
And the grace of the Great Mother.

One can see from the depth of these prayers and the hope embodied in them that the practitioners of the Old Religion were not easy targets for Christian missions. This makes the work of the early Christian missionaries even more remarkable. Unfortunately, this also made the conversion to Christianity a partial one in many cases.

Willibrord in Holland and Belgium

Willibrord (658-739) was a monk who studied under Wilfrid at Ripon. He won the confidence of Pepin II, king of the Franks, and had his support throughout his ministry. Pepin asked Willibrord and his twelve disciples to start work at Utrecht. Later Willibrord was made bishop of Utrecht. In 695, he traveled to Rome to receive that title.

For Willibrord, as in the case of most successful Christian missionaries of the seventh century, monasteries were the center of his missions strategy. He founded four monasteries—at Utrecht, Antwerp, Echternach, and Susteren. At all four places, Willibrord trained disciples in the arts of prayer and discipline. By the time of Willibrord's death, the Church had a foothold in what is now known as Holland and Belgium.

Boniface: Apostle to Germany

The greatest and most successful of the missionaries trained by Willibrord was Boniface (680-754). He is often called "the apostle to Germany." He spent the first forty years of his life under the tutelage of Willibrord and other teachers in a monastery. During this period, he wrote that his love for Christ was mixed with a desire for foreign travel.

In 722, Boniface was summoned to Rome and was ordained by Pope Gregory II as bishop for the German frontier without the benefit of a specific local support zone. While in Rome, Boniface was impressed with the strategy of filling converts in the new churches with an unswerving allegiance to Rome and the papacy. This was a relatively new idea in missions and became of great importance later in European missions.

Returning to Germany, Boniface made Thuringia his first center. He refused the papal offer to succeed Willibrord as bishop of Utrecht; he set out instead to evangelize Hesse. He was true to his oath to bind the new German Christians to the pope. He made each newly baptized convert swear this oath:

> I vow to thee, the first of the apostles, to thy vicar, Pope Gregory and his successors, that, with God's help, I will continue in the unity of the Catholic faith, . . . in close adherence to the usages of thy church.

Boniface was above all a Roman representative and wanted to burn himself out for the glory of the Church. He wrote to a Christian friend in England, "Since I am the last and most unworthy of all the messengers which the Romish Church has sent out for the publication of the gospel, may I not die without having brought forth fruit."

When Boniface began doing missions in Germany with earnestness in 724, he found that many of his early converts had returned to the worship of Thor, the Germanic god of thunder. Boniface determined to strike a blow for the Lord God Jehovah much in the style that Elijah had done with the prophets of Baal at Mount Carmel. In the presence of tens of thousands of angry Thor worshipers and half-converted Christians, Boniface chopped down the sacred grove of Thor in Hesse. The mighty tree crashed to the ground. Boniface was not stricken dead by lightning.

The people shouted, "The Lord, he is God." Later, a Christian church was built on that spot where Boniface presided over the baptism of ten thousand converts that same day.

Boniface was also effective in soliciting help from the churches in England. He wrote a circular letter which read, in part, "Have pity on the pagan Saxons." Multitudes of monks from English monasteries came to the German forests following Boniface's urging.

In 744, Boniface was called upon by the pope to execute a reform in the churches of the Franks. Boniface reported, after a brief survey:

> Religion is trodden under foot. Benefices are given to greedy laymen, or to unchaste and publican clerks. All their crimes do not prevent their attaining the priesthood; at last, rising in rank as they increase in sin, they become bishops.

Boniface called a series of councils to impose a series of reforms on the Frankish churches. These succeeded in removing the worst of the abuses.

Never one to give in to old age, Boniface went in 753 to the far side of the Zuider Zee, where the native Frisians were still nature worshipers. There was a great negative reaction when Boniface and his disciples arrived. Boniface and his party were finally attacked in 754 and killed. Boniface was holding a copy of the four Gospels in an attempt to stop the slaughter. That act was ineffective. Boniface died with fifty others.

The Benedictines

Benedict of Nursia (480-543) is often called the "patriarch of Western Monasticism." He set up a monastery at Mount Cassino, from which he could see the white pillars of the temple of Apollo. He transformed the old Apollo temple to a place of Christian worship and a simple monastery.

Benedict devised a rule for daily monastery life that was

soon adopted by most monks in Italy. The rule was taken to England by Augustine where it clashed somewhat with the orders of Columba and Iona.

Born at Nursia, Benedict retreated to the mountains of northern Italy to contemplate the immorality of his day. He established twelve monasteries near Rome and was regarded as a great counselor and instructor of youth.

Benedict wrote his "Rule of Life" which called for a disciplined soul, mind, and body. Each monk was to dig in the soil, read books, say his prayers, and eat only simple and nourishing food on a daily basis. The abbot was to be given complete obedience. As the prologue to the rule stated,

> If we wish to escape the punishment of hell, and attain to eternal life, we must so walk and so live only as to fit ourselves to eternity . . . that we may be worthy to be partakers in His kingdom.

The key person in Benedict's rule was the abbot. The whole group of monks was to choose him on the basis of obvious merit. The abbot was, however, instructed to rule with compassion and consideration. He was to deal gently but without compromise on any matter dealing with moral vice. The abbot could, according to Benedict, increase discipline by demanding even greater daily discipline in matters of food, drink, and sleep. The abbot had supreme authority in all matters of possible controversy.

Benedict made sure that one could not easily or flippantly join one of his monasteries. The potential initiate had to wait five days for an answer when he first came to the door of the monastery. At the end of a year, the rules were read to him and he could refuse to accept the conditions even at that point.

Daily discipline in a sixth-century Benedictine monastery was rigid by any standards. The monks were not allowed to own anything. All possessions were shared according to need. The day was rigidly divided to allow for a balance between work, study, sleep, and worship. There were only two daily meals. Each was accompanied by another monk's reading of the Bible or other devotional work. No meat was allowed except in the case of extreme illness. Fasts were called for by the abbot frequently. Silence was required at all times, even in the times of such emergencies as a fire.

The monks who proved disobedient were excommunicated without question after three warnings. The recalcitrant ones might be whipped. If all failed, they were expelled. A few applied for reentry, but the excommunication was usually final.

Benedict thus gave to the Church a most effective missionary tool. The monastery proved to be an effective spreader of learning, art, and disciplined worship in dark days. It was a ray of light for the Light of the world. In an age of disorder caused by threats within and without the Church, the Benedictine monasteries were centers of quiet, disciplined living, and gave the stability to the churches of the sixth and seventh centuries which they needed so desperately. The monks were effective missionaries for the Church.

Charlemagne

The Carolingian rulers had control in the seventh and eighth centuries over portions of what is known today as France, Belgium, Switzerland, Austria, and half of Italy. Charles the Great, or Charlemagne, and his brother took over that province from their father Pepin in 768. Charlemagne became sole ruler in 771. When he died in 814, Charlemagne had ruled for almost fifty years. His official coronation took place on Christmas Day in 800.

Charlemagne saw himself as ruling by Christian principles. He was a friend of the Church and was active in the improvement of that institution. He established monasteries whenever he conquered people and territories. Charlemagne also called and presided over synods and took a great personal interest in them. Even though he was illiterate, he deemed himself to be a theologian and took an active part in the debates at the synods.

Charlemagne also encouraged the repair and construction of churches and the reform of liturgy. He even told the clergy what to preach, especially on such matters as the keeping of the Ten Commandments.

Although unable to read and write, Charlemagne stressed the education of the clergy. He brought teachers from all over Europe to his monasteries. The most famous of these traveling scholars was Bede, the Venerable. Bede was interested in languages and writing. He wrote on many subjects but is remembered most for his ecclesiastical history of England. This work became the classic source of Christian records of this period.

Charlemagne treated the popes with respect. He sought to make his subjects follow strict religious laws to honor the papacy. He decreed the death penalty for eating meat during Lent or refusing to be baptized. Charlemagne also supervised the death penalty for killing a priest, bishop, or deacon or eating the flesh of a witch or demoniac.

Monastery residents under Charlemagne were forbidden to participate in gluttony, fornication, sodomy, or favoritism in promotions. He had an extensive system of reporting. Laymen were hired to investigate and report to him any injustices or disobedience.

Charlemagne is important to the history of missions, however, for another set of reasons. A historian of the times said, "He converted a greater part of the people to a faith in Christ, partly by the sword, partly by persuasion and partly through gifts."

Alcuin, paid by Charlemagne to be one his traveling scholars, was nonetheless one of his most severe critics. Alcuin condemned his king plainly for forced conversion. He wrote, "No grown-up person should be baptized until he has learned and accepted the truths of the Christian faith."

In spite of the criticism he received for merely nominal converts among his contemporaries, Charlemagne did sponsor the spread of the gospel into Scandinavia. This was in spite of fierce resistance to the spread of the Christian faith, especially by the Danes. The Danes built a wall across the Isthmus of Seesvig.

Actually it was Charlemagne's influence after his death that led to the conversion of the Scandinavians. Merchants at Birka in Sweden asked that a group of Christian missionaries be sent to them. King Bjorn received the missionaries with openness. He encouraged them to build a church, the first in Scandinavia.

The Byzantine Church

Justinian I reigned from Constantinople from 527 to 565, dying when an old man. He is remembered as being intelligent and industrious. Justinian was married to Theodora. She, too, was a person of great force. Theodora is remembered as a great reformer, especially for witnessing to the many prostitutes of Constantinople and surrounding territories. She founded convents to aid in the readjustment to life by former prostitutes.

Justinian was a great builder. He built roads and palaces. Most remembered is the famous Santa Sophia, the cathedral church in Constantinople. Justinian was deeply interested in theology. He did theology by condemning heresy. In 544, the Emperor Justinian issued a decree condemning Nestorianism, or the idea that there were two distinct natures in Christ with little interaction. When the edict was issued, Pope Vigilius of Rome vacillated on the issue. To settle the issue, Justinian called the Fifth Ecumenical Council. It met in Constantinople in 553. Much to the chagrin of Justinian, the council did not restore unity to the Church.

When the council failed, Justinian turned to force. He enacted new legislation to rid the empire of nature worship. He closed the pagan schools of philosophy in Athens.

But when Justinian died in 565, there was anything but unity in the East.

Justinian did, however, issue a number of laws dealing with the election of bishops, public worship, and the morals of the clergy. The bishops were given unprecedent power, dealing even with matters of secular polity.

Nonetheless, the Eastern and Western portions of the Church continued to drift apart. Both a cause and effect of the split was the council held in Constantinople in 692. The council members decreed, "The see of Constantinople shall enjoy equal privilege with the see of Old Rome . . . and second after it." This council was a clear sign of the widening gap between the Eastern and Western Churches.

The Eastern Church in the eighth century was torn by the iconoclastic controversy. The fight broke out in 726 and raged on into the ninth century. Emperor Leo III stirred the controversy, primarily out of a motive of religious reform. He set out to remove the icons, or images, in the churches of the East because he saw them as idolatry. Monks countered by arguing that the images were aids, not hindrances, to worship.

The Christians who supported the emperor's argument believed that most forms of Christian art were of the devil. They declared that "the only admissable figure of the humanity of Christ . . . is the bread and wine in the Holy Supper." Further, they argued that "to make the likeness of anything draws down the spirit of man from the lofty worship of God to the law and material worship of the creature."

Leo III issued an edict against the use of icons in 725. In 730, he called a council to invoke further measures against the icons. The Patriarch of Constantinople was deposed for failing to concur. Gregory III, the last pope of Rome to have election confirmed by an emperor from Constantinople, called a council to excommunicate those who supported Leo III.

When the icon controversy was settled, the effect was a lasting division between the Eastern and Western Christians. In practice, after 843 the Greek portion of the Church did not use sculptured figures, only one-dimensional representations of the holy family. The Church was split on the matter of icons.

The Vikings

The monks at Iona were attacked by the Vikings, those pirates from Scandinavia, in the middle of the ninth century. Forty monks were slain in front of the altar at the abbey. Then the marauding Vikings went to Lindisfarne and destroyed the monastery there, killing and looting as they went. The Vikings killed so many monks and missionaries in the remainder of the ninth century that they severely dented the earlier mission efforts of Columba and Boniface. The monasteries were easy and lucrative targets. The defenseless monks died by the hundreds.

But, the tide soon turned. In 878, a Saxon king of southern England, Alfred the Great, conquered a large invading Viking army and forced all the soldiers to convert to Christianity. The Vikings of that army then settled in England. By 1000, the Vikings had given three archbishops to the churches of England. The Viking terror was somewhat abated by the gospel.

There was a dramatic interchange between the Viking and English Christians during the ninth century. At the very time plundering armies of Vikings were pillaging the English countryside, the Christians of England were sending missionaries to Scandinavia.

Anskar: Prayer and Power

The most notable mission pioneer among the Vikings home territory was Anskar (801-865). He was born of Saxon stock in Flanders. Louis, the Pious, was the son of Charlemagne and a devout Christian emperor. Louis desired to spread his Frankish rule, and incidentally Christianity as well. He chose Anskar, who was being trained in a French convent near Armiens, to venture into Viking territory for the crown and the cross.

Anskar later wrote,

> When I was asked whether I would go for God's name among the heathen to publish the gospel, I could not decline such a call. Yes, with all my power I wish to go hence, and no man can make me waver in my resolution.

Anskar sailed with only one companion and headed for Sweden. They were attacked by Vikings along the way, but at last Anskar reached the court of Sweden's king. There he was accepted and eventually led dozens of nobles to faith in Christ.

The pope in Rome and King Louis, the Pious, made Anskar their vicar in all of Scandinavia. Anskar then opened in Schleswig a school to train young men for the ministry. Anskar is remembered for his courage, commitment, and depth of understanding of the Christian faith. He traveled widely. He set up a temporary training center in Sweden on Milar Lake. His nephew, Gauzbert, was named the first bishop in Sweden. He aroused the nature-worshiping Normans who sacked Hamburg and tried to expel all Christians from Sweden. This did not deter Anskar in his task.

Anskar persuaded King Horik of Denmark to let him build a church in his territory. When this task was completed, Anskar then reentered Sweden. The king of Sweden had lots cast before the nature gods to see if Anskar could preach the gospel in the Swedish court again. The lots answered in the affirmative. Then Anskar returned to Hamburg to train hundreds of young men to go to Sweden with the gospel. In the meantime, he opened a hospital in Bremen. Tales of miraculous healing at that hospital spread throughout Scandinavia. Anskar tried to disclaim such power, stating, "If I were thought worthy before my

God of that, I would beseech Him to grant me this miracle, that by His grace he would make me a holy man." He was also known as a friend to the slaves. He died in 865, urging his students to work hard to bring all Scandinavia to bow before Christ.

Anskar is significant in mission history because he is remembered as a medical missionary, friend to slaves and kings alike, and trainer of young missionaries to assume his task after his death. As the first specifically medical missionary, Anskar set the tone for the complete missionary, one who brings care for the total person along with the gospel.

Olaf Tryggvesson

The Viking Olaf Tryggvesson (969-1000) has been called the "Northern Muhammad" because of his violent attempts to rid Norway of nature worship. Many kings of Norway, reared in English Christianity, wanted to bring their people to faith in Christ. Such a person was Olaf Tryggvesson. He was born in Norway of a royal family but was captured by Vikings and sold as a slave. He was captured by other Vikings and as a young man helped those Vikings raid parts of England. There he was converted. He was then confirmed as a Christian by the Bishop of Winchester. In 995, he sailed to Norway with English priests and was soon elected king.

Olaf Tryggvesson brought his Viking tenacity into his Christianity and exiled or killed any of his subjects who refused to convert to the faith. His motto was "Baptism or Battle." By the last year of the tenth century, he had removed almost all opposition to Christianity in Norway. However, the king was creating ill will all across Norway. In the year 1000, he was trapped by a Danish and Swedish army of nature worshipers and swam into the sea rather than surrender.

His namesake, Olaf the Saint, entered Norway from England in 1015. He was able to bring all of Scandinavia under one rule and virtually eliminate the worship of Thor. Olaf the Saint was killed in battle in 1030 and has since been known as the patron saint of Norway. By that time, the Christian faith had a toehold in Scandinavia. In 1104, Denmark had an archbishop. That nation was followed in such an honor by Norway in 1152 and Sweden in 1164. Scandinavia was, therefore, nominally Christian by the end of the twelfth century, although there were still whole regions where the gospel was still unknown.

The Crusades: Triumph and Tragedy

The Crusades were launched in earnest with these words by Pope Urban II in the year 1095.

> All the world of Christianity is in dire peril. Stop fighting each other here in Europe. Go out shoulder to shoulder and fight the infidel. Go, recover the birthplace of our Lord in Bethlehem and his tomb in Jerusalem. To all who go I will give full absolution for all their sins and assurance of entrance into heaven.

"God wills it" was the war cry with which the brave Christians of Europe tried to recover from the Muslims the holy places in Palestine. Thousands were to die in that effort. However, one major impetus to missions came out of the Crusades. Heretofore ignorant Christians became aware of the foreign lands and faiths of the East and Middle East. This knowledge led later to the limited spread of the gospel into Muslim territory. These Christian gains were only temporary. Within fifty years, the Turks had reconquered most of Palestine.

The Crusades gave rise to military orders. The greatest of these were the Templars. They got their name because they were given quarters near the site of Solomon's Temple. They were founded by Hugo de Payens in 1119. The orders were set up on the model of the religious orders but

with the additional vows of fighting against infidels, protecting pilgrims, and defending the Holy Land.

These military orders gave rise to a kind of mind-set
which permeates mission societies today. Anyone who
could not join one of the orders was urged to give money
or pray for the warriors themselves. In that way, even those
who never joined an order felt themselves to be a part of
the movement. This missions-by-proxy has been a blessing
and curse in subsequent mission effort for the church.

The Crusades made no permanent impact on Christian
holdings in Palestine. The Crusades did not long deter the
spread of Islam in Asia Minor and the Middle East. Thousands of Christian and Muslim lives were lost.

The Crusades, however, were not a total loss for the
cause of Christian missions. They did unite the West and
prevent the takeover of all of eastern Europe by the followers of Muhammad. Knighthood orders were started to provide a necessary defense of the faith on into the fourteenth
century. Europe after the Crusades was awake to the reali-
ties of Islam and the possibility of mission effort across
newly discovered trade routes.

Vladimir's Baptism: A Turning Point

Vladimir I reigned in the Russian city of Kiev from 978-
1015. He was the grandson of Vikings who had looted the
area. An ancient Russian writing *The Chronicle of Nestor* tells
of the time Vladimir sent envoys in different directions to
test Islam, Judaism, and Christianity. He was determined
to adopt for his subjects that religion which he found most
suitable. Islam did not impress the envoys favorably at all.
They then traveled to the Khazors, the only example of a
people in that part of the world who had adopted Judaism.
They did not find Judaism attractive. The envoys then
traveled to Constantinople. There they found their answer
in the pomp and ceremony of the Eastern Church's worship forms. They reported to Vladimir.

> We did not know whether we were in heaven or on the earth. It would be impossible to find on earth any splendor greater than this . . . . Never shall we be able to forget so great a beauty.

The beautiful Cathedral of Santa Sophia was the scene. The envoys were impressed. The gold and mosaics, the chanting choirs, and the colorful vestments of the clergy filled the envoys with awe.

When Vladimir decided to adopt Christianity for his Russian people, it had far-reaching consequences. Vladimir went to work to spread Christianity throughout his provinces with four different methods. First, he destroyed the nature worship altars in Kiev. Second, Vladimir forced his subjects to be baptized into the church en mass in the nearby rivers. Third, he constructed church buildings and monasteries. Finally, and most important, the king sent missionaries to the rural dwellers. These methods were most effective, and Vladimir soon saw a Christian Russia.

After Vladimir's death, his son Yaroslav opted for a continuation of the Eastern form of Christianity in Russia. Yaroslav structured the church music in Russia in the Eastern tradition. This had lasting impact. The Christian faith was spread throughout Russia in the eleventh century mainly by Greek missionaries. Soon all the bishops and most of the clergy were Greeks. The work was spread by the Russian-recruited Greeks to Moscow and Novgorod. As they went, they spread Christian concepts of architecture from Constantinople. The tragedy was that the local Russian parish priests were uneducated in the faith except for the performing of the sacraments.

In spite of this early weakness, Russian Orthodoxy grew. Nowhere in the world was there created a greater welding of the belief that the church and the nation were to be one. Vladimir is remembered as the instigator of that phenomenon.

Boleslav, the Brave, of Poland

In 969, Boleslav II of Bohemia created a bishopric for Poland in the city of Pasen. This gave some early impetus to Christianity there.

The man most responsible for the growth of Polish Christianity was Boleslav I, the Brave, who ruled Poland from 992 to 1025. He encouraged missionaries, especially those from Bohemia and Germany. This early attempt to establish a sound Christian faith in Poland failed, however, mainly because of a failure to train qualified local bishops. Poland stands as an early lesson in how not to do missions. Rule from the outside does not have the lasting effect for the church as does the equipping of native leadership.

The Impact of Islam

The churches of East and West about 1200 had been greatly affected by Islam. In most of Asia, a majority of the Christians were either slain by Muslims or converted to Islam. In Persia, the kings were hostile to Christianity because they saw it as the religion of their enemy, the emperor in Constantinople.

In Egypt, the Coptic church survived the Muslim onslaught because the church was filled with architects and artisans willing to work for the Muslim invaders. However, large numbers of Egyptian Christians embraced Islam because it was the expedient thing to do.

The churches in Carthage and beyond gave way to Islam more than in any other part of the Christian world. The invaders found little resistance from the churches there, largely because the Christians were divided into so many rival factions.

In any land where Islam was the conquering force, Christianity was in deep trouble. No Christian was allowed to do missionary work, to ring church bells as a call to worship, or to propagate the faith among Muslims or even non-Muslims. The churches were shut off from all power of self-expression. Huge hunks of Christian territory were lost in the Muslim advance and have never been recovered by Christian missionaries. The Church was never to be the same.

The Church about 1200 was a house divided. Gradually power had shifted from Rome to Constantinople, and the final break began with the iconoclastic controversy of the eighth century. There was little unity between emperor and pope or even between pope and the patriarch of Constantinople. The fledgling unity which was beginning to be felt in 500 had now virtually disappeared. The Catholic Church was splitting, a contradiction in terms and nature.

But, the Christian churches were not without bright spots in 1200. The monks were the backbone of the missionary effort as they spread the gospel with their accompanying emphasis on discipline and education. They did well by the Church. There were outstanding courageous individuals during the three centuries prior to 1200. Their influence was still being felt in far-reaching regions of the empire. Patrick, Columba, and Boniface had left an impact never to be forgotten in Ireland, Scotland, and Germany. Europe was to be at least nominally Christian in the wake of their efforts.

The church in 1200, then, was beset from within by disunity and from without by Islam's incursions. From within it was finding the strength for more than survival. The cause of Christ was advancing.

Christianity About AD 1200: Fightings and Frustrations

By the year 1200, Christianity had won the nominal allegiance of most of the people of northwest and central Europe. Russia was Christian in the Eastern Orthodox tradition. The Christians were spread geographically into most of Europe and Asia, including the China coast. Christianity was definitely in a period of geographical expansion.

But, the Church had effected a trade-off which would prove costly later. In all the territories, the Church was controlled to some degree by the kings and nobles. Secular rulers were in positions to make or break the Church. Nominal discipleship was helping to make this possible.

Fightings were still taking place between the Eastern and Western churches. Russia was apparently given over to Eastern Orthodoxy, but Poland, Bohemia, and other Slavic states were still for the taking. The Eastern Church was frustrated by the stubborn refusal of most Muslims to convert and were turning north to seek more communicants. Different groups within the Western Church were still fighting among themselves for such prizes as Scandinavia. The popes were being controlled even more by such rulers as the emperors of the Holy Roman Empire.

These were bad times for the Church. They were also good times. Persons were emerging from the rubble of nominal Christianity to become examples of Christian virtues. Such men as Francis of Assisi were about to make their influence felt. The Dark Ages were passing away, for the world and the Church. The power of the gospel was still there, smoldering among the ruins of the fighting and frustrations for the bride of Christ. A great new day was about to dawn for missions.

Case Study: Bernard of Menthon, Rich for Poor

Bernard of Menthon (923-1008) was born into a rich family of noble blood. In his teen years, he refused an honorable marriage urged upon him by his parents. Instead, he received ordination into the clergy. He started a monastery near the southern end of a major pass through the Alps. Bernard won hundreds of people to Christian faith from among the residents and travelers there.

Questions

1. Why is it so difficult to contemplate giving up worldly possessions for missionary service?

2. What are the trade-offs when one does so?
3. Is it more important to be remembered or to be an humble minister?
4. What areas do you know where a kind of ministry to tourists can be done?
5. Bernard risked the ire of his parents to do mission service. Is this morally correct? Why?

Time Line: AD 500-1200

500?	Baptism of Clovis
542	Benedict of Nursia died
550	
597	Columba died
600	
632	Muhammad died
650	
700	
732	Battle of Tours
750	
754	Boniface died
800	
850	
900	
950	
1000	
1016	Knut made king of Denmark
1050	
1096	Crusades begin
1100	
1119	Templars founded
1139	Otto of Bamberg died
1150	
1153	Bernard of Clairvaux
1200	

4
Fragmentation, Failure, and Success:
AD 1200-1500

The beginning of the thirteenth century was one of great anticipation for the churches of Europe. Great movements of renewal were about to occur from many sources. People who were despairing of the future of European Christianity at this time would have lost that despair if they could have seen the future.

Monks and Renewal

Monastic life fell to a low level in the tenth century. Monasteries by the dozens lay in ruins. Hundreds of monks were killed by invading Vikings and other powerful forces. As the thirteenth century dawned, however, new forms of monasticism were beginning to emerge. They were to stress ideals of poverty, chastity, and living with possessions shared in common. Even more important, monks were to be missionaries to remote regions of the globe.

Cities and their growth greatly aided the growth of vitality in the old and new orders. The orders were now unable and unwilling to be found only in the deserts. They wanted to minister where large numbers of humanity were to be found. The orders which blossomed in the thirteenth century were to bring renewal to the Church through specialized ministries, such as teaching and nursing. The Church was on the march through the least likely of soldiers, those who stressed the conquering power of love.

The Franciscans

Francis was born in 1182 in Assisi. It was a time and place of great slavery. Most of the people were either enslaved to the land or to each other. If a serf did not produce the quota his lord had set, his possessions could be confiscated. Numbers of serfs tried to go to local courts to disprove the obligations claimed by the lords. Most of the time the serfs lost.

Saint Francis's father Pedro Bernardone was an exceedingly rich cloth merchant and one of the most prominent citizens of Assisi. He profited from the fact that Assisi was located on a major trade route. The elder Bernardone was described by one of his peers as, "Dominated solely by the instinct of lucre, master of swindles and interested always in increasing his business."

Francis entered school at the Church of San Giorgia, run by the rulers of the cathedral at Assisi. A biographer, Thomas of Celano, wrote of Francis's early life:

> From his earlier years he was brought up by his parents proud of spirit, in accordance with the vanity of the world; and imitating their wretched life and habits for a long time, he became even more vain and proud.

Francis became a tradesman at age thirteen. At age fourteen, he was initiated by his father into the cloth trade. Despite his inherited wealth, Francis was moved by the plight of the poor. Beggars often came by his shop. They wept as they asked for food. A turning point came one day when Francis was busy with the matters of the day. He sent a poor man away without food. He later wrote:

> If that poor man had come in the name of some count or baron, certainly I would have listened to him. How much I should have done, then, seeing that he spoke to me in the name of the King of kings.

Assisi was known as a city of pleasure and parties. Thomas of Celano wrote of Francis:

He was the admiration of all and strove to outdo the rest in the pomp of vainglory, in jokes, in strange doings, in idle and useless talk, in soft and flowing garments, for he was very rich.

In 1202, in battle with Perugia, Francis and hundreds of other young warriors from Assisi were taken prisoner. It was a turning point in his life. In a semiconscious state, Francis had a dream. In the midst of it his friends in the cell heard him say, "The men of Perugia have done many evil things to their neighbors, and their hearts are filled with ignominy. However, the revenge of the Lord is approaching and his hand is on his sword."

When the war was over and he had been released, Francis returned to Perugia on a festival day and gave the warning he had seen in his dream, plus many more. He said, "The lord has glorified you above all neighbors. . . . Yet your heart is puffed up with arrogance, audacity and pride . . . . Wrath will teach you, for kindness has not taught you."

There was a truce declared between Assisi and Perugia in 1203. Francis gained strength after the war. In 1206, he went on a pilgrimage to Rome. There he saw a large number of poor. On his way home he met a leper and was greatly moved with compassion. Suddenly the leper disappeared. Francis took it as a sign. His whole world was now changed. He would work for and with the poor. His life of meditation was beginning. He put aside his rich velvet mantle and took one that was torn and old.

The name of Francis's first companion is lost in history. However, Francis chose another from Assisi, Giles, to go with him on his first recruiting journey. Often Francis would stop and say to those along the way, "Love and fear God and make worthy penitence for your sins." Francis's first rule for his companions was to "pay no heed to money, whenever you find it, any more than you would to the dust under your feet."

In 1209, the noble Francis went to visit Pope Innocent III. He wanted the approval of the powerful pope to start a new order of monks. Innocent objected when he heard the stringent requirements Francis would have for the new order. Francis replied that total poverty could only come as a gift from Christ. Innocent told Francis and his small party to pray about their decision to know God's will. The pope later ruled in Francis's favor.

Francis returned happily to Assisi and started a small monastery where his followers lived in bliss. Francis taught them patience and humility. Francis began to preach in the countryside. One of his peers said, "His heavenly words seemed like sharp arrows shot from the bow of divine wisdom; they pierced the hearts of everyone."

Every day in 1210 more citizens dropped out of their life of the world to join Francis and increase his small company. The crowds that gathered to hear him every Sunday at the cathedral of San Rufino grew rapidly.

Francis spent from 1212 to 1215 on the road. While traveling, he was credited with healing lepers and aiding the poor. Now Francis had followers of his order spread all over Europe. He called for the first of annual international gathering in 1216. These meetings were called "chapters."

In the 1217 chapter meeting, Francis officially ordained missionaries to go to Constantinople, Egypt, Syria, and Palestine. From the chapter meeting of the next year, Francis sent missionaries to Tunisia and Greece. From the 1219 meeting, Francis sent six volunteers to Morocco. On that occasion, Francis gave this missionary advice:

> My dear sons, so that you may better fulfill the commandment of God, look to the health of your souls and see that there is peace and concord and a link in indissoluble charity among you. Flee from envy. . . . Be patient in tribulation, humble in success, and thus always in battle be the victors. Be imitators of Christ in poverty, obedience and chastity.

In 1221, Francis formulated some rules for the journey which were to guide all Franciscan missionaries of the future. Rule number 1 was to take nothing for the journey. Rule 2 was that money is worse than mud, and the friars were to consider it as dung. He said more on that subject, "If any of the friars collects or keeps money, except for the needs of the sick, the others must regard him as a fraud and a thief and a robber and a traitor." Francis continued, "Having food and sufficient clothing, with these let us be content."

For Francis, chivalry required and produced joy. He said, "The knight must be joyous because this is the life of warriors: happiness in the field and joy in the castle." For Francis, sadness was an illness of the soul. "Then the Devil rejoices most when we can snatch away spiritual joy from a servant of God."

Francis was perhaps most remarkable for his love of the birds. He once addressed them:

> My little bird sisters, you are much to God your Creator, and you must always and everywhere praise him, because He has given you freedom to fly anywhere . . . and your food is ready without your working for it, and your singing that was taught to you by the Creator.

Francis knew he was dying and prepared himself for the last farewell. As he lay dying, he called his brothers, and they knelt around him. His eyes were dim but he took time to bless them: "May the Lord be mindful of your work and your labor, and may a share be reserved for you in the reward of the just. May you find every blessing you desire."

Francis died and was buried in sackcloth, a sign of his eternal vow of poverty.

Francis is remembered as founder of the Order of Little Brothers, or the Franciscans. They are still known as caring, intellectual ministers to the poor and sick. The sacrificial life of Francis had set Christian missions ahead considerably. He encouraged women to join his order. He gave specific instructions to missionaries. Above all he helped to wed the Christian faith to all of creation. His was an unforgettable life.

The Dominicans

The Dominicans, or Preaching Brothers, also arose early in the thirteenth century. However, there were great dissimilarities between the Franciscans and the Dominicans. The Dominicans were greatly concerned about scholarship and teaching. They were the seedbed for Thomas Aquinas. The Dominicans came mainly from the wealthy classes, as an antisecular university movement.

Dominic was not as colorful a character as Francis. He was born in 1170 in Castile and was an older contemporary of Francis. Dominic is remembered primarily for his disciplined scholarship. In his early thirties, Dominic was shocked by his visit to southern France where he saw moral corruption and ignorance among laity and clergy alike. With his bishop, Diego, Dominic started a nunnery near Toulouse in 1206. Dominic and Diego trained and sent dozens of missionaries to southern France. In 1215, Dominic moved to Toulouse and set up a house with his followers. That same year Dominic decided to get approval for a new order from Pope Innocent III. It was the approving pope who suggested the title of the Preaching Brothers.

Dominic met Francis in Rome in 1218 and even attended the general chapter meeting of the Brothers Minor that year. Dominic died in 1221. By that time his order already had sixty houses. The order is remembered today as having teachers with greatly disciplined minds. They have produced hundreds of outstanding scholars through the centuries. That scholarship, however, was always for the purpose of training missionaries to the masses.

The Carmelites

In the twelfth century, a few pilgrim Crusaders stayed at Mount Carmel where Elijah had his successful contest with the prophets of Baal. By 1210, those pilgrims were given official sanction and a rule to follow by the Patriarch of Jerusalem.

When the Muslims recaptured Palestine, the Carmelites scattered. Many went to Cyprus where they found refuge. In 1229, the Carmelites got papal recognition as beggars. Simon Stock became ruler of the order in 1247 and led most of the monks to study in emulation of the Dominicans. The Carmelites began to frequent the universities of Europe. There the Carmelites were able to make their most lasting contribution, along with the Dominicans.

All in all, the new monastic orders of the thirteenth century pumped new life into Western Christianity. The discipline therein rubbed off on other movements, even some denounced as heretical in the decades to follow. The emphasis on the intellectual side of Christian commitment gave cause for Christian scholars to influence the religious and secular universities of Europe in the two centuries before the Reformation. Anselm, Abelard, and Aquinas were heirs of the monastic movements. They made Christian conversion more intelligent and committed, especially among the literate. The aristocracy could not escape this academic emphasis, plus the constant reminder of their obligation to the pope.

The monastic movement of the thirteenth century also demonstrated the room for a variety of expressions of the Christian faith. Here, unknown to the monks, were the roots of the Reformation, in such matters as freedom of choice in life-style and types of discipleship. The movement also gave rise to a deeper consideration among the masses for the working out of individual salvation. One did not have to profess Christianity merely because one's king had demanded it. There was the choice of deeper discipleship.

The monastic movement raised the consciousness of Christians to missions. Monks were dispatched with specific instructions to regions uncharted. The products of those mission efforts were finally grateful for the abbots and clerics who had an expanding vision. The journey inward brought the inevitable journey out of the monastery. The pattern was set for the great Spanish, Italian, and Portuguese conquests of the fifteenth century to follow.

The Heretics

Other reform movements (that is, nonmonastic), arose also during the thirteenth and fourteenth centuries. They were made possible by the mass conversions to Christianity in Europe of an earlier age. There was an obvious need for deeper discipleship for the laity and extensive reform of the clergy.

The Waldenses

Peter Waldo (d. 1218) preached a simple, Sermon-on-the-Mount kind of religion. This led him to criticize the pope and bishops for not being "poor in spirit." Peter was a wealthy merchant of Lyons who was much impressed with the self-denial of Saint Alexis, who lived for many years as a beggar under his parents' porch. Waldo became convicted about the size of his wealth, sold all his goods, left enough for his wife and family, and started a career as a traveling beggar and preacher. He lived by the rule based on Matthew 19:21: "If thou wouldst be perfect, go, sell that thou hast, and give to the poor and thou shalt have treasure in heaven, and come, follow me."

Waldo was a powerful preacher largely because he had memorized huge portions of the New Testament. Large crowds, including a handful of full-time followers, flocked to hear him preach. Waldo went to Rome during the Third Lateran Council and sought official sanction for his efforts. He was accompanied by his followers, who were called the "Poor in Spirit." Pope Alexander III praised Waldo for taking the vow of poverty but reminded him that he must preach only under local clerical supervision. The local clergy of Lyons refused to give Waldo permission to preach in public. The leader of the "Poor in Spirit" charged that this was the voice of man not God. He and his followers continued preaching in defiance of the order. In 1184, the Council of Verona excommunicated the Waldenses. The Waldenses then quickly spread into Northern Italy and Germany. They became famous for preaching on mission tours two by two and rejected all oaths and wars. Ecclesiastical persecution drove them to develop strong communities where they held possessions in common and commissioned some to be missionaries while others worked to support them. They were persecuted by the papacy, and some were burned at the stake. Those who were caught even listening to their sermons could have their property confiscated.

The Waldenses were remembered by their contemporaries as being humble people, temperate, sober, truthful, and avoiding the accumulation of wealth. They were respected even by their neighbors who chose to remain faithful to the papacy.

The Waldenses were joined by the Humiliati, who were active in the Milan area. They were excommunicated in 1184 by Pope Lucius III for disobedience to Pope Alexander III. They went about preaching under the shaky protection of the Waldenses, clad only in simple wool robes and begging for their food. They fasted on Mondays, Wednesdays, and Fridays. They defended lay preaching by both men and women. The Humiliati were gladly received by the Waldenses.

The Waldenses did not start out as heretics but were forced to be so by the pope. They were forerunners of all mission societies who stress freedom of religion and the necessity of evangelization. The Waldenses still exist today in the area of Turin and around Valdese, North Carolina, the only extant medieval sect, although their practices have mellowed somewhat. They are still known as honest, hardworking people, proud of their heritage of defiance of authority when they deem such defiance necessary and right.

The Albigenses

The Albigenses were so-called because of their main monastery being located near Albi, in France. They are also known as the Cathari, or "Pure Ones." They were most numerous in the twelfth century in the northern portions of Spain and Italy and in southern France.

In 1167, the Cathari held a widely attended council near Toulouse. The participants in that council were very critical of the wealth and power of the Church and the pope soon heard of it.

The Cathari were dualists in theology. They held that God had two sons, Satan and Christ. Satan rebelled and Christ was obedient. They also held to the existence of two gods—one good and the other evil. This visible world was held by the Cathari to be the work of Satan. The greatest sin is the one committed by Adam and Eve, that of human reproduction. The problem with procreation is that it increases the number of souls held in the prison house of the body. The higher class of the "Pure Ones" subjected themselves to "endura," a slow process of starvation through which the soul was purified. Salvation was held to be through self-denial. When salvation was achieved, it must be kept by remaining perfect. To do so, the redeemed must abstain from the eating of meat, milk, or eggs since they are the products of the reproductive process. An unusual belief among the Cathari was the one that those who died unredeemed could be reincarnated in human or animal bodies until they could be purified and brought to salvation.

The Cathari were of high moral character and were diligent missionaries. They recruited mainly from the lower classes but included a few scholars who specialized in Bible translations, especially their beloved Gospel of John. The Cathari were a moral and theological threat to the church in Rome. Their missionary efforts increased their visibility, and they were seen as a dangerous enemy to the papacy. The pope responded.

The Inquisition

In 1179, the Third Lateran Council proclaimed a crusade against heretics. Pope Alexander III (1159-1181) put together an army and had it march into southern France. The crusade accomplished little and the heretics were as strong as ever in the favorite territories by 1185. It was up to Innocent III (1198-1216) to wield the weapons of punishment. Simon de Montfort was named as general of the papal army. Years of warfare followed. The Cathari and their defenders were made helpless. Innocent III declared heresy to be a capital crime and ordered a massacre. In 1209, the "Slay all, God will know His own" massacre occured at Beziers. About twenty thousand of all ages were killed, including some faithful Catholics. At Minerva, more that a hundred of the Cathari were burned. Innocent III bestowed remission of sins and material wealth on the soldiers who lighted the torch.

The Fourth Lateran Council in 1215 provided for the punishment of heretics and excommunication for all protecting them. In 1220, the Inquisition was turned over to the Dominicans.

The Synod of Toulouse was called in 1229 for the purpose of codifying the Inquisition. The synod forbade the laity from possessing the Scriptures and denounced all unofficial translations into the vernacular. The synod gave birth to a systematic inquisition. Thereafter, the Inquisition was a well-organized instrument of punishment for the heretics. The accused were allowed no trial since they were stripped of all legal rights. The accused heretics were tortured as their hearings progressed with the certainty that their tongues would confess the truth.

In 1233, Pope Gregory IX ordered the Dominicans to exterminate the Albigenses. The Inquisition was to continue with vengeance during the time of the Protestant Reformation, proof that torturous suppression does not die out easily. The Cathari were virtually eliminated, but the Waldenses held on stubbornly. Their missionaries continued to proclaim the scriptural truths as they saw them in spite of persecution. The Inquisition was an early attempt by the Catholic church to control dogma and propagation.

Marco Polo and China

In 1260, two Venetian brothers, Nicolo and Maffeo Polo, made the long journey overland to Peking to trade with the Mongol rulers there. They were received by Kublai Khan. In 1271, Marco, the son of Nicolo, went back with them. Marco stayed in the service of the Mongol court until 1295. Marco's father had returned from his first visit with a letter from the khan. It read, in part,

> Send me a hundred Christians, intelligent men acquainted with the sacraments, able clearly to prove by force of argument to idolaters and other kinds of folk that the law of Christ was best, and that all other religions are false and naught. If they would prove this and all under me will become Christians and the church's servants.

The Christians of Italy responded only nominally to this appeal, thus missing a wide-open invitation to evangelize China.

The Mongols were tolerant religiously, but the majority were followers of nature priests who led in veneration to and manipulating of the elements. The gospel did not have a great planting among the Mongols of the thirteenth century, in spite of Kublai Khan's request.

John of Monte Corvino

John of Monte Corvino was an Italian Franciscan. He left on mission assignment to Peking in 1291 and had started a church there by 1300. He was appointed archbishop of China by Pope Clement V in 1310 and eventually had six bishops serving under him. John won about six thousand converts before his death and had translated the whole New Testament into the Tartar language. At his death, John had gathered more than a hundred young men around him and was training them in doctrine.

At his funeral in 1328, there was a huge crowd. One observer wrote:

> To his . . . burial there came a very great multitude of people, both Christian and pagan. Those pagans sent their mourning garments as their manner is; and both Christians and pagans devoutly laid hold of pieces of the clothing of the archbishop and carried them off as relics with great reverence.

Ramón Lull: Master Strategist

Efforts were made in the thirteenth century to reach the Muslims living outside of Europe but with very little numerical success. An example is Francis's preaching to the Sultan of Egypt in 1219. But, there was almost no response until the time of Ramón Lull (1232-1315).

Ramón Lull is remembered as the first and best missionary to the Muslims in the modern era. Lull determined to see Muslims come to the gospel "by love, by prayer, by proclaiming the word of truth rather than by force of arms."

Ramón Lull was born on the island of Majorca and reared in wealthy and scholarly circles. In his early thirties, Lull had a series of visions of Christ on the cross. He wrote the story of his call to missionary service in *On Divine Contemplation*. In it he records how he prayed,

> To Thee, O Lord God, I offer myself, my wife, my children, and all that I possess. May it please Thee, who didst so humble thyself to the death of the Cross, to condescend to accept all that I give and offer to Thee, that I, my wife and my children may be thy lowly servants.

Ramón Lull started the study of Arabic in 1266. He wrote his *Ars Magna* and designed it to persuade thinking

Muslims of the superiority of the truths of Christ. Lull's chief concern was to convert all peoples to Christ. He tried to convince European Christians to send missionaries to Muslims and Mongols before their faith was too established to make Christian conversion possible. He traveled extensively over Europe and tried to convince Church leaders to start more monasteries to train missionaries for ventures among the Muslims. He made three missionary journeys to North Africa. On the third, at more than eighty years of age, he was stoned so severely that he died.

Lull wrote:

> Let us win the whole world for Christ. Let the church give a tenth of its wealth to missions. Let our best preachers be trained as missionaries. Let them learn all the languages they can speak, so they can speak to them of Jesus Christ. He who loves not lives not: he who lives by the Life cannot die.

Ramón Lull has had a lasting impact on missions, especially work among Muslims, because he was a master mission strategist far ahead of his time in at least three areas: apologetics, language, and active mission service.

Apologetics. Lull devised a philosophical system for persuading nonbelievers of the superior truth of Christianity. Lull's primary apologetic method was to seek to prove the harmony between the truths of Christianity and those in the natural mind. This he did in his *Ars Magna.* Less well known is the fact that Lull also wrote an apologetic volume entitled *On the Discovery of Truth.* In it, he reasoned:

> We have composed this treatise in order that believing and devout Christians might consider that while the doctrine of no other religious sect can be proved to be true by its adherents, and none of the truths of Christianity are really vulnerable on the grounds of reason, the Christian faith cannot only be defended against all its enemies, but can also be demonstrated.

Language. Lull studied Arabic for nine years before he

embarked on his first missionary journey. This gave him the idea of founding missionary colleges for the study of linguistics. He wrote, "The monks should learn various languages. Monks of holy lives and great wisdom should form institutions in order to learn various languages, and to be able to preach to unbelievers." This was near the modern idea of mission societies and their accompanying resources for training.

Ramón Lull visited the pope twice, trying to get him to order a missions institute established in Rome to train both men and women for missions. In 1311, Lull persuaded the Council of Vienna to pass a decree ordering professorships of Oriental languages to be established at the universities of Paris, Oxford, and Salamanaca. This emphasis on linguistics continues whenever mission work is successful today.

Active Mission Service. Ramón Lull's first act in Tunis was to invite the Muslim scholars to a conference. Lull was so effective in defending the Trinity that he was placed in prison. Three more times he was imprisoned in Muslim lands and was finally stoned to death.

Lull was more than a theorist. He was willing to put his ideas to the test. No missionary since has been more original in plan and creative in consecrated service for Christ.

Missions to the Jews

The Inquisition was introduced in Spain in 1478 to deal with Muslims and Jews and any Christians whom Rome cared to denounce as heretics. By 1502, the Moors, or Muslims, were expelled from Spain.

The Jews were not spared. In 1481, Seville was the scene of the burning of almost three hundred Jews. In the rest of the fifteenth century, the notorious Torquemada burned more that ten thousand Jews at the stake. In 1492, Queen Isabella issued a decree expelling all Jews from Spain. This joined the previous orders in France in 1182 and in England in 1290. It should be noted that when these decrees were issued, all ruling popes opposed them immediately.

Missions among the Jews was made extremely difficult by anti-Semitism in Europe in the fourteenth and fifteenth centuries. There were a few, however, who labored rather unsuccessfully for their salvation. An exception to this rule is considered in the following section.

Vincent Ferrer: All Israel

The Dominican Vincent Ferrer (1350-1419) labored among Jews in Spain. Under his forceful preaching, more than twenty thousand Jews were baptized. Scholars of the era wonder, however, how many of those were coerced by the setting and threatened persecution of the Jews. This number is further clouded by the attraction of secular advantages to conversion, such as the removal of taxes.

Ferrer had an extensive education in theology and philosophy and was a master apologist. His major themes were sin and the necessity of repentance. Drunkenness, gluttony, and profanity were denounced and the saints were praised. The people, especially the Jews, responded well to the message. Ferrer was an apologist to be emulated.

Medieval Synthesis Breakdown

Deterioration of the Western Church was underway by 1350. The decline of the papacy, the rise of Eastern Orthodoxy, the popularity of the mystics and other factors entered into breakdown of the medieval synthesis.

The *medieval synthesis* is a phrase used to describe the sameness of thought and practice which permeated the churches in Europe about the middle of the fourteenth century. Features of the synthesis included:

1. Dogma is demonstrable by the use of reason;
2. The pope has supreme power in matters of doctrine;
3. Local bishops serve as representatives of the papacy;

4. Local secular rulers treat the Church with special consideration;
5. The monastic life-style is to be employed as a special means of grace;
6. To be excommunicated from the Church is to risk losing salvation; and
7. Grace comes only through the sacraments of the Church.

This synthesis was about to crumble, making the doing of missions more difficult, complicated, and fragmented.

Decline of the Papacy

Marsiglio of Padua (1276-1342) popularized the theory that the emperor had control over the pope. In 1328, he installed an antipope and gave him the name Nicolas V. This move by Marsiglio came after the removal of the papacy to Avignon in 1309. Because Rome was in danger of attack, the popes lived in Avignon where they found existence almost intolerable. Most of the commoners in the Avignon area had little respect for the Italian popes and believed that the emperor should have power over them. In fact, the first Avignon pope, Clement V, admitted publicly that he was subservient to the king of France. That king, Philip IV, had been responsible for the death of the previous pope, Boniface VIII, in a dispute over the right of the emperor to tax clergy.

Seven different popes ruled from Avignon from 1309-1377, all giving allegiance to the French monarch. One of the Avignon-based popes, Urban V, tried to return to Rome in 1367 but soon returned to his residency in Avignon. His successor, Gregory XI, returned to Rome for good.

The Great Schism

What is known as the Great Schism started in 1378, after the death of Gregory XI. Urban VI was elected by a council dominated by the French, the rest made up of Italians. He was soon denounced as an Antichrist by the cardinals and other clergy from Avignon. They insisted that they could declare the post vacant immediately. The French cardinals were in the majority in the council which was empowered to elect the pope. They called a council and elected a Frenchman who took the name of Clement VII and settled in Avignon. Urban VI refused to step down and continued to rule from Rome. Spain and Germany joined France in supporting Clement VII. England, Poland, and Portugal supported the Italians who followed Urban VI.

Therefore, a church council to settle the issue was called in Pisa in 1409. It was attended by neither the pope from Avignon nor from Rome. The council declared both of them deposed and elected Alexander V to be the new pope. For the six years that followed, the Church had three popes, a ridiculous and scandalous situation.

Finally, the Council of Constance was called in 1414. The council deposed all three reigning popes. A new pope, Martin V, was elected. He set about immediately to restore the power of the office. He returned to Rome and helped to restore the city. However, he was unable to effect much change as in the reforms outlined in the Council of Constance.

The papacy reached its lowest ebb under Alexander VI (1492-1503). He was elected by open bribery of the electing cardinals. But, he is remembered even more clearly for his advancing his own family members in Church offices and favors. Alexander VI was almost devoid of moral fiber.

The papacy was an embarrassment to moral and pious Christians in the century and a half leading up to 1500. This was a major factor in the breakdown of the medieval synthesis. Missionaries during this period either had to ignore or disobey the pope, or even multiple popes, to be effective in the spread of the gospel.

The Mystic: Catharine of Siena

Catharine of Siena (1347-1380) was an outstanding example of the movement called mysticism which led to the breakdown of the medieval synthesis. Mysticism defined Christian discipleship in terms of piety and seeing beyond the philosophical truths in a search for the miraculous among the mundane. This movement gave honor to such attributes as humility, sacrifice, and discipline.

Catharine took the vows to become a Dominican as a teenager. In her early twenties, she decided to reenter the world as a helpful minister. Thereafter she was remembered as a "practical mystic." For years she served the poor, the sick, and the imprisoned.

Catharine was deeply embarrassed and grieved by the Great Schism and wrote letters of protest to the French cardinals whom she blamed for the confusion. She was summoned by Urban VI to Rome and served as a special assistant to him until her death.

Catharine is remembered as deeply meditative and joyous. She was a major figure to those searching for a moral model in a time of spiritual depravity among church leaders.

Mystics: Wycliffe and Hus

John Wycliffe (1330-1384) was trained at Oxford where he proved to be an outstanding scholar. While he is remembered as a radical reformer, he was, above all, a scholar.

Wycliffe made his opposition to the wealth of the Church and the attempts by popes to rule political life known in 1376. He lectured that year at Oxford *On Civil Lordship.* In 1377, he was summoned to appear before William Courtenay, the bishop of London. That same year Pope Gregory XI issued five bulls against him. Wycliffe continued to write. He argued that the Bible is the only law of the Church. The Church is centered in the believers, not in the pope. Its only true head is Christ.

A major contribution of Wycliffe's was the translation of the Bible into English from the Vulgate in 1384. This act led him to become the "patron saint" of the modern Wycliffe Bible Translators. The translation was widely heralded as easily understandable and yet it satisfied the pious.

To further the gospel even more, Wycliffe encouraged the sending out of what he called "poor priests." They had great success in the English countryside, seeing thousands of new converts to the Christian faith. They were a striking picture of sacrifice, clad in long robes and carrying staffs. They traveled in twos in obedience to the New Testament model.

Wycliffe is credited with starting the Lollard movement. He attacked the dogma of transubstantiation in 1379 and argued for what was later called consubstantiation. In 1382 the Archbishop of Canterbury held a synod in London which condemned some twenty-four of Wycliffe's teaching. He was no longer allowed to lecture at Oxford. His "poor priests" were arrested throughout England as they did their mission work.

Today Wycliffe is called "Doctor Evangelicus" for his contributions to the spread of the gospel, including his deep personal piety, Bible translating, and the sending out of the "poor priests."

When John Hus was born in 1373 in southern Bohemia, the Great Schism of the papacy was about to occur. At age eighteen, young John went to the University of Prague. There he was known as a good student, driven by his ambition to learn as much as possible. He wrote:

> From the earliest time of my studies I have set up for myself the rule that whenever I discern a sounder opinion in any matter whatsoever, I gladly abandon the earlier one. For I know that these things I have learned are but the least in comparison with what I do not know.

The masters under whom Hus studied had learned much from Wycliffe. He started teaching at Prague in 1396. During the first two years he lectured on Aristotle.

In 1402, Hus was named rector and preacher of the Bethlehem Chapel at the university. There he distinguished himself as a chaplain to the students. He preached twice every Sunday. Hus was loved as a devoted pastor.

The archbishop of Prague, Zbynek (1403-1411) noted Hus's agreements with the heretical Wycliffe. He was reported to the Council of Constance. The council ruled that every Christian was bound to submit to its decisions, especially on dogma. The council members insisted on Hus's complete and public submission to their rulings. In July of 1415, he was condemned and burned for heresy.

Hus advocated the New Testament alone as the law of the Church with Christ at its head, not the pope. He argued that God had predestined a Church of the elect. His ideas lived on after him. When the news of his execution reached Prague, the nobles determined to keep his reform movement going. Armed bands attacked monasteries and churches. By early 1416, all the churches in Prague were in the hands of Hus's sympathizers. The revolt spread throughout the regions around Prague.

Hus's influence lived on all across Europe in the fifteenth century. His followers made a powerful spiritual and military attack on the papacy. The medieval synthesis was in its last days.

The Renaissance

The final disintegration of the medieval synthesis came with the wide movement called the Renaissance. Industry was advancing with new methods of producing cloth and military arms. New forms of land and corporation ownership were emerging. Mercenaries were replacing vassals as the dominant form of military service.

The Renaissance was basically a humanization of the life processes. In art, sculpture, and literature, the themes were no longer basically Christian or even religious. A symbol of this was the work by Dante (1265-1321) who is remembered as Italy's greatest poet. He was exiled from Florence for antipapal activity in 1301. In 1318, he published *On Monarchy* in which he called for a worldwide emperor who would bring world peace. His most widely read work has been *The Divine Comedy.* A recurring theme is that good works without religion will never merit salvation.

For the most part, the popes of the fifteenth century were unaware or unable to stem the tide of the Renaissance. Social change was so rapid that they were powerless to try to stop it. The dissolution of the medieval synthesis was complete.

The Rise of Eastern Orthodoxy

In 1453, Constantinople fell to the Ottoman Turks. The Turkish ruler, known as Muhammad II, entered the city and held a Muslim worship service in the Cathedral of Santa Sophia. The church was later fully transformed into a mosque. Yet, Christianity did not die in the East. Muhammed II allowed the election of a patriarch. Other Orthodox bishops were made subservient to him. The Orthodox churches still had their clergy and monks among Byzantines. This was in spite of harsh treatment by the Muslim rulers.

The Russians

The Orthodox churches, in spite of the fall of Constantinople, continued to grow in Russia. The churches were a sign of Russian unity in the fifteenth century. Most of this new life in the Russian churches centered around Moscow. In 1480, Ivan III, the ruler of Moscow, threw off Mongol rule and led his people to full independence. He also claimed to be the true heir to the patriarchs in Constantinople since that city had fallen while he was still a young man.

The heartline of missions in fifteenth century Russia were the simple monks. They were responsible for spreading the word to northeast Russia. They founded monasteries which became schools, hospitals, and hospices. Some of their numbers were even canonized for outstanding service to the church, including Servius.

The monks split into two types of servants late in the fifteenth century. One group was started by Joseph Volotsky who insisted that monasteries should be characterized by hard work, fasting, and study. His followers were called Josephites. The second model was influenced by Nilus Sorsky (1433-1508) who started the Transvolga Non-Possessors. These monks lived alone and devoted themselves to meditation and prayer. They practiced complete poverty and celibacy.

Christianity had firm rootage in Russia by 1500. Russians were even seeing themselves as rightful heirs to the fallen patriarchs of Constantinople. Russian Orthodoxy was flourishing on the eve of the Protestant Reformation.

The Final Rift

A strong effort of the papacy to bring the Eastern Christians into union with it was a council held at Florence in 1439. Pope Eugenius IV (1431-1447) wanted to assert his authority in both East and West. The Byzantine emperor came to the meeting along with the patriarch of Constantinople and a score of Eastern bishops.

The most thorny question was the authority of the pope. An ambiguous statement was passed. The decree, published in 1439, read in part, "We recognize the pope as sovereign pontiff, vice-regent and vicar of Christ, shepherd of all Christians, Ruler of the church of God; saving the rights and privileges of the patriarchs of the East." This final clause was not defined clearly. In 1472, a synod in Constantinople was called and repudiated the action of the council at Florence.

The popes after Eugenius strove to reassert their control

over the Eastern Christians. The Eastern churches, especially the strong ones in Russia, refused to succumb to such pleas. The two largest arms of the Church were split when the Reformation was about to dawn.

This rift was to have tremendous repercussions for the history of Christian missions. Catholics of the West were to operate without reference to the Orthodox churches of the East. The New World churches were to be formed without the theological and liturgical balance which a unified Catholicism could have presented. The Eastern churches were to have limited success with missions, quite impotent in comparison to what could have happened by linking with their Western brothers in Christ. The Eastern emphasis on the Holy Spirit and the Western stress on Christology could have been unified to bring a world-changing redemption to the known world of the fifteenth and sixteenth centuries. Instead, a divided Catholicism was the basic reality in the era just before the Reformation. In spite of the rift, the branch of Catholicism centered in the West remained active in mission causes.

Roman Catholic Missions

Fifteen hundred is an artificial separation date for the phenomenon called Roman Catholic missions. The period just before and after the start of the sixteenth century was one of extensive exploration and activity among European powers who saw to it that the priests went along to Christianize the natives found in newly discovered territories. When the swords of the fighting Spanish and Portuguese went to the New World, they were accompanied by the liturgy book of the Catholic monks and nuns. From the beginning, the conquest of the New World was a missionary effort. Even the king of Spain described himself as protector of the Indians.

In 1493, Pope Alexander VI issued three bulls. He recognized the exclusive right of the Spanish rulers to trade with the lands of the Atlantic. The papal statements included the order "To bring to Christian faith the peoples who inhabit these islands and the mainland . . . and to send to them wise, upright, god-fearing and virtuous men who will be capable of instructing the indigenous peoples in good morals and in the Catholic faith."

The monks went along with the conquerors to teach the natives a European language, music, writing, and agriculture. They used the people to build new church buildings and trained them in Roman Catholic ritual. Throughout the sixteenth century, thousands of natives in the New World were brought only a shallow and debased form of Christianity. There were few native clergy trained to preside over ritual. This made for few examples of native leadership in the New-World churches. Some of the Catholic clergy openly disgraced the name of Jesus by helping to reduce the natives to slavery and claiming vast territories of land for the Church.

The priests set up for their Spanish and Portuguese colonists a replica of the Church structure they had known in their European homelands. Only a few women came on the conquest. The soldiers produced a new racial mixture, the mestizo. These people were often baptized en masse with little knowledge of why they were converting.

The Portuguese carved Brazil out of South America with its almost three million square miles of jungle. With the conquerors went Franciscan and Dominican priests. However, their task was made difficult by the dense rain forests inland.

Bartholome de Las Casas

Bartholome de Las Casas was the son of a man who had sailed with Columbus on his second voyage across the Atlantic. De Las Casas at first settled on a large estate on the island of Hispanola in the Caribbean. He was converted by a vision and became a monk. In 1516, he sailed to Spain and convinced the king of Spain to make him the "Protector-General of the Indians." In 1520, de Las Casas was given even more power by Spain's king. He traveled extensively through Mexico, Peru, Guatemala, and Nicaragua. Everywhere he went, he set up mission work among the natives.

In 1542, de Las Casas sailed again for Spain where he forged the "New Laws" to protect the Indians of the New World. He returned as Bishop of Chiapa, in Mexico. There he ordered the priests to refuse absolution of sins to any slave owner. De Las Casas died in 1566 at the age of ninety-two. He fought to the end for the beloved natives. At his death, he was made patron saint of all the "colored" peoples of the New World. One can imagine de Las Casas meeting a slave ship with medical aid for the injured and a Christian funeral for the dead. This scene was typical of de Las Casas's willingness to serve those whom he loved in Christ's name. Unfortunately, there were not many of de Las Casas's caliber in the mission forces sent to the New World under the flags of Spain and Portugal.

Christianity About 1500: The Synthesis Crumbles

The era preceding the sixteenth century was one of fragmentation, failure, and success in mission effort. The success was in terms of spiritual renewal among the monastics of the faith. Poverty and chastity gave rise to a willingness to do missions among the monks. A pillar in this movement was Francis of Assisi, the founder of the Franciscans. The renewal was also given impetus by the Dominicans and Carmelites.

From the Catholic perspective, the "heretics" were a threat to be squelched. Attempts to do so led to the infamous Inquisition. The "heretics" continued to spread their message, in spite of, or perhaps because of, the Inquisition. The very attempts to stop the heretics gave them zeal to do itinerant preaching and teaching.

In the meantime, the Christian gospel was being spread by such pioneers in geography and methodology as Marco Polo and John of Monte Corvino. Ramón Lull and Vincent

Ferrer were working hard to bring the message of Christ to the difficult audiences of Muslims and Jews. These were quite successful, in spite of strong odds against them.

Fragmentation was occurring among European Christians because of the breakdown of medieval life-styles and attitudes. Alexander VI became the symbol of the decadent papacy during this pre-Reformation era. John Wycliffe and John Hus were thorns in the flesh of the Church's highest authorities because they questioned papal supremacy and openly called Christians to allegiance to other sources of spiritual authority. They were symptomatic of an era primed for change.

The devastating rift between Christians, East and West, dealt a severe blow to universal and cooperative mission effort. In spite of that rift, missions based in the West remained active.

Albrecht Dürer engraved *Melancholia* in 1514 and captured the spirit of the times. Mankind was pictured as being afraid to enter the future. There was conflict between the old and the new. This conflict was symbolic of the pre-Reformation age. This long-awaited Reformation was soon to be.

Case Study: Marsiglio of Padua

In 1324, Marsiglio of Padua, an Italian physician, wrote the *Defensor Pacis.* In it he attacked the claims of the pope for claiming supremacy over both church and state. In his *Defensor,* Marsiglio called for all clergy to practice complete poverty. Canon law was denounced. The ruling pope condemned the book. Marsiglio was removed as rector of the University of Paris.

Questions

1. Is there ever a right time to challenge church authority?
2. Should the church rule over political leaders?

3. Should a pope remove a priest for criticizing the papacy?
4. Is the cause of missions ever advanced by revolt against church leaders?
5. How was Marsiglio like Amos?
6. To what degree must a missionary be prophetic on behalf of his charges?

Time Line: AD 1200-1500

1200	
1210	Francis of Assisi started his order; Carmelites started
1218	Peter Waldo died
1221	Dominic died
1229	Synod of Toulouse
1250	
1300	
1315	Ramón Lull died
1328	John of Monte Corvino died
1342	Marsiglio of Padua died
1350	
1377-1378	End of Avignon papacy and Great Schism
1380	Catharine of Siena died
1384	John Wycliffe died
1400	
1419	Vincent Ferrer died
1450	
1453	Fall of Constantinople
1478	Inquisition in Spain
1492	Alexander VI became pope
1500	

5
Reformation and Revival: AD 1500-1792

In a sense, the Reformation may be viewed as home missions at its best. It was the intention of such giants as Martin Luther and John Calvin to have a purer gospel proclaimed and followed. Indirectly, the Protestant movement became a spur to foreign missions because it forced Roman Catholic leaders to look to the New World to replace adherents they were losing in Europe and its environs.

Erasmus wrote in the midst of the Reformation, "I see no end of it but the turning upside down of the whole world." This is remarkable in that this is exactly how the Book of Acts described the early missionaries in 17:6.

Yet, the Reformers were less than missionary at the beginning. There were reasons for this, including:

1. There was a limited understanding of the nature of the kingdom of God, both biblically and geographically;
2. There were still the prejudices of Europeans against the outside world (it was deemed to be dangerous and filled with "primitive" peoples).
3. The eschatology of the Reformers slowed their missionary progress. There were many who saw the end of the age fast approaching and even went as far as to specify the date. This worked in an antimissionary sense.
4. Luther and Calvin had an internalized view of their value to the church. They saw themselves as history

has designated them (that is, Reformers and not apostles to the unredeemed).

Erasmus

Erasmus (1467-1536), from his youth on, believed and preached that the gospel had to be proclaimed to those he called "heathen," as well as to Muslims. In the pursuit of such a dream, Erasmus gave to the scholarly world a New Testament in Greek along with his own translation in Latin. This text was the basis for Luther's translation in 1534. Erasmus wrote,

> I wish that even the weakest woman should read the gospels . . . I would rather hear unlearned maidens talk of Christ than certain Rabbis who pass for men of high attainments. The Scriptures ought to be read by clowns and mechanics and even by the Turks. . . . The Scriptures should be translated into all tongues.

In 1535, Erasmus of Rotterdam wrote *On the Art of Preaching.* In it he expounded on the virtues of the preacher and pastor. It read as a missionary manual, in part:

> Everlasting God! how much ground there is in the world where the seed of the gospel has never yet been sown, or where there is a greater crop of tares than of wheat! Europe is the smallest quarter of the globe; Greece and Asia Minor the most fertile. . . . Oh how these would turn to Christ if noble and faithful workers were sent among them, who would sow good seeds, remove tares, plant righteous trees, and root out those which are corrupt. . . . But now speak of nations who stray as sheep without a shepherd, because they have never had any Christian teaching. . . . Travellers bring home from distant lands gold and gems; but it is worthier to carry hence the wisdom of Christ, more precious than gold, and the pearl of the gospel, which would put to shame all earthly riches. We give too much attention to the things which debase our souls. . . . Some excuse themselves on the ground that they are ignorant of foreign languages. Shall princes have no difficulty in finding men

who, for the purpose of human diplomacy, are all well
acquainted with various tongues? . . . And shall we not show
the same zeal in so noble an enterprise? . . . I have not dealt
with the last excuses, that of the risk of death. Indeed, since
men can die but once, what can be more glorious and
blessed than to die for the gospel? . . . How much better
it is to die as Paul did, than to be wasted by consumption,
or to be tortured for many years by gout, to be racked by
paralysis, or to suffer a thousands deaths by the disease of
the stone? . . . Death is not to be feared under the protection of Christ. . . . It is the first duty of an apostle to spend
his life for the gospel. . . . Better yourselves, then, ye heroic
and illustrious leaders of the army of Christ. . . . Address
yourselves with fearless minds to such a glorious work.
. . . Do not, however, make earthly gain the object of your
labors, but strive to enrich the heathen with spiritual trea-
sures. . . . It is hard work I call you to, but it is the noblest
and highest of all.

Erasmus was a bright light in the Reformation age devoid generally of such vision.

The Reformation's Setting

The Reformation had deep roots in the rapid social
change going on in Europe about 1500. Part of this was
perpetuated by the capture of Constantinople by the Muslim Turks. That home mission field became a foreign one.
The church was split and fearful of losing even more territory.

Nationalism, with its accompanying rise of secular
power, was a threat to the power of the church. Absolute
monarchs became the pattern in Europe. The kings were
seeking new powers over the church and were partly successful in obtaining them.

Science was replacing theology as the basic way of viewing the world. For example, Isaac Newton (1642-1727)
made major advancements in the fields of physics and

mathematics. Man was ready to study and try to master his natural environment.

Another root of the Reformation was in the new discoveries of the conquistadores. There was the temptation of Christians to succumb to material wealth. Commerce was booming, and persons profiting from it seemed to have less time and respect for the Church.

Regionalism was a root to the Reformation. The Teutonic peoples of the north were growing tired of Latin control from the south. The Holy Roman Empire had played its part in the growth of that regionalism.

The times were ripe for Martin Luther.

Martin Luther

The world's history was changed radically by Martin Luther. His was a movement growing out of his deep Christian commitment and stubborn determination to stand up for what he was convinced was right.

Luther was born in 1483 in Eisleben, where his father was a poor miner. Luther entered the University of Erfurt in 1501. He was graduated from that school in 1505 and fully intended to enter law school. However, the Lord intervened with a bolt of lightning (literally), and Luther was ordained to the priesthood. In 1508, he enrolled at the University of Wittenberg. The next year he was graduated with the Bachelor of Theology degree.

In 1510, Luther made a life-altering trip to Rome. There he encountered the corruption of the papacy of which he had previously only heard. He reenrolled at Wittenberg and received the Doctor of Theology degree in 1512. He was named lecturer in the Psalms, a post which he filled until 1515. In 1516, he began to lecture on Romans, Galatians, Hebrews, and Titus.

All this study of Scripture served to stir his soul as he saw the obvious gap between the standards of the Church and those of the Bible. He became convinced that salvation is a new relationship with God based on full forgiveness of sin. Luther had a personal salvation experience in 1516 which convinced him that a believer could, indeed, have a personal assurance of forgiveness of sins.

In 1517, Luther felt compelled to cry out against an abuse of the Church in his region. Pope Leo X gave to one man three bishoprics in exchange for a large payment in money. In return, the holder of those three bishoprics, Albrecht of Brandenburg, agreed to sell indulgence for the forgiveness sin. Luther preached against such sales.

On October 31, 1517, Luther posted on the door of the church in Wittenberg his famous "Ninety-five Theses." In that document, Luther argued that repentance is a lifelong frame of mind, not a series of acts.

Luther got immediate response. Johann Maier of Eck (1486-1543) was professor of theology at the University of Ingolstadt. He charged Luther with heresy. In April of 1518, Luther was ordered to appear before a hearing in Heidelberg. There he testified that he desired no quarrel with the pope. Later in 1518, Luther was summoned to appear in Rome. A decision was reached on Luther's case two months later. It read, in part, "He who says that the Roman Church cannot do what it actually does regarding indulgences is a heretic." At this stage, Frederick the Wise, the territorial ruler in Germany, stepped in to protect Luther. This he was able to do until the following year.

In 1519, Luther went to Leipzig to debate the master, Johann Maier of Eck. Eck maneuvered Luther into admitting that he was influenced by John Hus and skeptical of the authority of both popes and Church councils. In 1520, a papal statement of condemnation was issued against Luther.

1520 was the year in which Luther decided that he could not remain silent. He published *To the Christian Nobility of the German Nation*. In it he argued that all believers are priests and that a free and open church council should be called by the secular authorities.

Later that year, Luther wrote *The Babylonish Captivity of the*

Church. In it he argued that there should be only two sacraments in the church, the biblical ones, baptism and the mass. Luther attacked the idea that the Eucharist is a sacrifice to God.

In 1520 also, Luther came out with the work entitled, *On Christian Liberty.* He wrote, "A Christian man is the most free lord of all, and subject to none; a Christian man is the most dutiful servant of all, and subject to everyone."

Luther was summoned to the Diet of Worms in 1521. There he was allowed the chance to recant statements made in his writings. On the next day, he refused to do so, uttering these famous words, "I cannot do otherwise. Here I stand. God help me, Amen."

Frederick again came to Luther's aid and hid him in Wartburg Castle. There Luther translated the New Testament into a very readable, popular German. He omitted Hebrews, James, Jude, and Revelation as inferior.

Luther's marriage to Katharine von Bora, a former nun, in 1525, set the pattern for married clergy among Protestants.

Luther died in 1546 at Eisleben, his birthplace. Scholars have since argued about his place in church history. It is not fair to say that without Martin Luther there would never have been a Protestant Reformation. It is, however, accurate to observe that he was the strongest personal force behind it.

As to the history of missions, Luther made a series of valuable contributions. His challenge to the papacy led others to launch out on missions of faith. His was a spirit of bold independence. Further, Luther's emphasis on Bible study was to have lasting impact on such people as William Carey and Adoniram Judson. For Luther, it was imperative to base all activity for God on his written Word. The Bible has since been the chief handbook on missions. Finally, Luther's life work split world missions into its two major camps today, Catholic and Protestant. The wounds have never healed. While the early Lutherans were not expressly missionary, their founder had affected missions indelibly.

Philip Melanchthon

Philip Schwarzert or Melanchthon (1497-1560) was by temperament more of a missionary theologian than Martin Luther, his contemporary. Melanchthon is remembered as forming the link between Luther and Erasmus in his interest in Greek and Latin literature.

Melanchthon was a renowned scholar and colleague of Luther. Melanchthon hailed Luther in 1520 as a second Elijah or apostle Paul. In order to protect his friend, Melanchthon wrote and presented the Augsburg Confession in 1530. It became the statement on which most other Protestant creeds have been based. The central theme is justification by faith. Faith is held to be more important than works for salvation. Ultimate authority for Melanchthon rested on the Bible interpreted by conscience. Those principles have given missions theology among Protestants its base for the past four and a half centuries.

John Calvin

John Calvin was born in 1509 near Paris. Never ordained, Calvin entered the University of Paris in 1523 to study Latin. He was graduated in 1528, whereupon he went to the University of Orleans to study law. He took a law degree but was more interested in the classics, including Greek and Hebrew. Calvin reported a "sudden conversion" in 1534. Calvin understood through the Bible that God's will is to be obeyed without question.

In 1534, Calvin moved to Protestant-controlled Basel. There he completed his major work in 1536, the *Institutes of the Christian Religion*. In this monumental work, Calvin argued that God has elected certain things to be and that obedience to that election is central. God's knowledge comes to the believer through the Bible and the accompanying witness of the Holy Spirit. Salvation is not an end unto itself but is for the sake of righteousness.

Calvin's system, based on the Bible, left room for only two church sacraments, baptism and the Eucharist. On the presence of Christ in the elements of the Lord's Supper, he wrote, "Christ, out of the substance of his flesh, breathes life into our souls, nay, diffuses his own life into us, though the real flesh of Christ does not enter us."

John Calvin moved to Geneva in 1536. In 1537, he presented to the city council a rule for living to reform the citizens. He proposed that certain persons should look through each quarter of the city to report of those needing church discipline. This initial attempt was a failure, and Calvin fled to Strassburg. There he married in 1540.

After an upheaval in Strassburg, Calvin was invited back to Geneva in 1541. As soon as he arrived, Calvin presented another form of his civic rule. He assigned to deacons the care of the poor and the supervision of the local hospital. Calvin desired to make Geneva the model of the perfect Christian community.

Geneva was not without its heretics. The most serious threat was one presented by Michael Servetus. In 1531, Servetus published *On the Errors of the Trinity*. In it he argued that the Church was being corrupted by its teaching on the Trinity. He also took Calvin's *Institutes* to task. He was finally arrested in 1553 and burned at the stake by Calvin's court. Calvin reigned supreme in Geneva. In 1559, he was successful in starting what was to become the University of Geneva. When he died in 1564, he was justly called the "only international reformer."

Calvin's contribution to mission theology was threefold. First, he stressed perfection in community. The Christian world caught a vision that the gospel could actually produce the ideal community, given proper formulation and supervision. Second, Calvin's emphasis on election was one which brought comfort to the redeemed. He is wrongly remembered as one who stressed the eternal lostness of the damned. The assurance of salvation has motivated thousands in mission service since Calvin's death. Finally, the Calvinistic system emphasized the sovereignty of God and the importance of submission to him. Obedient missionaries have crisscrossed this planet with that assurance.

Menno Simons

The largest sixteenth-century group of Anabaptists (see later section) to survive persecutions were the Mennonites, named for Menno Simons (1496-1561) their founder. He was ordained as a priest in 1524. Based on personal Bible study, Simons came to the conclusion that infant baptism was wrong and only the baptism of responsible adults has scriptural base. In 1536, he publicly renounced his Roman Catholic priesthood and was baptized by a group of Anabaptists. He was ordained as an Anabaptist minister and became a traveling missionary. In 1543, he traveled as a missionary to Germany, although he knew he was likely to be hunted by both Catholics and Lutherans. At his death, there was no doubt that he was to be remembered as the outstanding traveling missionary among the early Anabaptists, a spirit transferred to the modern Mennonites today.

Ulrich Zwingli

Ulrich Zwingli (1484-1531) was born in Wildhaus, Switzerland. He was educated in the humanist tradition at the universities in Vienna and Basel. In 1506, he was appointed a parish priest at Glarus. He was forced out of that pastorate in 1516. The charges were primarily those of Zwingli's being antipope. In 1516, he moved to a pastorate in Einsiedeln. There he preached openly against the sale of indulgence and other papal infractions of Bible teaching.

In 1519, Zwingli became the pastor of the largest church in Zurich. He got into more trouble in 1522 when he preached against Lenten fasts and rules. In 1524, he married a wealthy widow.

Zwingli was summoned to a debate in 1523 for which he wrote his *Sixty-Seven Articles.* In these he denied that priests can mediate between God and man. He argued also against what was becoming the popular idea of purgatory. For the mass, Zwingli wanted to substitute a love feast. Instead of transubstantiation, Zwingli argued that the elements in the mass are purely symbolic.

Zwingli's main theological work was published in 1525. It was called *A Commentary on True and False Religion.* In it he argued that every Christian should reject anything not specifically taught in the Bible. He rejected the traditional Catholic view of original sin, arguing instead that Adam and Eve's acts did not involve the personal guilt of persons in contemporary society.

Luther and Zwingli disagreed on the presence of Christ in the mass at the Marburg Colloquy in 1529. Each said the other was inspired by Satan. Zwingli died in battle in 1531.

Zwingli was a major contributor to subsequent mission effort for at least two reasons. One, he was a forerunner of the Anabaptists. Further, Zwingli's reform efforts stirred the independent spirits of those active in missions following the sixteenth century.

John Knox

John Knox was born in 1510 in the Edinburgh area. He was graduated from a university in Scotland and was ordained to the Roman Catholic priesthood and into a church desperately in need of reform. He served as a chaplain to King Edward VI of England but went to Geneva and became a disciple of Calvin.

Knox returned to Scotland in 1556 and became a popular preacher in the southern part of that small nation. By 1560, he had written a confession of faith adopted by the Parliament in Scotland. It was patterned after Calvin's *Institutes.* Knox next drew up the *First Book of Discipline.* It called for a widely supported system of public schools, parish ministers to be nominated by the people, and the relief of the poor. Knox also authored *The Book of Common Order* in 1564. It was to remain official until 1645.

Knox died in 1572, smiling broadly at the advances made by the reformed churches during his lifetime. He had given his stamp to the form of church polity called Presbyterianism. Presbyterians today remain mission minded largely because of the brave spirit of their founder, who spread his gospel in spite of heavy persecution.

The Anabaptists

Balthasar Hubmaier (1480-1528) was an evangelist-missionary from the start of his career. As a priest, he did much public preaching in Waldshut. He joined Zwingli in Zurich but disagreed with him about infant baptism. Zwingli challenged Hubmaier to a public debate before the city council. Hubmaier lost the debate but was publicly rebaptized. This was in spite of numerous threats and persecutions from every side: the Catholics, Zwinglians, and Lutherans. By the time of Hubmaier's death, more than twenty thousand Anabaptists (rebaptizers) had been put to death.

Hubmaier was imprisoned in Zurich in 1525 and tortured. He faked a recanting and was released. Thereupon he fled to Moravia where his preaching was to have great impact two and a half centuries later. In 1528, he was captured, taken to Vienna, and burned at the stake. Three days later his wife was drowned in the Danube River. This was most ironic because a few years earlier Hubmaier had written a tract arguing that burning heretics at the stake was contrary to Scripture and even satanic.

Conrad Grebel (1498-1526) and Felix Manz (1498-1527) worked very closely together in the early Anabaptist movement. They started out by working with Zwingli in Zurich on town reform. Like Hubmaier, they broke away from Zwingli on biblical grounds, arguing that infant baptism was unscriptural. In 1524, they were both insisting that baptism should be administered only to adults who confessed belief in Christ without coercion. Grebel and Manz were imprisoned in 1526. Grebel escaped but died soon thereafter. Manz was killed by drowning in 1527.

Michael Sattler led the Anabaptists in Strassburg from 1526 to 1533. He had been exiled from Zurich in 1525. In 1527, he presided over a conference at Schleitheim which produced the first confession of faith for Anabaptists. There were several major sections of the confession:

1. Baptism for adults who have repented;
2. Banning from the Lord's Supper on moral grounds;
3. Exclusion from the Lord's Supper of anyone not "united in baptism";
4. Separation from the evil and wickedness of the world;
5. Pastors to lead the faithful;
6. Nonuse of the sword; and
7. Rejection of all swearing and oath taking.

Three months after this conference at Schleitheim, Sattler was burned at the stake as a heretic. Sattler's wife was drowned a few days later.

The creed written by Sattler was a threat to both Catholics and Protestants in sixteenth-century Europe because it called for a separation of church and state on such matters as participation in war. The Anabaptists were setting up their own protest group based on the Bible. This was a threat to all after organized government and religion. Their spirit lives on wherever men follow God rather than men.

The Apocalyptists

Unfortunately, the Anabaptist movement was discredited near its beginning (as it continues to be even in the present) by a movement called Apocalypticism. An early predicter of the end was Hans Hut, a contemporary of Hubmaier, who predicted the end of the age in 1528. Hut never lived to see the failure of his prediction. He was burned at the stake in 1527.

Melchior Hofmann (1495-1543) was a Lutheran minister

who became an Anabaptist. He announced that Christ's second coming would be in 1534. He counseled his converts not to be baptized as the times were not expeditious. He was arrested in Strassburg in 1533 and died a disappointed man a decade later.

Hofmann's madness lived on through one of his disciples, Jan Mathis, who seized control of Munster in 1534. There he was able to control a military-led, communal-type of living for almost a year. He decreed death or banishment from the city for all who refused rebaptism. Hundreds fled to Munster, believing the end was near. Mathis was killed trying to repel a seige. His followers included the one chosen leader, Jan Bockelson, who legalized polygamy and took fifteen wives. The city fell in 1535. All the men were massacred by Catholic and Lutheran soldiers.

The large family of Baptists in the present world owe their being to the first Anabaptists. Their insistence on the separation of church and state helped to frame an important question for missions theology: what is the desired relationship between Christ and culture? This emphasis has allowed mission strategists from every denomination to forge new definitions of how the gospel can be enfleshed in each new culture it penetrates.

More Roman Catholic Missions

The sixteenth century, in spite of and because of the Reformation, was a time of Catholic renewal and a new interest in mission activity. Part of this was because of the rise of the Catholic Reformation. This movement had its center in Spain and Italy. It is unfair to call this movement the Counter-Reformation as it started before the Protestant movement and existed more concurrently to it than as an alter ego to it.

Cardinal Francisco Jimenes de Cisneros (1436-1517) kept the reform fires burning in Spain. He was known for his hatred of heresy and removal of heretics in the name of orthodoxy. The cardinal also enforced the most severe laws for the monastics in Spain. A lasting impact was his establishment of the University of Alcala. In 1507, he became the Grand Inquisitor of the Spanish Inquisition. In his term of office, he executed about twenty-five hundred heretics and tortured some forty thousand prisoners.

Just as important as the reform movements in Spain and Italy as an impetus to Catholic missions in the sixteenth century was the Council of Trent. This council (1545-1563) was a sign that the papacy was on its way back to respect and renewed power. At that council, only Church officials could vote. The council was dominated by the pope and his representatives. Not one concession was made to the Protestant demands. Tradition was, for example, placed on the same level of authority as Scripture. The Apocrypha was given canonical standing. The council also reaffirmed the seven sacraments of the Church. Latin was to be used in the mass by all priests and communicants.

The Jesuits

The Society of Jesus or the Jesuits came out of the Catholic Reformation. It was largely the work of Ignatius of Loyola (1491-1556). He had a deep spiritual experience in his youth which led him to deepen his commitment to the pope and the Church. He wrote in his *Spiritual Exercises,* "Man was created to praise, reverence, and serve God our Lord, and by this means to save his soul." He grew up in a military career and was severely wounded in 1521. He recovered in a Benedictine monastery in which he read Christian literature. Upon his recovery, Loyola confessed past sins and dedicated himself as a soldier of Christ.

Loyola went on a pilgrimage to Palestine. There he felt called to spend the rest of his life in Jerusalem witnessing to the Muslims. He was denied that privilege by the Franciscans there and returned to Spain. But he never forgot his vision for world missions. He studied at the University of Alcala where he became proficient in Latin. From there he went for further study at the University of Paris. He received a Master of Arts degree in theology there in 1535. At the University of Paris, a small group gathered about him to learn more of spiritual discipline. One of these young men was Francis Xavier (1506-1552). Xavier was to become one of the greatest missionaries of any age. In 1534, Xavier and Loyola took vows in the initial meeting of the Society of Jesus. They received official acceptance and approval by Pope Paul III in 1540.

Loyola put final form to his *Spiritual Exercises* in 1548. In it he recommended a four-week exercise to assure a disciplined Christian life. The first week concentrated on the confession and removal of sin. The second week focused on the life and example of Jesus. The third week zeroed in on Christ's passion. The final week focused on the victorious resurrection of Christ. Throughout the work is the conviction that any human finds meaning only in the life of Christ.

The new society focused on education. By 1630, the Jesuits had almost five hundred colleges in the world and almost forty seminaries. They had a rigid curriculum with grammar, poetry, and rhetoric.

The society defined itself as an army whose members were to behave as soldiers of God. They took a special vow to their commander-in-chief, the pope. They were "to acknowledge and reverence him, as is befitting, as they would Christ, as if He were present in person."

The new society had phenomenal early growth. They gave more of their sons to missions than any other order. By 1600, they had pushed into India, Japan, China, Indochina, Morocco, Peru, Brazil, Paraguay, Canada, and the United States of America.

The strong personal force behind the Jesuit missionary effort was Francis Xavier. In 1541, he set out for Goa on the west coast of India. He was in Japan by 1549. Under his ministry, more than one million persons were baptized. A mission expert centuries later summed up Xavier's missionary success:

He had grasped the social and political situation in Japan, and had settled on the methods which could ensure success. . . . The only way to secure permanent results was to win over the local rulers with their almost complete independence. . . . He had understood that if this people was ever to be won, it would be necessary to send missionaries of the highest quality, flexible enough to adapt themselves to the customs of the country to the limit of what was permitted by their faith.[3]

The Jesuit missions of the sixteenth century were a bright spot for the Catholic Church in the midst of the Protestant Reformation. They were joined by others later.

An outstanding Jesuit missionary was Roberto de Nobili (1577-1656) whose primary work was done in the seventeenth century. He was born of a noble Italian family. Sent by the Jesuits to India, he was shocked to discover that the Roman Catholics were only making headway among the lower classes in India and were considered to be a part of the lower social classes by most Indians. He quickly realized that he had to devise a way to reach the upper classes of India, where the people who were still greatly being affected and controlled by the caste system. He aimed his missionary efforts thereafter at the Brahmins, the highest social class in India. He moved to the center of Madura and began to dress and eat as the Brahmins. De Nobili became familiar with the ancient Sanskrit language so he could converse with the religious teachers. In 1623, the papacy ruled in favor of this missionary procedure, although de Nobili was charged with compromise by some of his missionary peers. By the time of his death, the total Christian community in the Madura area numbered about one hundred thousand. De Nobili still stands as a fine example of identifying with a culture sufficiently in order to win respect and converts.

Matteo Ricci (1552-1610) was the most famous of all the Jesuit missionaries to China. Born in Italy, Ricci first served as a seminary teacher for the Jesuits on the Portuguese-controlled island of Goa. In 1579, he went to Macao where he set about to learn the Chinese culture and language. In 1583, he settled in a provincial capital. By 1600, he was welcomed into the Chinese imperial capital. He was allowed to work among the Chinese only after a persuasive speech before Emperor Wan-li. The speech, in part, read:

> Your Majesty's servant comes from a far distant land which has never exchanged presents with the Middle Kingdom. Despite the distance, fame told me of the remarkable teaching and fine institutions with which the imperial court has endowed all his peoples. I desired to share these advantages and live out my life as one of your Majesty's subjects, hoping in return to be of some small use.

Ricci was liked by the emperor because he could repair clocks. He lived in the imperial city for a decade, producing many volumes of Christian literature in Chinese dialects.

The problem of translation of Scripture into Chinese was a thorny one. For example, *Sheng* was used for holy. This later opened Ricci to the charge that he was compromising too much with the ancient Chinese religions, including Taoism and Confucianism. Ricci advised his new Christian converts to give homage to family members as in the Confucianist tradition. His strategy was to allow the Chinese Christians to decide later how they would relate to the ancient customs.

The Chinese Jesuit mission flourished under Ricci's leadership. By his death in 1610, the Church around the imperial capital had almost two thousand members. His strategy was simple: present the gospel without demanding a radical break with Confucianism and Taoism. This allowed the Chinese, including their leaders, to become Christians without offending their families and clans. In turn, Ricci was allowed to enter and influence the royalty in Peking while it was still closed to most foreigners. This mission principle has been used by those most successful in mission history. The secret is in the learning of the language and culture and in allowing the new converts to adapt their faith to their culture without forcing them to become too European or American or allowing them to revert too far to their previous religious commitment.

Alexander de Rhodes (1591-1660) was a French Jesuit who went to Indochina and mastered the Anamese language. His strategy was to introduce Christianity to the educated and wealthy. He was so successful as to have more then two hundred Buddhist priests to become Christians. Besides theology, de Rhodes also taught some of his converts to care for the sick so as to honor Christ by ministering "to the least of these." In 1658, he returned to Paris where he was the main force in the establishment of the Paris Foreign Missions Society. By the end of his lifetime, he and his trainees had baptized more than three hundred thousand new disciples.

In the same pattern as de Nobili and Ricci, Alexander de Rhodes had lasting impact on the nations of Indochina because his was a strategy starting at the top but neglecting no segment of society.

A Note About Eastern Religions

The Jesuits who entered India, China, Japan, and Indochina in the sixteenth and seventeenth centuries encountered what were already old and well-established religions. This made the work difficult and the development of a workable mission strategy important. Five religions were encountered.

The religion endemic to Japan is called Shinto. The Japanese call it *Kaminuchi*, "the way of the gods." The origins of Shinto lie in the hazy sea mists of the dawn of Japanese history. The ancient Japanese were familiar with a feeling of awe and mystery in the presence of the unknown. This gave rise early to the development of a type of nature worship combined with clan mores.

In traditional Shinto, creation is described as beginning with a spontaneous generation of an original trio of gods:

"The lord who fills heaven" and two fertility gods. Man is seen as good and responsible for acting in such a way as to enhance order and harmony in society and in the universe.

Shinto proved to be difficult to penetrate by the gospel because of its high degree of nationalism and attachment to the emperor or local lords.

The dominant religion in India is Hinduism. It can be defined simply as the religion of the Indian people. The word *Hindu* comes from a Persian word meaning *Indian.*

There is no more important belief in all of Hindu thought than that of karma. Karma means "action" or "doing" and is an ethical interpretation of the law of causation which reasons that every action is the effect of a cause. Bound up with karma for the Hindu is the idea of reincarnation. According to the law of karma, a person may be reborn up or down the caste system according to every word, deed, or thought in previous lives. Also, karma in this life determines the acts appropriate to each caste. What is right for the Brahmin might be wrong for the water carrier. What persons desire most is moksa, or deliverance from the endless cycle of reincarnation.

Into this system came Roberto de Nobili, who quickly saw that the system could only be approached effectively from the top.

Buddhism started in India. The word *Buddha* was the title carried late in life by one born Siddhartha Gautama of the Sakyas (b. 563 BC). He carried this title after being "enlightened." His converts were mainly from the young nobility class, just as Gautama had been. His converts came quickly after the first five, who came upon hearing his first sermon.

The "Buddha" was concerned primarily with the pain and frustration of human life. For him, each person is to work out his own escape from this anxiety. His teachings are often summarized in the "Four Noble Truths":

1. Natural human existence is filled with pain;

2. The cause of this pain is false attachment to this world;
3. This pain can be stopped;
4. Stopping the pain can be done by amending ones' actions and attitudes.

An ancient Buddhist proverb reads: "All desires should be abandoned; But if you cannot abandon them, let your desire be for your salvation."

Into this Buddhism came the Jesuits who went to Ceylon, India, and Japan.

Taoism features belief in all sorts of gods, in the spirits of ancestors, and in a supreme power called the "Lord on High."

The ancient Chinese operated on the premise that only the virtuous were favored by this "Lord on High." It was assumed that the most important component of a person's being was moral character or integrity.

The founder of Taoism, called Lao-tzu, was born LiTan about 600 BC. He taught that there is one unifying principle underlying all of reality, namely the Tao. The ideal person for Lao-tzu would be one who operates in harmony with nature and society, including the family.

Taoism was deeply planted in China when Matteo Ricci was allowed entrance into Peking. He was wise enough not to disrupt it too completely or too quickly as he taught the principles of Christ.

Confucianism is embedded in the total thought patterns and life-styles of the ancient Chinese.

Kung Fu-tzu was born in 551 BC into an empire he later called filled with decadent luxury and oppression. His was a poor family in the province of Lu. At age twenty-one, he gathered several disciples around him and began to teach them history, philosophy, and other areas in the humanities.

Confucius, as he was called by the Catholic priests who came to China, taught that the "ideal man" could be described in four qualities. First, *yi*, or the way things go when they behave according to their own nature. Second, *jen* is goodwill, or willingness to do what is best socially. *Li* is propriety, or the appropriate way of giving overt expression to inner attitudes. Fourth, *chi* is both wisdom and power. This is the definition of personal behavior which Matteo Ricci encountered in China and tried to emulate.

Confucius assumed that heaven stood as the cosmic counterpart to man's ethical responsibilities. For him, when religion is properly pursued, it offers human disciples moral aspiration and emotional satisfaction. Confucianism never had a churchly organization, a priesthood, an emphasis on God, divinely revealed Scripture, or rites of initiation. Confucius taught that there is a divine order which works for love and welfare and that only in obedience to that divine order will persons find their highest good.

Methods Examined

In 1622, Pope Gregory XV (1621-1623) founded the Congregation for the Propagation of the Faith. It became the official papal tool for supervising Catholic missions service overseas. A major statement on mission policy was made by the strategists of the Sacred Congregation in 1659. It reads, in part, "Do not make any effort toward and do not for any reason persuade the people to change their customs unless they should be patently opposed to religion and morality." Some critics of Roman Catholic mission strategy of the seventeenth century and following have questioned openly that strategy. These critics maintain that this view makes the Catholic faith little more than a thin veneer over these conquered cultures. That judgment is aimed primarily at Latin America where the work has been a little more cursory. What was needed earlier were many more leaders such as Bartholome de Las Casas.

However, the charge was unfounded in such places as India, China, Japan, and Indochina where the very effective first-generation missionaries used cultural identification to win converts. Such men as Matteo Ricci knew precisely what they were about. They realized that limited access is better than none. They were patient enough to allow the second generation of new Christian converts to decide what the gospel would mean to their families and society. The Jesuits made a lasting, positive impact on missions.

Early Protestant Efforts

Early Protestantism did not produce many missionaries. It was growing into a "movement": a flexible and sometimes amorphous collection of sects which focused on beliefs about God, Christ, the Bible, and freedom of expression. Common to all of these was the emphasis on salvation through faith. This they saw as the essence of the gospel.

The Peace of Westphalia came in 1648. It was formed without much input from the papacy, a revolutionary concept at the time. Catholic rulers were to permit Protestant worship in their provinces where it had existed prior to 1824 and vice versa. A curb was placed on Roman Catholic missions among Protestants by the rule that no religious order founded since the Reformation was to be introduced. It was a blow to the Jesuits. The Protestants were glad of this new rule. The pope condemned the Peace of Westphalia. Yet, it became the basis for religious toleration in Europe. It gave Protestantism room to breathe, even the fresh air of missions.

Yet, about 1600 the famous Roman Catholic author Robert Bellarmine remarked that the Protestants had little missionary activity:

> The Lutherans compare themselves to the apostles and the evangelists; yet though they have among them a very large number of Jews, and in Poland and Hungary have the Turks as their very near neighbors, they have hardly converted even so much as a handful.[7]

Protestants were beginning to stir from their lethargy as such charges filled the air. There were some signs of life.

Hugo Grotius

Hugo Grotius (1583-1645) wrote his work in Latin entitled *The Evidences of Christianity.* It was designed as a textbook for the Dutch Reformed missionaries on their treks with the Dutch East India Company. A seminary was set up by that corporation in Leyden in 1622 to train missionaries. About twelve went to Ceylon and Indonesia. The ministers were paid a cash bonus for each new convert. Special political favors were given to new converts. These two factors made for many converts.

John Eliot

John Eliot (1604-1690) was a Presbyterian who became the pastor of a congregation in Massachusetts. He immediately started to study the Iroquois language. By 1651, he had baptized a number of Indians. Eliot gathered the Christian Indians into separate congregations and by 1671 had about fourteen such gatherings. All Indians who joined these communes had to make this pledge: "The grace of Christ helping us, we do give ourselves and our children to God to be his people. He shall rule over us in all our affairs of the church, but also in our works and affairs of this world."

John Eliot translated the New Testament into Mohican in 1661. The Old Testament was completed two years later. He is remembered as the "apostle to the Indians."

David Brainerd

David Brainerd (1718-1747) labored among the North American Indians most of his adult life. His diary is a classic in mission chronicles. When he died as a young man from tuberculosis, he had taken the gospel to the Indians of the Delaware and Susquehanna Rivers area. His diary was read by such greats as Henry Martyn and William Carey.

Protestant missions were on the verge of a launching to affect the known world. The cause was a movement called Pietism.

Missionary Pietism

Pietism had its roots in the Protestant Reformation of a century earlier. Pietism as a movement stressed the need for personal conversion and daily discipline. Small groups for Bible study were part of it. Personal witnessing responsibility was a key component, along with an expectation of the return of Christ to come soon.

Baron von Welz

Freiherr Juatinianus Ernst von Welz (d. 1675?) was a generation ahead of his time in missionary vision and practicality. In 1664, this precursor of Francke and Spener wrote two pamphlets:

1. A Christian and Loyal Reminder to all Right-Believing Christians of the Augsburg Confession, regarding a Special Society, through which with Divine Help, our Evangelical Religion could be extended." and
2. Invitation for a Society of Jesus to promote Christianity and the Conversion of Heathendom."

Von Welz also urged missionary departments and courses in Oriental languages in all Protestant colleges in Europe. He found little acceptance for his ideas, so he went to the mission field himself, to Dutch Guyana. Von Welz was a man ahead of his time who was willing to match action with theory.

Jacob Spener

The one able to draw these components together at a critical time was Jacob Spener (1635-1705), a Lutheran pastor in Strassburg. He gathered together a group of church members in his home for Bible study and prayer.

Spener was aware that most church services tended to be dry and formal. He began to disdain sermons on dogma, desiring rather to stir commitment to Christ by emphasizing personal conversion and a warm, personal, continuing faith. In 1675, Spener published his *Pia Desideria,* in which he said that no true Christian would be involved in cards, dance, or the theater. The movement was born!

Spener moved to Dresden in 1686 but was not accepted by members of the court there. In 1691, Spener moved to Berlin. He died later in Halle. Spener had crystallized a movement that was never to leave missions alone.

August Francke

August Francke (1663-1727) was greatly influenced by Spener. In 1686, at the University of Leipzig, Francke formed a group for the study of the Bible. The following year Francke had a new-birth experience. He preached that new Christians ought to be disciplined in such matters as Bible study. He got so much criticism that he left Leipzig in 1690 to go to Erfurt.

At that point, Spener invited Francke to Halle to help him. He started immediately to influence the church folk of Halle in matters of piety. He became a faculty member in 1698. For the next almost three decades, Francke made Halle the center of the Pietist movement. He started a school for young children. More than two thousand children were enrolled in the school at the time of Francke's death.

All of this pietist activity at Halle aroused great missionary interest. Pietism there also had lifted the lay participation in the churches and promoted the devotional study of the Bible. A long-lasting impact on what was to become evangelical missions came with the Pietist insistence that entrance into God's kingdom comes only with the new birth.

Count Ludwig von Zinzendorf

Count Nicolas Ludwig von Zinzendorf (b. 1700) gave the movement called Pietism some stability in the eighteenth century and missions a secure base at the same time.

He grew up in a home atmosphere bathed in prayer and Bible study. At age ten, he left home to enter the school for children run by Francke at Halle. There he met missionaries sent out by the Danish-Halle Mission.

Von Zinzendorf was a genius, who at age fifteen could read the New Testament in Greek. He completed his education at the University of Wittenburg.

In 1721, he purchased from his grandmother a large estate at Berthelsdorf. He married in 1722 and shared with his wife his dream of making a Christian commune there. Late in 1722, he welcomed the first group of ten Moravians seeking refuge. He dedicated the place as "Herrnhut," meaning "under the Lord's watch." In 1724, the first new building was dedicated. By 1726, some three hundred Moravians were living at Herrnhut.

In 1731, the count attended the coronation of Christian VI in Copenhagen. There he met a man calling for missionaries to the Danish West Indies. Zinzendorf went back to Herrnhut and told the people of the need. Two Moravians volunteered to go. They had already been trained and spiritually prepared for such service while at Herrnhut. The two were commissioned.

As Zinzendorf lay dying in 1760 he said, "Did you suppose, in the beginning, that the Saviour would do as much as we now really see?"

Karl Barth called Zinzendorf "perhaps the only genuine Christo-centric of the modern age." The count wanted to be remembered as being like his Lord. He is.

Count Ludwig von Zinzendorf provided a training base, daily inspiration, and vision to dozens ready to go to foreign fields for Christ's sake. He was an enabler who used his riches for the sake of others, a giant in eighteenth-century missions.

The Danish-Halle Mission

In 1704, the king of Denmark, Frederick IV, urged the court chaplain to found a missionary college. This was done in Copenhagen by one Dr. Lutkens. He sent to Herrnhut to see if there were any missionaries ready to be sent out.

Bartholomew Ziegenbalg and Henry Plutschau were sent out to India. They arrived in 1706 and began to translate the catechism into Tamil. In 1707, they baptized their first five converts. In 1708, Ziegenbalg began his Tamil translation of the New Testament, the first concerted attempt to put major portions of the Bible into a native Indian dialect.

Plutschau returned in 1711 and Ziegenbalg four years later. King George I wrote of the latter:

> I express satisfaction not only because the work undertaken by you of converting the heathen to the Christian faith doth, by the grace of God, prosper; but also because, in this our kingdom, such a laudable zeal for the promotion of the gospel prevails.

Ziegenbalg died in 1719, leaving behind more than three hundred converts in India, a completed Bible in Tamil, a dictionary, a seminary, and numerous other schools. Alexander Duff wrote, "He was . . . inferior to none, scarcely second to any that followed him."

Plutschau and Ziegenbalg worked with five sound missionary principles in India. They were:

1. Training of a native clergy;
2. Personal evangelism;
3. A study of Hinduism;
4. The Bible made available in the native language; and
5. Investment in Christian education.

No sounder missionary strategy has evolved since.

The Birth of Methodism

As the eighteenth century dawned, England was ripe for religious revival. Rationalism and Deism had penetrated the scholarly circles. Evangelism among the masses was almost nonexistent. Illiteracy was a widespread problem. Prisons were coarse and unrefined. Most of the people were caught in spiritual apathy.

The Moravians at Herrnhut affected the rise of Methodism. A Moravian missionary asked John Wesley the burning question, "Do you know Christ?" Another Moravian, Peter Boehler, taught Wesley to define true faith as "dominion over sin, constant peace and a sense of forgiveness." Pietism was about to burst onto the British scene through John Wesley.

John Wesley

Samuel Wesley (1662-1735) was rector of a rural parish at Epworth. His wife, Susanna, was a deeply devoted Anglican, as was her husband. Nineteen children were born to the Wesleys. John was the fifteenth and Charles the eighteenth.

John Wesley was born in 1703. In 1714, he entered the Charterhouse School in London, where he excelled. In 1720, he entered Christ Church College at Oxford. There he became interested in the church fathers, Thomas a Kempis's *Christian Patterns* and Jeremy Taylor's *Rule and Exercise for Holy Living and Holy Dying.* His favorite was William Law's *Serious Call to a Devout and Holy Life.*

In 1726, John was chosen a fellow at Lincoln College. He was ordained a deacon. He served also as his father's assistant in the parish. In 1728, John was ordained as an Anglican priest. He returned to Oxford the following year for further study and joined a newly formed book discussion club. John soon became the leader of the group. They were called the "Holy Club" by other students; and, later, the "Methodists" for their stern discipline.

In 1735, John Wesley sailed for the new colony of Georgia. He met on ship a company of more than two dozen Moravians. He was impressed by their calm and joy during a savage sea storm. He would never forget that experience. In 1736, John started a little "Holy Club" in Savannah, patterned on the Oxford model. He was unsuccessful as a missionary there, a bit too high church even for the Anglicans. In 1738, he returned home. His life was to be altered drastically.

In May of 1738, John Wesley met Peter Boehler, a Moravian, who was preaching the necessity of a sudden conversion. John was convinced. He went to a meeting on Aldersgate Street in London and heard Martin Luther's preface to his *Commentary on Romans* read. John later recalled:

> I felt my heart strangely warmed. I felt I did trust in Christ, Christ alone, for salvation; and an assurance was given me, that He had taken away my sins, even mine, and saved me from the law of sin and death.

In 1739, John started a preaching ministry among the coal miners of Kingswood. He organized societies among them and taught against those who were advocating that nothing should be done to grow faith. Wesley wrote tracts fighting those who would tend to let salvation lead to antinomianism. For John, justification by faith meant forgiveness of sins and newness of life displayed in loving acts on behalf of others.

This conviction in theology took root the year before when Wesley spent two weeks at Herrnhut. He appealed to their piety by calling for more action by dedicated Christians.

Late in 1739, George Whitefield invited John to preach at Bristol. Wesley quickly became known as a preacher without peer, with the possible exception of Whitefield himself.

But, John Wesley is best remembered as an organizer.

Originally, he did not intend to leave the Church of England. He wanted only to organize "societies" to train Christians in the disciplines of the Christian faith. He came up with the idea of distributing "society tickets" to the more mature Christians. Others were on probation in attending meeting. The tickets were renewed quarterly, and each person had to have those renewed. Wesley organized each "society" into classes of twelve each with a class leader assigned to collect a penny a week from each member. John also named "stewards" to care for property and "visitors of the sick." By 1744, there were so many societies that Wesley decided to have an annual conference of society leaders. In 1746, John divided the societies into "circuits" with traveling lay preachers. More stationary leaders were assigned "to assist chiefly in one place." A "superintendent" was placed in charge of each circuit. Persons were invited to join a Wesleyan society if they had "a desire to flee from the wrath to come, to be saved from their sins." Members of the societies were to abstain from cursing, ribald songs, racy reading, theft, and drunkenness. They were urged to feed the hungry and live frugally. They were, in their meetings, to hear the Word, take communion, fast, pray, and study the Bible.

Wesley's societies moved only very slowly from affiliation with the Anglican churches. Gradually his societies acquired property. By 1759, the movement was being referred to as the Methodist Church, but over Wesley's objections.

In 1784, Wesley ordained Thomas Coke as the Methodist bishop of Baltimore, the first in the United States. Meanwhile, Wesley was winning many sympathizers from among the Anglicans.

In 1795, the "Plan of Purification" marked the official beginning of the Methodist church. John Wesley had died four years earlier in London. His work had already affected the working classes in England and was about to do so in America.

In the last five decades of his life, Wesley had traveled more than a quarter million miles. He had given the world of Christendom emphases on the new birth, deep piety, discipline, fervent preaching, warm fellowship, and hymn singing. John Wesley is still bearing spiritual grandchildren. Whenever Bible reading, social concern, missions, and hymnody are stressed, the spirit of Methodism's founder lives on. That is especially true in the field of missions, wherever evangelical fervor is king.

Other Early Methodists

Charles Wesley (1707-1788) was a close ally of his older brother John. Charles preached in London the last eighteen years of his life. Charles was more Anglican and conservative than John. He is remembered as the premier hymn writer of the early Pietists.

Francis Asbury (1745-1816) was the dominant figure in the founding of the Methodist Episcopal Church in the United States. He arrived in America in 1771 and came out boldly for American independence during the Revolution. He remained celibate to give himself more time for the churches. He traveled constantly, going from Maine to Georgia and to the frontiers of Ohio and Kentucky. By the time of his death in 1816, the Methodists in the United States numbered about one-quarter million.

The Methodists of that first generation were determined that the world, old and new, would know of the values endemic to personal belief in the gospel. They got the word around.

Friedrich Schwartz, Lutheran

Friedrich Schwartz was born in Germany in 1726. He landed in India in 1750 and served there without a break until his death forty-eight years later. At first he served as British chaplain to the forces at Trichinopoly. He finished his career at Tanjore. Time and again he stopped wars between Indian feudal lords. He was called the "priest-king of Tanjore" by the natives. At his death, India had twenty thousand new Christians who had been baptized by this saint.

A British officer wrote of Schwartz, "The knowledge and integrity of this irreproachable missionary have retrieved the character of Europeans from imputations of general depravity." A man of integrity and intelligence, Friedrich mastered Portuguese, English, Tamil, Farsi, and Hindustani.

The epitaph on Schwartz's tomb was written by a young rajah:

> Firm wast thou, humble and wise,
> Honest and pure, free from disguise;
> Father of orphans, the widow's support;
> Comfort in sorrow of every sort.

Friedrich Schwartz was a man of moral integrity who could do no less than his best for his beloved Jesus. Gifted was this man, but he never forgot the source of his gifts.

Christianity About AD 1792: Bright Promise

The new Christian movements of the seventeenth and eighteenth centuries gave Christianity a much-needed boost. These movements were built on the earlier movement called Protestantism. The pope had been challenged successfully. In Protestantism, the Bible was central as the source of authority for beliefs and practices. Salvation was declared to be a matter of personal faith, indeed, by definition. Portestantism challenged the Roman Catholic Church at its roots.

The Roman Catholic Church responded. Clergy were called to moral reform. The Jesuits called for discipline and went scattering the word to such faraway places as China and Japan. The Catholic Reformation had life of its own.

The Pietists and Moravians came together at Herrnhut. Their work was to burn brightly across the globe, from

Iceland to India. Even John Wesley went to Herrnhut to warm in the glow.

In 1792, even the Eastern churches were showing signs of life. The laity were being exposed to Pietist themes in Russia. Special spiritual attributes were being cultivated in the monasteries. There was even a movement whose members were known as the "Spiritual Christians." Mennonites were coming into Russia with their spiritual nurture. As the nineteenth century neared, there was bright promise for the churches and missions, just beyond the horizon.

Case Study: Conrad Grebel

Conrad Grebel (1498-1526) worked closely with Ulrich Zwingli in Zurich. When Grebel joined the Anabaptists, he pushed hard for such quick reforms as the dropping of five of the sacraments. Grebel later fought Zwingli on the matter of infant baptism and lost. In spite of warnings by Zwingli, Grebel baptized his friend Felix Manz. He was jailed for baptizing and preaching. He was sentenced to life imprisonment. Grebel escaped from prison and died of the plague while being hunted down for execution. His few years were dedicated to the spirit of God-led rebellion when necessary.

Questions

1. When is it right to go against a spiritual leader's authority?
2. Is a missionary to go against the authority of those over him? Why?
3. Where are missionaries today being persecuted for their beliefs and practices?
4. How would a person like Grebel fit into the executive committee of a mission board today?
5. What part does Bible study play in forming church polity? Why?

Time Line: AD 1500-1792

1500	
1507	Spanish Inquisition
1517	Luther posted ninety-five theses
1540	Jesuits recognized
1561	Menno Simons died
1572	John Knox died
1600	
1610	Matteo Ricci died
1648	Peace of Westphalia
1656	Roberto de Nobili died
1660	Alexander de Rhodes died
1690	John Eliot died
1700	
1705	Jacob Spener died
1722	Herrnhut dedicated
1747	David Brainerd
1791	John Wesley

6
The Birth of Modern Missions:
AD 1792-1914

The modern mission movement had deep roots in the Pietism and calls to commitment of the Protestant and Catholic Reformations. The stage was set for an actor to call for mission action. Such a one was waiting in the wings in England.

When William Carey spoke and wrote with fervor, he was not speaking in isolation. Other broad movements were afoot in England.

"The fullness of time" had come. The "father of modern missions" was about to be heard.

The British Revival

George Whitefield (b. 1714) came into contact with John Wesley in 1735. Whitefield had a religious experience earlier that year which gave him a joyous peace with God. He started his career as a preacher the following year. He is ranked with John Wesley as one of the greatest pulpiteers of that time. The chief theme of his sermons was the forgiving grace of God. He is described by his peers as being an impressive and dramatic speaker. He died getting ready to preach in Massachusetts in 1770. Whitefield did not have the organizational skills of a John Wesley, but he certainly had the unction.

William Wilberforce (1759-1833) made great strides in bringing evangelical emphases to Oxford. He fought against slavery and was instrumental in having that institution abolished in England by 1833. Wilberforce served as a member of Parliament. He reported an adult "new birth" experience in 1784. Three years later he wrote the popular *Practical View of the Prevailing Religious System.* He had a major impact in Anglicanism.

William Wilberforce pled the cause of missions at a critical moment in history. Britain was in revival.

William Carey

The life of William Carey falls naturally into two periods. The period in England where he faced and overcame the hostility to missionary effort was the first. This was followed by the period in India where he proved himself to be a very effective missionary. It is often stated that he was perhaps the most versatile and greatest missionary sent out in the modern era of missions.

William Carey was born in 1761 in the county of Northamptonshire. His parents were weavers who valued industry and thrift. His home was pervaded by a deep and simple Christian piety. Bible study and family altar was a daily occurrence in the Carey home. At age six, William entered the village school. His sister wrote: "He was from childhood intent in the pursuit of knowledge. Whatever he began, he finished; difficulties never seemed to discourage his mind; and as he grew his thirst for knowledge increased."

When William Carey was eleven, he heard men talk of slavery, the burning social issue of the day. In 1772, the Lord Chief Justice Mansfield's decision was that no man could be a slave on English soil. William started studying Latin at age twelve. From his youth up, he was an avid reader. He read of the explorations of Captain James Cook. Cook became young Carey's hero. He read *The Pilgrim's Progress* as well.

At age sixteen, William went into an apprenticeship to a local shoe cobbler named Clarke Nichols. That master had a commentary on the New Testament in his home library. William read it and became quickly interested in studying Greek.

In 1779, Carey went through a deep personal crisis. Carey was opposed to the war Britain had declared on the American Colonies. He joined a group of Dissenters and became active in their cause, his first public move away from village mores.

Carey was also affected by the great evangelical revival which was sweeping through England. By the time Carey was twenty, the Methodist societies had some forty-five thousand members.

In 1779, Mr. Nichols died, before Carey had completed his apprenticeship. In 1781, Carey married Dorothy Plackett, a member of a pious Christian family. In 1783, he opened his own shoe shop.

In 1782, Carey attended his first meeting of the Baptist Association at Olney, where he met John Sutcliff, John Ryland, and Andrew Fuller. He was invited to preach in Olney two weeks later. He was so well-received that they called him to be their preacher at a Baptist church. This preaching led him to deep and regular study. This in turn led him to study Hebrew.

In 1785, Carey was called to be schoolmaster at Moulton. There he lived for more than four years. In 1785, he presented himself as a member at the church in Olney. In 1786, that church licensed Carey to preach.

In 1786, Carey attended a Baptist ministers' meeting at Northampton. The group was shocked when the inexperienced young minister stood to declare that they should consider: "Whether the command given by the apostles to teach all nations was not obligatory on all succeeding ministers to the end of the world, seeing that the accompanying premise was of equal extent."

Carey was immediately told to sit down by the moderator, Dr. John Ryland, who said, "When God wants to convert the heathen, he will do it without your help or mine. You are a miserable enthusiast for asking such a question."

Carey sat down, but he was not silenced for long. In all the ministers' meetings from 1787 to 1790, Carey reintroduced the subject of missions. Gradually he started making an impression on his fellow ministers.

In 1787, the little Baptist church at Moulton called Carey to be their pastor, and he was ordained by his old friends Ryland, Sutcliff, and Fuller. While at Moulton, Carey heard the call to missions. He later wrote, "My attention to missions was first awakened after I was at Moulton, by reading *The Last Voyage of Captain Cook.*" In his heart there arose the thought, "Those South Sea Islanders need the gospel." Carey began to devour every book he could on foreign lands. He soon concluded, "The peoples of the world need Christ." He read on. His peers report that he most surely read Jonathan Edwards's *Life and Diary of David Brainerd* and a book by the Danish missionaries Plutschau and Ziegenbalg.

The most influential work Carey read during his time at Moulton was a pamphlet by his friend Andrew Fuller. It was entitled, *The Gospel Worthy of All Acceptation.* Carey translated the sentences in this pamphlet into its missionary implications. He wrote in the margin, "If it be the duty of men to receive the gospel . . . then it is the duty of those who are entrusted with the gospel to endeavor to make it known among the nations."

In 1789, Carey was called to the Baptist church at Leicester. He was officially ordained to that pastorate only in 1791. At that ordination, Carey read a pamphlet he had written. It was published in 1792 under the title, *An Enquiry into the Obligations of Christians to Use Means for the Conversion of the Heathens.*

The brief introduction began:

> As our blessed Lord has required us to pray that his kingdom may come and his will be done on earth as it is in heaven, it becomes us not only to express our desires of that event by our words, but to use every lawful method to spread the knowledge of his name.

Section 1 was on the Great Commission. In it Carey argued that Christians ought not to neglect embracing openings around the world to preach the gospel.

Section 2 was a mission history, from the early apostles on. The chapter closes by talking about "the late Mr. John Wesley in the West Indies." Section 3 was a graphic survey of Carey's known world. He estimated the world population in 1791 at 731 million. Section 4 was a practical section. He argued, "The uncivilized state of the heathen, instead of affording an objection against preaching the Gospel to them, ought to furnish an argument for it."

The final section was concerned with even more practical matters. For the financial support of missions, Carey argued that the rich should give a good portion of their income, those with moderate income one-tenth, and the poor should give "a penny or more per week."

The pamphlet concluded with a call to action:

> What a heaven will it be to see the many myriads of poor heathens, of Britons among the rest, who by their labors will be brought to the knowledge of God. Surely a crown of rejoicing like this is worth aspiring to. Surely it is worth while to lay ourselves out with all our might, in promoting the cause and kingdom of Christ.

Carey preached to the spring meeting of the Baptist ministers' Association in Northingham. From his sermon came the immortal words, "Expect Great Things from God, Attempt Great Things for God."

The following morning Carey called upon his brothers to form a missionary society. The proposal was turned down and the meeting adjourned. In distress, Carey grabbed Fuller and asked if they would postpone a decision yet again.

In October of 1792, the fall meeting of the association was held in Andrew Fuller's chapel in Kettering. The evening of the first day fourteen men met at the home of Widow Wallis, called the "Gospel Inn." Carey pulled out a copy of a little booklet entitled, *A Periodical Account of Moravian Missions.* He cried out, "If you had only read this and knew how these men overcame all obstacles for Christ's sake, you would go forward in faith." The men finally agreed and the Baptist Missionary Society was launched. It was called "The Particular Baptist Society for Propagating the Gospel Among the Heathen."

Carey was chosen by the society as its first missionary. Early in 1793, he wrote his father:

> I consider myself as devoted to the service of God alone, and now I am to realize my professions. I am appointed to go to Bengal in the East Indies, a missionary to the Hindus. . . . I hope, dear father, that you will be enabled to surrender me up to the Lord for the most arduous, honorable, and important work that any of the sons of men were called to engage in. . . . I have set my hand to the plough.

William Carey, his son Felix, with Mr. and Mrs. John Thomas set sail. They had to set anchor in a cove in the English Channel and hide from French privateers for weeks. Finally they had to return home. But, William Carey never lost his vision. He bid his wife a second farewell and left again. He landed in Calcutta late in 1793.

Upon arrival, Carey learned that to serve as a chaplain to the East India Company he had to learn some native dialects. He set about to master several at once, being a proficient linguist. To this he added two of his own principles from the *Enquiry:*

1. Live among the people in the simplest manner possible, and
2. Support oneself by agricultural, industrial, or some other work.

Carey soon moved to Hoogbly, about thirty miles from Calcutta. Although he was hungry and discouraged, he wrote: "Bless God, I feel peace within and rejoice in having undertaken the work, and shall, I feel, if I not only labor alone, but even if I shall lose my life in the undertaking."

Carey soon found a job at a factory near Malda. There he spent the next six years. Carey was a factory supervisor with almost a hundred people under his control. He saw them as a mission field. He preached the gospel quietly and expected results. Within a year, he was writing back to England, "I now rejoice in seeing a regular congregation of from 200 to 600 people of all descriptions—Muslims, Brahmins and all other classes of Hindus." A little Baptist church was started at Malda with four members.

In 1796, he wrote for help. The letter said: "I think it very important to send more missionaries hither. We may die soon, and if we have no successors in the work, it will be a lamentable circumstance." John Fountain was sent out by the association to help Carey.

In 1799, Carey bought a printing press. He set out to print the New Testament as he had translated it into an Indian dialect. William Ward arrived in 1800 to help with the task. The band transferred to Serampore, a small place on the west bank of the Hooghly River. There they constituted themselves into a Baptist church with Carey as their pastor and John Fountain as a deacon.

While Ward was printing, Carey was preaching in the area. Carey recorded: "There appears to be a growing familiarity between us and the natives. They receive our printed papers and books with the greatest eagerness, and we cannot doubt that they are pretty extensively read." The first Indian convert was baptized late in 1800. The first Hindu woman was immersed early in 1801.

In 1801, Carey jumped at the chance to become a professor of Bengali at a new college in Calcutta. He wrote, "It would open a way to preach to the Hindus in Calcutta and its environs, and would put a number of respectable Hindus under my direction."

With the professorship as leverage, Carey started crying out against the social abuses of the Hindus. One was the practice of suttee, the burning of Hindu widows upon the funeral pyres of their dead husbands. He was successful in having this practice officially reconsidered.

Carey dreamed of starting a Christian college in India. He was convinced that India would be won to Christ only by the Indians. Carey believed that: "Those who are to be employed in propagating the gospel should be familiar with the doctrines he is to combat and the doctrines he is to teach."

Carey issued a prospectus for a college in 1818. A piece of land was purchased. The college was completed in 1821. It was the first college in Asia with the power to confer degrees.

By the time of Carey's death, India was very open to missionaries. He lived to see many of his dreams realized. His tombstone reads, "A wretched, poor and helpless worm, on Thy kind arms I fall." That inscription speaks of William Carey's humility. He deserves the title given him by missions scholars, "the father of modern missions" as well. Carey was a pioneer in vision, persistence, and sacrificial service. There has been no greater since the Galilean.

Andrew Fuller

Andrew Fuller was born in 1754 at Wickes, England. His parents were Particular Baptists. He started preaching at age sixteen and started pastoring four years later. In 1781, Fuller became the pastor of the Kettering Baptist Church and remained in that post until his death in 1815. For twenty-three of his thirty-four years at Kettering, Fuller served as secretary of the new Baptist Missionary Society.

In 1785, Fuller wrote *The Gospel Worthy of All Acceptation.* In it he argued that the gospel must be preached to all people everywhere. This theology clearly influenced William Carey.

In 1793, Fuller became general overseer of the daily affairs of the new missionary society which had sent Carey to India. He was unafraid to discipline disobedient missionaries. Fuller was forced to write to William Carey in 1798, "It is absolutely necessary that missionaries should confine themselves to their work, and not meddle in politics."

Fuller remained constant in his devotion and advice to his beloved missionaries. He wrote to a dejected missionary in 1796, "Do not, my dear brother, give way to a spirit of dejection. Look forward to your reward. You are sowing a seed." Mr. Fuller wrote a similar note to William Carey in 1803, "Let us . . . pray for each other in the Lord. . . . God has honored us not a little by employing us in this great work."

Fuller was also involved for more than a score of years in raising money for the new Baptist society. He traveled over England, Scotland, Ireland, and Wales. He collected more than thirteen hundred pounds in 1805.

Andrew Fuller never went as an active foreign missionary but provided a stability to the Baptist Missionary Society which made the continuing efforts of William Carey and others possible.

The Missionary Societies

The time of William Carey and Andrew Fuller is considered as the time of the beginning of missionary societies, although there were a few before then. The missionary society was a form of mission support which was dependent on a loose-knit group of individuals who gave prayer and finances to the missions movement.

Carey went out with the Baptist Missionary Society in 1793. That effort was heir to earlier similar organizations. The Society for the Propagation of the Gospel in New England was formed because of the pleas of John Eliot. It was brought into existence by an act of Parliament in 1649. That society financed the printing of the Bible which Eliot had translated into Mohican, one of the Iroquois dialects.

The Society for the Propagation of the Gospel in Foreign Parts was started in 1701 by Thomas Bray to send chaplains overseas to instruct the soldiers and colonials and "to win to the Christian faith of the aborigines and Negro slaves." This did not keep others from sending missionaries but did sound the alarm for needed religious instruction in the colonies.

In 1699, Bray had been instrumental in the beginning of the Society for Promoting Christian Knowledge. Its avowed purpose was to spread the knowledge of Christianity by books and school. This group paid for the press which printed the New Testament in Tamil at the place run by Ziegenbalg. The movement was also instrumental in supporting Christian missions in India during the seventeenth century, where it was called the "English Mission." This society operated internationally until 1829, when it was taken over by the Society for the Propagation of the Gospel.

The Society for the Propagation of the Gospel was started by the Moravians in 1797 as an outlet of the Herrnhut mission training center. It had great staying power and was famous for coordinating the work of Pietists and Evangelicals in such lands as India.

The London Missionary Society (LMS) was formed in 1795, only three years after the one started by William Carey. It was started with the intention of being free from control by any specific denomination but was later taken over by the British Congregationalists. The LMS was one of the first to recognize the problem of transplanting culture instead of Christ. Its declared intention was to have the gospel preached without being tied to Western culture. The missionaries of the LMS failed in the intent, but they were at least aware of the problem. The LMS started work in Ceylon in 1814, as it had done in the South Seas in 1796. The LMS entered Madagascar in 1818. There was no missionary society so widely involved geographically in the early nineteenth century.

The Church Missionary Society (CMS) was started by Anglican Evangelicals in 1799. This society had as its aim the establishing of self-governing churches. In 1816, the CMS sent a contingent to help the Church of the Saint Thomas Christians in India. A party of four was sent to help train native priests. The CMS College was formed in Kottayam. Christians were educated and unbelievers evangelized.

At times CMS missionaries even encouraged native converts not to become Anglicans. The wishes to that effect were recorded by CMS strategists in 1836 when they decreed their "decided conviction that we ought to preserve their identity and not attempt to amalgamate them with the Church of England."

The CMS honor roll of missionaries includes Alexander Mackay, Edward Stuart, and Valpy French. The society in 1900 had almost six hundred mission stations with over four hundred missionaries.

The Scottish Missionary Society (SMS) came into being in 1796. Presbyterians and others were appointed. Their first missionaries were sent to Sierra Leone. One of the first sent was Peter Greig, who was martyred by native traders around Foulah. In 1798, the society sent missionaries to Moslems in Russia, where the New Testament was translated into Russian. The SMS sent envoys to India in 1822.

The London Society for Promoting Christianity Among the Jews was started in 1809 on an ecumenical basis at first but was affiliated with the Anglicans in 1815. In 1825, Michael Alexander was baptized and became the first Anglican bishop in Jerusalem. A remarkable missionary was Joseph Wolff, who worked for forty years in Ethiopia and called himself the Protestant Xavier. Similar in purpose, the British Society for the Propagation of the Gospel Among the Jews was started in 1842 and worked throughout the nineteenth century in all major European cities.

The China Inland Mission was started as a transdenominational effort in 1866 by Hudson Taylor, a missionary to China. At its height, the society had almost eight hundred missionaries in China with almost six hundred paid native clergy or helpers. They have been instrumental in starting almost one thousand new churches in China.

The American Board of Commissioners for Foreign Missions (ABCFM) was started in 1810 and sent Adoniram Judson to India in 1812. The ABCFM at its apex sponsored more than three hundred missionaries with a similar number of native pastors in twenty-five nations.

The Religious Tract Society was started in 1799 for the circulation of Christian literature in the British provinces. Five years later the British and Foreign Bible Society (BFBS), similar in intent but broader in scope, was organized. This latter group sponsored Carey's Serampore translations. More than two hundred languages saw the Bible under this society's ministry. More than one-quarter billion pieces of literature have been distributed by the BFBS.

One of the early directors of this British society reasoned:

> Where would the Missionary Societies have been without the Religious Tract Society; the preacher and the teacher might have used their voices within a very limited circle; they could do little with their voices alone in comparison with that which they could do with the aid of such literature as the Tract Society provides.

The American Bible Society was started in 1825, the brainchild of W. Allen Hallock. It is currently a home agency for distribution within the USA but has aided in work in Turkey, India, China, and Japan before becoming affiliated with the worldwide work of the United Bible Societies.

The Paris Society for Evangelical Missions (PSEM) was started in 1824 to send French Christian missionaries to such places as South Africa. Major Malan was one such missionary to that region for the PSEM. Perhaps the most effective missionary sent out by this group was Francois Caillard, who spent time in Basutoland and Rhodesia.

The Norwegian Missionary Society was started by Evangelical Lutherans in 1842 in Stavanger where a missionary college was also established. It has been active in Madagascar.

The American Tract Society was started in New York City in 1825. In 1982, the organization printed more than 160 million pages of printed material. More than 2 million pieces of Christian literature are printed weekly. The headquarters are now in Garland, Texas.

The Home Mission Board of the Southern Baptist Convention

On May 12, 1845, a resolution was passed at the first meeting of the newly formed Southern Baptist Convention. It read, in part:

> *Resolved,* that the Board of Domestic Missions be instructed to take all prudent measures, for the religious instruction of our colored population. . . . *Resolved,* that this convention recommend to the Board of Domestic Missions, to direct its effective attention to aid the present effort, to establish the Baptist cause in the city of New Orleans.

Thus was born what we now know as the Home Mission Board of the Southern Baptist Convention (HMB, SBC). From 1845 through 1859 the total receipts were $266,000, an average of only $19,000 per year.

The Civil War proved to be a major disruption to the work. In 1860, there were just over 100 missionaries on the field serving almost 400 churches. A total of 12 hundred converts were baptized that year. During the Civil War, Southern Baptists employed at one time or other more than 130 missionaries to work among the soldiers.

By 1870, the work was in full swing again. There were more than 90 missionaries in the states of Tennessee, Mississippi, Alabama, Georgia, and Virginia.

In 1882, the board was moved from Marion, Alabama to Atlanta, Georgia.

This chart shows the HMB, SBC's growth through the years:

Year	Missionaries	Cash Receipts
1846	7	$1,800
1856	100	$23,000
1866	53	$23,000
1876	26	$19,000
1886	255	$80,000
1896	411	$215,000
1906	880	$176,000

Woman's Missionary Union of the Southern Baptist Convention

The Woman's Missionary Union of the Southern Baptist Convention (WMU, SBC) was formed in 1888 in Baltimore. The power behind the organization was Annie Armstrong. She made the motion which set the organization into being.

The preamble to the constitution of the WMU, SBC reads:

> We, the women of the churches connected with the Southern Baptist Convention, desirous of stimulating the missionary spirit and the grace of giving among the women and children of the churches, and aiding in collecting funds for missionary purposes, to be disbursed by the boards of the Southern Baptist Convention, and disclaiming all intention of independent action, organize and adopt the following.

The first elected president was Martha E. McIntosh of South Carolina. She served from 1888 to 1892.

Annie Armstrong served as corresponding secretary from 1888 to 1906. She was born in Baltimore, the daughter of wealthy and cultured parents. She was converted at age twenty under the preaching of Richard Fuller. From that moment of conversion, she took the motto "Go Forward." Miss Armstrong brought to the movement deep missionary zeal and experienced leadership.

Annie Armstrong was a businesswoman of unique capacity. She once wrote a Convention leader, "I have always had an idea that if I had been a man, I would have been successful in business, for I believe I have some ability in that line."

"Miss Annie" became a household word among Southern Baptists. On the day the WMU was formed, Annie Armstrong had in her hand a letter from Dr. Tichenor of the HMB, SBC, asking to raise five thousand dollars for a church building in Havana. Late in 1888, the WMU took a Christmas offering of two thousand dollars to go to China.

The WMU started a literature department in 1906. That year a publication was started. It was called *Our Mission Fields* and was to be published quarterly.

The Southern Baptist Theological Seminary in Louisville admitted women starting in 1902. A WMU training school for women was set up in Louisville in 1907. The WMU's annual meeting passed a resolution which read, in part, "To open a Training School the coming fall, though it has neither house nor equipment . . . neither faculty nor pupils." The women pledged to raise ten thousand dollars. The buildings were occupied in 1917 by fifty-seven young women.

Annie Armstrong was replaced by Edith C. Crane in 1907. Miss Crane had just previously been an executive officer in New York City for the Young Women's Christian Association (YWCA). She served for four years with distinction.

Kathleen Mallory took over as corresponding secretary for the WMU in 1912. She served for thirty-six years. Miss Mallory was responsible for the name of the WMU magazine being changed from *Our Mission Fields* to *Royal Service.*

The *WMU Year Book* published first in 1912 had a page on mission study. It contained this suggestion:

If the conditions do not favor a mission study class, a reading circle might be formed to meet from house to house, having one member read some mission textbook while others sew. Many bypaths of research will open up and the informality will encourage discussion and merriment. It follows that the next missionary meeting will be less solemn.

The WMU's first annual meeting in 1889 was the scene for this statement:

Profoundly impressed with the importance of early training for the young in mission work as a material aid in the missionary cause, Home and foreign, it is recommended that young people's societies and Bands be organized and fostered in all states.

The recommendation was adopted. In 1896 the WMU took the responsibility for the Sunbeam Band work.

In 1907, WMU gave the name of Young Women's Auxiliary to the six hundred young ladies' missionary groups scattered throughout the churches of the SBC. The Girl's Auxiliary was started in 1913.

The missionary societies of the nineteenth century, following in the footsteps of William Carey, set the tone for the doing of missions in the modern era. Early Southern Baptist efforts reflected the parallel work being done by the various societies, from the London Missionary Society to the American Tract Society. These early ecumenical and loose-knit organizations stressed:

1. Voluntary cooperation;
2. Pooling of financial and spiritual resources;
3. Specifically targeted emphases and goals;
4. Transdenominational efforts with ecumenical governing bodies; and
5. Ambitious desires for the conquest of the world for the gospel's sake.

These early efforts at cooperative mission work are still being reflected today, particularly among Evangelicals. These societies contributed significantly also to their own day by providing support for such outstanding individuals as John Vanderkemp and others.

The period between 1792 and 1914 saw a colorful parade of giants in the modern mission efforts. These individuals are still remembered for their sacrificial lives in lands viewed by other nineteenth-century "moderns" as unbearable. These brave few still stand as examples of daring discipleship to those who tread similar paths in 1984. Such names as David Livingstone and Henry M. Stanley will never be forgotten.

John Vanderkemp

The pioneer missionary for the London Missionary Society was John Vanderkemp, M.D. (b. 1747). He arrived in Cape Town, South Africa, in 1799. There he worked among the Mbutis, Hottentots, and Zhosas. He concentrated his work among the Hottentots. He died in 1811, having made an indelible impression on the peoples of South Africa. He is still remembered and beloved by the black peoples there because he fought against white rulers on their behalf and married a black African wife.

Robert Moffat

Robert Moffat (1795-1883) was sent at age twenty-one to Africa by the London Missionary Society. He had no theological training. He served for almost fifty years among the Bechuana peoples. Moffat was successful mostly because of his mastery of the native languages, especially Tswana. This was extremely difficult because Tswana was an unwritten language. He first had to develop an alphabet. By 1857, he had translated the Bible into Tswana. Moffat is remembered for his patience and love for the African peoples.

David Livingstone

David Livingstone (1813-1873) was Robert Moffat's son-in-law. He is by far the most well-known Christian missionary to Africa. He was reared by Scot parents in the Reform tradition of hard work and godly discipline. They were poor but gave young David a deep love for Christ. He went to Africa in 1841, appointed by the London Missionary Society. His training was in theology and medicine, a perfect combination for missionary service. Livingstone joined Moffat and soon married his daughter. For ten years he served with Moffat, learning the Tswana language and staying put with one group of people.

When Livingstone started making longer and longer journeys into the bush, he kept careful records. In 1853, while among the Makololo peoples, he wrote:

> I took thence a more intense disgust at heathenism than I had before, and formed a greatly elevated opinion of the latent effects of missions. . . . I place no value on anything I have or may possess, except in relation to the kingdom of Christ. If anything will advance the interests of the kingdom, it shall be given away.

David Livingstone's conscience was greatly bothered by the slave trade he saw; some Africans were even selling others. Livingstone gave an address at the University of Cambridge in 1857: It was a masterpiece. He said:

> Do you carry on the work which I have begun. I leave it with you. . . . Can the love of Christ not carry the missionary where the slave trade carries the trader? . . . I beg to direct your attention to Africa. I know that in a few years I shall be cut off in that country, which is now open. Do not let it be shut again! I go back to Africa to try to make an open path for commerce and Christianity.

The world remembers Dr. Livingstone as a great explorer, but he was, above all, a missionary. He did trace the Zambesi River to its source, but his purpose in traveling was to treat the natives and win converts to Christ. Along the way, he tried to train the Africans in legitimate trades so they could be less vulnerable to the slave traffickers.

When Livingstone died, his heart was cut out and buried in his beloved Zambia. The remainder of his body is buried at Westminster Abbey. He was a man beloved by those who sent and those who received him alike.

Henry M. Stanley

Henry M. Stanley was a young newspaper reporter sent out by the *New York Herald* to find Livingstone. He found him and was greatly impressed with the doctor's devotion and the needs of the African people. In 1874, he came back to Africa and explored what is known today as Uganda. There he found the Buganda peoples, a vigorous Bantu people. That year Stanley was able to convert the king of the Buganda people. His name was Mtesa, and he was about half Moslem and half nature worshiper. When Stanley left the Uganda region, his work was carried on immediately by the Church Missionary Society (in 1877).

Johann Krapf

An Anglican missionary to Abyssinia was Johann Krapf (1810-1881). He was sent there in 1838 and went in 1844 to Mombasa in Kenya. When his wife died within a few days of his arrival in Kenya, he wrote the directors of the Anglican Church Missionary Society:

> Tell our friends that in a lonely grave here on the African coast there rests a member of the Mission. This is a sign that they have begun the struggle with this part of the world; and since the victories of the Church lead over the graves of many of her members, they may be more convinced that the hour is approaching when you will be called to convert Africa, beginning from the East Coast.

Krapf made a dozen or so journeys inland and is credited with discovering Mount Kenya and Mount Kilimanjaro, the two highest peaks in all Africa. He was instrumental also in the translation of the New Testament into Swahili. Johann Krapf was a pioneer who saw few converts but made the way easier for the Christian witnesses who followed.

Alexander Duff

Alexander Duff (1806-1878) was a notable pioneer in Christian higher education in India. He went to India in 1829 as the first official missionary of the Church of Scotland. As Roberto de Nobili before him, Duff sought to win the Brahmins. Alexander soon won the friendship of Ram Mohan Roy, who had organized the Brahmo Samaj in 1828. That group was an attempt to syncretize Hindu, Christian, and other religious beliefs.

When Duff started Christian schools for instruction in English and in Christian beliefs, it was definitely with evangelistic intent. He made friends with hundreds of young Bengalis. In 1833, he was able to baptize four of them. For the first time in the history of India, Duff's school in Calcutta was teaching young Hindu scholars that Western science and Christian theology were the forces to bring India into the modern era. Duff believed secretly that the two forces could crush Hinduism. Bible study was a central part of the curriculum.

From an evangelism standpoint, Duff's work was disappointing. He reported only about thirty converts in a score of years' work in Christian education. However, the subtle Christian influence on India's young elite was a deep and lasting one.

Ida Scudder

John Scudder II was Ida's father. He arrived in India in 1861 to join the Arcot Mission founded by three of his brothers. He immediately wrote to individuals supporting the mission and complained about low missionary salaries.

Dr. John served at Tindivanam, near Madras. It was a city about 90 percent Hindu and less than 10 percent Muslim. He served as pastor of the small local school and principal of a boarding school for one hundred boys.

Ida was born in the mission compound in India in 1890. She did not have to leave the compound at Tindivanam to see Hinduism. Only a few hundred feet away was a temple to the goddess Kali. She learned to pity the Hindu women who were discriminated against.

In 1892, Dr. John moved his household to Vellore, eighty miles west of Madras. There Ida assumed control of the two day schools for Hindu girls.

She sailed on furlough with her father in 1894 and enrolled in the Women's Medical College in Philadelphia the following year. There she was able to study bacteriology, public health, preventive medicine, and sanitation. All were desperately needed in India.

In 1898, Ida moved to Cornell Medical School in New York state. She was one of the first women to study medicine there. It was not easy. She worked hard and was graduated near the top of her class. The new Dr. Scudder decided to intern with her father at Vellore in South India for a year instead of remaining in the USA. She arrived to find that her father was not well. He died shortly after her arrival. Ida was gripped with grief. She had lost her best friend and close counselor. She handled her grief by staying busy.

In 1901, Ida Scudder recorded that she visited in 177 Hindu and Muslim homes. Later that year she presided over the opening of the Memorial Hospital in Vellore. It was to enhance her work greatly. The hospital grew rapidly. By 1906, there were 150 more inpatients than the year before. By the fall of that year, Dr. Scudder had supervised the core of almost 30 thousand outpatients over a 5 year period.

Ida was concerned about the role of the women in Indian society. A woman's husband was her god. She was taught to have no desires or thoughts apart from her husband. Early marriage was considered a religious obligation.

Nearly half the Hindu girls were married before age fifteen. She tried to change the system by teaching Christian principles and using her medical skills to train the ignorant midwives.

In 1907, Ida went to America on furlough. When she came back to India in 1908, she started plans for a boarding school. There was great difficulty in recruiting students. Nonetheless, the school was going by the next year. The bright girls usually became teachers.

In 1909, Ida secured an automobile and started making numerous visits to neighboring villages for clinics and public health training. By 1913, she and the newly trained nurses were making about five hundred visits a year.

Ida came to America in 1914 to solicit further financial support. She got little as World War I was raging in Europe. She was successful, however, in spreading information about her work.

In 1918, Ida performed the miraculous feat of opening a new medical school for women. It was an ecumenical endeavor of several Christian groups. The school was open to all, regardless of class, caste, or creed. Eighteen was the minimum age.

Her worst problem was the feeding of her new female students. Finally she divided the Hindu, Muslim, and Christian students into three categories: vegetarians, meatarians, and eggarians.

Ida's Tuesday Bible classes were most effective in providing Christian witness and training. Her one course was "The Life of Paul." By 1920, Ida was running a hospital, two weekly drug dispensaries, and a medical college.

In 1922, Dr. Scudder came back to America for fund raising. She made speeches and wrote dozens of letters. Also, she drafted new recruits to go to India to help her. She set the almost unbelievable goal of raising two million dollars and she reached it.

Dr. Ida Scudder's mother died in August 1925. Hindus,

Muslims, and Christians came bearing gifts. This helped to relieve her daughter's deep grief.

In 1927, Mahatma Ghandi visited Ida's medical school and hospital. He spoke to the students on the maintenance of high standards of morals. Two greats met that day.

By 1936, Ida's hospital was running far behind in financial obligations. That year she wrote in her diary:

> First ponder, then dare. Know your facts. Money is not the most important thing. What you are building is not the medical school. It is the Kingdom of God. Don't err on the side of being too small. If it is the will of God that we should find some way to keep the college open. It has to be done.

As a result of that diary entry, Ida was no longer fearful of the future of her work. Later that year she received the good news that her friends were starting a worldwide prayer fellowship called the Friends of Vellore.

1950 was Ida's jubilee year in India. She started public health services in Kavanur and stressed leprosy rehabilitation. She did not look or act eighty years old. Her enthusiasm was contagious.

In 1957, Ida's eighty-seventh year, great progress came to reward her efforts. A new rural hospital complex was started. It was a project close to Ida's heart.

When Ida died, it was difficult to calculate her contributions to India in Christ's name. They included:

1. Women's liberation;
2. Medical education;
3. Bible teaching;
4. Personal witnessing;
5. Public health instruction;
6. Secondary education; and
7. Personal devotion.

Robert Morrison

Robert Morrison (1781-1834) was the son of a devout Scottish farmer. He became in 1807, when he reached

Canton, the first Protestant missionary to China. He distinguished himself immediately as a master of Cantonese. In 1809, he was appointed the official translator for the East India Company. He spent some of his time writing pamphlets about Christianity and translating the Gospels. The New Testament translation was complete by 1814 and the Old Testament in 1819. His lifework was the compilation of a Chinese dictionary.

Morrison saw less than a dozen converts in his quarter century in Canton. He ordained only one, whose name was A-fah. A-fah was the first Protestant Chinese to be ordained and distinguished himself as a writer of Christian literature for his people.

Robert Morrison's most lasting achievement was the founding of the Anglo-Chinese College in Malacca in 1820. Morrison recorded his hopes for the college, that "the light of science and revelation will, by means of this institution, peacefully and gradually shed their lustre on the eastern limit of Asia and the islands of the rising sun."

Morrison was effective especially because of his identifying with Chinese customs. When he died at age fifty-two in Macao, his influence was just beginning.

Timothy Richard

Timothy Richard (1845-1919) was a fiery young man of Welsh background. He arrived in China in 1870 and served there until his death almost fifty years later. He was a Baptist who had great appreciation for the necessity of conversion and the new Christian's disciplined growth.

Richard moved into the Shantung province in 1875 and found himself in the midst of a great famine. Nearly twenty million people died in the next three years in that province while most parts of China had plenty of food. He became convinced that Western forms of agriculture, transportation, and communication could prevent such tragedy from recurring in his beloved China. He tried to persuade his sponsors to help start a Baptist college in Shantung but they did not respond. He was angry and disappointed and resigned from missionary appointment in 1899.

But, Richard's work was just beginning. He was convinced that China could be Christ's through the wide distribution of Christian literature. Timothy started the new Christian Literature Society for China. He felt that the literate should be reached first since converts from the educated would be effective as missionaries among their own people.

Timothy Richard was a prolific author. His works were read by Chinese leaders in every field. The titles of Richard's works included: *Famine, Disease and Poverty and How to Prevent Them; Freedom and How to Win It;* and *Education for the New China.*

A most revealing occurrence reflective of Richard's influence in China happened in 1890. No less than ten thousand young Chinese political reformers approached the emperor demanding changes. The reformers, under questioning, revealed that they had gotten most of their ideas from Timothy Richard's writings. The emperor then sent his prime minister to see Richard. The envoy returned to the imperial court with the word from Richard. China would be better if reforms were made in four areas: education, economics, internal and international peace, and spiritual renewal. Richard refused the emperor's offer to assist in possible reform, replying, "If I did become advisor to the Emperor I should not have time to be a missionary, and the greatest of these four reforms is spiritual rebirth."

Timothy Richard was stubborn when necessary but concerned about the spiritual welfare of the Chinese always. He is to be honored as one who kept education and evangelism in proper perspective. Richard's ministry was effective overall because the Chinese knew this man's love extended to all areas of their lives.

Hudson Taylor

Hudson Taylor (1832-1905) was trained in medicine so he could go to China. In 1853, he arrived in China, put on Chinese dress, and headed for the interior. It took him seven years to learn Chinese, but his patience paid huge dividends later in his career.

Taylor was originally sponsored by the Chinese Evangelization Society. It was poorly organized and lasted less than a decade. It is not surprising, therefore, that Hudson Taylor resigned from the society and designed to depend solely on God. In 1865, he formed his own China Inland Mission (CIM). It was organized to hire conservative Evangelicals to be "willing, skillful workers." By 1914, the organization had more than one thousand missionaries serving in China.

In 1860, Taylor was forced to return to England because of ill health. While there, he had time to write a short book, entitled, *China's Spiritual Needs and Claims* and to solicit financial support. He also had time to frame the kind of mission society he knew would work in China. He called for the new organization to be:

1. Involved in evangelism;
2. Encouraging of Chinese dress for the missionaries;
3. Directed by Christians in China, not England;
4. Hiring of native clergy with little or no education; and
5. Interdenominational.

The China Inland Mission was remarkable in its success. Recruits for mission service showed up by the hundreds. Most proved to be highly successful. They went even to the people of the far west of China and up to the borders of Tibet. All corners of China were reached with eager, native Chinese missionaries. The CIM missionaries were characterized by mobility, devotion, and simple life-style and message.

Hudson Taylor's impact on China was a great one because of his personal devotion and sharp thinking on the establishment of the China Inland Mission. But, his influence is far greater than just his work in China proper. Evangelicals have learned in the last century and a quarter that church extension in all regions coupled with open recruitment of all willing Christians can make for rapid church growth.

One of his diary entries shows that he saw missions as a combination of his personal involvement and the calling out of other helpers. This one is from January 27, 1854:

> Asked God for fifty or a hundred additional native evangelists and as many missionaries as may be needed to open up the . . . cities still unoccupied in Chekiang, also for men to break into the nine unoccupied provinces. Asked in the name of Jesus.
>
> I thank thee, Lord Jesus, for the promise whereon Thou hast given me to rest. Give me all needed strength of body, wisdom of mind, grace of soul to do this Thy so great work.

Lottie Moon

Charlotte (Lottie) Digges Moon[4] was born in 1840 in Virginia. Hers was a home where Baptist beliefs were firmly established. Her parents at her birth were involved in trying to get a Baptist church started in nearby Scottsville. When only ten, Lottie watched her uncle go off as a missionary with the Disciples of Christ. He was sponsored by the American Christian Missionary Society.

When Lottie was thirteen, her father died. Her mother, Anna Maria Moon, was godly. She allowed no gossiping. There was no cooking on Sunday.

Lottie's older sister Orianna was one of the first Southern women to earn a medical degree. Lottie was sent to the Virginia Female Seminary near Roanoke in 1854. There she studied Latin, French, math, and English. When she returned the next year, the school's name had been changed to Hollins Institute. She was graduated in July 1856. Lottie Moon heard the valedictory message urging women to seek their rights. Lottie heard what was said and never forgot it. This was in a day when the "proper" Baptist woman was to keep silent in the churches.

Lottie Moon then enrolled in the new Baptist school for women in Charlottesville, Albermarle Female Institute. One of the faculty members was H. H. Harris, later to serve as president of the Foreign Mission Board of the Southern Baptist Convention. By 1858, Lottie had earned a diploma in Latin.

In December 1858, Lottie made a profession of faith in Christ. One of her peers wrote, "She immediately took a stand as a Christian. She was different in all those details of the daily life which at last afforded the most delicate test of the Christian character."

John A. Broadus kept before all the students in Charlottesville the possibility of foreign missions. He stressed the whole world's need for the gospel and God's desire that we take the gospel to every land. Every time Lottie Moon heard Broadus speak about foreign missions, she knew that he was speaking mainly to men and only to those women who might go as wives. But, Lottie was responding in the affirmative.

At the institute, Lottie took Greek, Latin, Italian, French, and Spanish. She received a special Master of Arts degree from the University of Virginia. She was only the fifth woman to receive such a degree.

The Civil War had begun by the time Lottie graduated. She returned home where she found life dull. Yet, she remained two years. She went away to tutor private students in Alabama and Georgia for a while and was back home by the end of the war in 1865.

In the fall of 1866, Lottie went as an instructor to the Danville Female Academy in Kentucky. There she taught for three years.

A Southern Baptist missionary to China, G. W. Bunton, came to Danville. He was to influence Lottie all the time she was in Danville.

In 1870, Lottie went home to care for her mother. After

her mother died, Lottie wrote to a friend, "She died peacefully and happily . . . I think I can never fear death after watching her triumph over it."

Lottie returned to Danville for the fall term of 1870. She was troubled about what the churches were calling the "woman question." Lottie wrote a letter to the *Religious Herald.* She argued, "Our Lord does not call upon women to preach, or to pray in public, but no less does he say to them than to men. 'Go work today in my vineyard.' "

Lottie had a distant cousin who was a merchant in Cartersville, Georgia. She moved there for the school year beginning in 1871. She was made associate principal of the Cartersville Female High School.

In 1872, Lottie's younger sister, Edmonia, went to China as a Southern Baptist missionary. Early in 1873 Lottie began to inquire about personal appointment. In July, she was officially appointed. Georgia Baptists were asked to assume the bulk of her support.

Lottie wrote to friends for help:

> Young brethren, can you, knowing the land call for laborers in the foreign field, will you settle down with your home pastorates? . . . For women, too, foreign missions open a new and enlarged sphere of labor and furnish opportunities for good which angels might also envy. Could a Christian woman possibly desire higher honor than to be permitted to go from house to house and tell of a Saviour to those who have never heard his name?

She sailed for China in September 1873. Lottie was assigned to Shantung Province, the most densely populated spot on earth. She served in the city of Tengchow for thirty-three years. She moved in with her younger sister, Edmonia, and was soon at work learning Mandarin Chinese. She learned faster than most new missionaries.

At once Miss Moon noticed the Chinese women and their hesitancy to become Christians. She wrote home, "Their deformed feet and tottering walk are but a type of their narrow minds and degraded morals. The greatest blessing we could bestow upon this people is the Christian education of the future wives and mothers."

Lottie returned home for a furlough late in 1876. Edmonia had decided not to return, and Lottie was given the news that she would have to raise her own support. She was able to raise such support and was back in China in November 1877.

Upon returning to China, Miss Moon started a Christian school for girls. The courses included reading, math, and geography. She had the students memorize all of Matthew and Mark. In the first year, three of the girls were baptized into the new Tengchow Baptist Church.

Lottie Moon was also instrumental in starting new churches in outlying provinces, unheard of for a woman in the 1880s. She went to Pingtu in 1885, more than a hundred miles from Tengchow. After her first trip there, she wrote:

> If experience teaches anything in China, it is that the gospel succeeds much better in the country than in the cities. Preaching in a city chapel has a fine sound or looks like work. In point of fact, it is the easiest and least productive kind of missionary work.

In her church extension work, Lottie had a definite strategy. She wanted to establish a permanent Christian presence in Pingtu, so she did not draw immediate attention to herself by preaching in the streets. Rather, her strategy was to become a friend and neighbor. She wanted to be a teacher and counselor on a personal basis. She wanted to demonstrate a Chinese-Christian life-style, win the people's confidence first and then speak of Christ. She wrote to the missionaries back in Tengchow, "We must go out and live among them, manifesting the gentle, loving spirit of our Lord. We need to make friends before we can hope to make converts."

In the meantime, Lottie Moon was busy writing home

urging Southern Baptists to give more to mission causes. In a widely-distributed letter, she wrote:

> I wonder how many of us really believe that it is more blessed to give than to receive. A woman who accepts that statement of our Lord Jesus Christ as a fact, and not as impractical idealism, will make giving a principle of her life. She will lay aside sacredly not less than one-tenth of her income or her earnings as the Lord's money.

Encouraged by her success in church extension, Lottie adopted more of the Chinese life-style. She was no longer too squeamish to eat a Chinese meal. She learned to sit in filthy conditions in order to teach about Jesus. She wrote back home, asking for human help:

> We do not ask people to come out and live in costly style, hardly touching the heathen world with the tips of their fingers, but we ask them to come prepared to cast in their lot with the natives.

In 1888, the fledgling WMU, SBC was taking its first Baptist Christmas offering for missions. The women set a goal of $2000 and collected $3315. It was announced that this was enough to send three young women to help Lottie Moon. Within a year Fannie Knight, Laura Barton, and Mary Thornton were on their way. The coming of these three women to China did not slow Lottie Moon down in asking for more help. She wrote to friends in Virginia:

> The hard pioneer work has been done . . . There is now a wide-open door . . . I am trying honestly to do the work that ought to be done by young men. The men are not here, nor as to that matter, the women either.

In 1891, she returned home for a much-needed furlough. She was the center of attention in the annual meeting of the WMU in 1892.

When she returned to China late in 1893, it was agreed that she should concentrate on rural evangelism. She visited more than eighty villages within the next year, instructing the people in Christian doctrine. She wrote:

> I have never found mission work more enjoyable. To go out daily among a kindly people, among enchanting views of nature . . . all this to me is most delightful. I constantly thank God that he has given me work that I love so much.

On a typical day, Lottie would visit two villages, usually six to eight miles apart. She was greeted at the edge of the villages by those who called her Kiang, or "Mother Teacher."

In 1898, Miss Moon started a coeducational school back in Tengchow, the first one in China. She described it as being like Sunday School every day.

The Boxer Rebellion brought grief to the Chinese Baptist Mission in 1900. Many missionaries left. Lottie served as a missionary in Japan from mid-1900 to mid-1901. She then returned to her beloved China.

In 1902, Lottie came to the US for furlough again. By 1904 she was back to resume her work in China. She worked with faithfulness until illness overcame her.

Lottie Moon died on her way home from China on Christmas Eve, 1912. The captain wrote: "Tuesday, December 24, 1912, Harbor of Kobe, Japan. Miss Lottie Moon, age 72, died of melancholia and senility. The remains were cremated at Yokohama on December 26."

In Tengchow Christians and non-Christians alike gathered for a memorial service. A monument was erected. It read: "To bequeath the love of Miss Lottie Moon, an American missionary. The Tengchow church remembers forever."

Southern Baptists and most evangelical Christians have never forgotten the pioneer work of Lottie Moon. In her name, more than 450 million dollars have been gathered. Every penny has gone directly to mission effort. Lottie Moon lives on wherever women are unafraid of being free in Christ and wherever sacrificial giving of time, treasure, and talents are done in foreign lands.

The cause of Protestant missions in the nineteenth century was, indeed, blessed with outstanding pioneering individuals. From John Vanderkemp to Lottie Moon, these pioneers manifested these common characteristics, which left indelible marks on Christ's cause around the world. These included:

1. A deep compassion for and identification with their adopted people;
2. A realization of the need to solicit prayer and financial support (with the exception of J. Hudson Taylor) from the Christians in the nation from whence they came;
3. A committed advocacy on both the national and international level on behalf of the suffering people among whom they ministered;
4. A commitment to the targeting of previously overlooked peoples; and
5. A concern that the persons in contact with their ministry end up better off both spiritually and physically.

Nineteenth-Century Roman Catholic Missions

The Roman Catholics in Europe suffered severely from the French Revolution and the military triumphs of Napoleon Bonaparte. Both Spain and Portugal were declining and becoming less important as sending bases for the monks as missionaries.

A severe blow to Roman Catholic missions came also with the loss of prestige of the Jesuits. They had caused jealousy by some of the other religious orders because of their wide success on the mission field. By 1759, they were expelled from all Portuguese-held territories. France followed suit in 1764 and Spain in 1767. Finally, the pope dissolved the society in 1773. Undaunted, the Jesuits continued to work in Russia where they could escape the influence of the pope. By 1814, the pope had restored their official status in all parts of the world.

The French Revolution broke out in 1789. It arose out of a seething discontent among the middle class about social conditions in the major cities. Also, the French had aided the colonists in the American Revolution and were touched by the ideas found in the Declaration of Independence and other American documents. Paris was the most populous city of western Europe and whatever happened there was bound to affect the rest of the continent.

In the early stages of the French Revolution, direct attacks were made on the institution of Roman Catholicism. In August 1789, tithes were outlawed. Later that year all church property was confiscated. In 1790, the monasteries were officially dissolved. The French Constitution of 1791 gave complete religious freedom to all citizens. This cut into the privileges which had been enjoyed by the Catholic churches.

In 1794, in effect, a new national religion was created in France, a form of Deism. It was decreed that the French people affirmed the existence of the Supreme Being and the immortality of the soul. Christianity was announced as primitive superstition. In 1798, Pope Pius VI was captured and brought to France, where he died.

At that time, Napoleon Bonaparte (1769-1821) came to power. In 1804, he turned France into a republic and had himself declared emperor. Napoleon was a nominal Catholic but had little personal faith. He had a new pope elected, who called himself Pius VII, and returned him to power in Rome. But, Napoleon decreed that no decrees were to be published by the new pope without the emperor's approval. Finally, in 1808, Pius VII excommunicated Napoleon as "a robber of the patrimony of Peter."

The duo of the French Revolution and Napoleon brought Roman Catholic missions to a virtual standstill. For the three decades following 1789, there were very few new missionaries sent out. The Sacred Congregation of

Propaganda was taken over by Napoleon and reduced to a small advisory council rather than a training center.

In spite of these severe setbacks of French origin, Roman Catholics were to have a highly successful nineteenth century of mission efforts for several reasons.

New Orders

In 1800, Madeleine Sophie Barat founded the Society of the Sacred Heart of Jesus. It was a congregation of women devoted to education.

From France came the Congregation of Pigsus, founded by Condrin, a priest who had been faithful under persecution in France. It got official papal support in 1817. From the beginning, it was an order given to missions.

In 1802, Edmund Rice started the Christian Brothers of Ireland, carrying on the tradition of Patrick to bring the gospel to the villages of the Emerald Isle through traveling clerics.

These new orders pumped new life into Roman Catholic missions at a time when such life was needed desperately. They were part of a larger context of renewed life of all the Catholic monastic orders during the early nineteenth century.

In 1816, Charles de Mozenod (1762-1861) started the Oblates of the Immaculate Virgin Mary. He designed the order to be missionaries among the skeptics in France. The order got official papal approval in 1826.

1816 also saw the beginning of an order popularly known as Society of Mary. It was started by Jean Colin (1790-1875). It received papal approval in 1836. The islands of the South Pacific were its primary targets for missions during the last three quarters of the nineteenth century.

Gaspare del Bufalo (1786-1837) started The Congregation of the Most Precious Book in 1815. Bufalo was often called the "little apostle of Rome." He was a very powerful traveling preacher. The order was especially effective in France, Italy, and some parts of North America.

Vincent Mary Palloti (1798-1850) started the Pious Society of Missions. The order became known for its care of the poor and sick on the mission field. The order was officially begun in 1835. The major mission work was done by Pallotines in Italy, England, Germany, and in some parts of Africa and North Africa.

The Society of the Holy Ghost was reconstituted in Paris in 1816 and got the pope's official approval eight years later. The chief mission field of this society was in the French colonies of North America. In 1846, the Society of the Holy Ghost was merged with the Congregation of the Immaculate Heart of Mary. This latter society had been started by a Christian Jew named Jacob Liebermann. With the merger, the new group began missions also in West Africa.

John Bosco (1815-1888) was instrumental in beginning the Salesians Fathers. The Salesians devoted themselves at first to aiding orphaned boys in the Turin area. Within the first generation of their existence, the Salesians were also busy at work in the French colonies in North America.

These new orders gave new life to Catholic missions by supplying new personnel, vision, papal loyalty, care for the sick, coverage of new colonial territory and inspiration for devoted Catholics on the edge of despair in the early nineteenth century.

Deepening Lay Piety

The nineteenth century saw a rise in devotion to the Virgin Mary among European Catholics. Finally, in 1854, Pope Pius IX formally declared the Immaculate Conception of Mary to be an official teaching, or dogma, of the Church. Mary was declared to "immune from all taint of original sin."

In 1858, the famous Bernadette announced that the virgin Mary had appeared to her almost twenty times in a grotto near Lourdes, France. Thousands of pilgrims came there within the decade that followed. More than five million faithful Catholics came to Lourdes to adore Mary before the end of the nineteenth century.

Joseph, the earthly father of Jesus, also received honors during this period. Pope Puis IX declared him to be patron saint of the whole church.

The Sacred Heart of Jesus became the center of adoration, emphasizing the passion and sacrifice of Christ. The symbol was the bleeding heart of Jesus. Several new orders or societies took the name Sacred Heart of Jesus.

Laity in the Church were also aided in their daily devotion to the holy family by a revolution in sacred music. In 1903, Pope Pius X issued a decree on church music, declaring that the Gregorian chant or form should be standard. It was restored to the central place in Catholic church music through most parts of the world during the six decades which followed.

Groups of laity in the Catholic Church were encouraged during the latter half of the nineteenth century to aid local bishops in doing the work of the Church. Catholic schools and political action were encouraged through this lay renewal movement. This broad but unnamed movement gave impetus to lay involvement in piety and the mission of the Church, especially in Italy.

Adoration of Canonized Saints

One outstanding person honored as a saint in the nineteenth century was Jean-Baptiste Marie Vianney (1786-1859). He started a school and orphanage for the care of girls in Lyons. After 1827, thousands of people came to him for spiritual discernment, counseling, and healing.

One pope was canonized during this period. He was Pope Pius X (1835-1914). He reigned as pope the last eleven years of his life. The people called him the "peasant pope" because of his humble background and identification with the masses. He was officially canonized in 1954.

This emphasis on saints gave Roman Catholic missions a boost in the period between the French Revolution and World War I. Clerical and lay missionaries were inspired by the saints' examples and encouraged by the slight possibility that they, too, could be canonized after death. New churches and mission stations were named for those recently canonized. The new orders were particularly fond of this practice. Deep personal piety was increased. Mission effort grew. The Roman Catholics missionaries were on the march, with the whole world their parish.

Increased Papal Authority

With the popularity of Napoleon, the nineteenth century did not begin well for papal authority. But, as the century moved on, the matter of the pope's power was greatly improved. The primary reason with that the Catholic Church was indeed becoming catholic (that is, worldwide). The Congregation for the Propagation of the Faith was restored in 1814 and became truly the instrument through which the pope supervised and directed missions.

The major reason for the enhancement of the pope's power in the nineteenth century was the actions of Vatican Council I. There had been no general council since Trent closed in 1563. The council met in 1869 and 1870. The key issue was that of papal authority. The council decreed, "The primacy and jurisdiction over the universal church of God was immediately and directly provised and given to Blessed Peter the Apostle by Christ the Lord." The council went even further:

> To the jurisdiction of the Roman pontiff, all, of whatever right and dignity, both pastors and faithful, both individually and collectively, are bound to submit, not only in matters that pertain to faith and morals, but also in those which appertain to the discipline and government of the church throughout the world.

The issue was settled. The pope's authority was even

asserted to be over that of an ecumenical council. The question of infallibility was settled thusly:

> It is a dogma divinely revealed that the Roman Pontiff, when he speaks ex cathedra, that is, when in the discharge of the office of pastor and doctor of all Christians, by virtue of his supreme apostolic authority he defines a doctrine regarding faith or morals to be held by the universal Church, by the Divine assistance provised to him in blessed Peter, is possessed of that infallibility with which the Divine Redeemer willed that His Church should be endowed.

The result of the Vatican Council I was to produce a Church that was close knit. This aided the cause of missions greatly because it could be provised confidently that new converts were, indeed, joining the worldwide Church.

The Church as Antimodern

The tendency of nineteenth-century popes to declare publicly against modernistic trends in society started with Pope Leo XII, who ruled from 1823-1829. He issued statements against Bible societies, restored the Inquisition to an official status, opposed Freemasonry, and denounced the movement toward individual freedom of choice.

Pope Pius IX came to the papal throne in 1846 and stayed there thirty-two years. He was an ultraconservative who proclaimed the dogma of the Immaculate Conception of Mary, called Vatican Council I, and affirmed the supremacy of the pope over all parts of the Roman Catholic Church.

In 1864, Pope Pius IX issued his now famous *Syllabus of Errors,* in which he listed under eighty categories the errors of his day. Among those he listed are:
1. The idea that God equals nature;
2. That human reason is the only judge of truth;
3. That Divine revelation is imperfect;
4. That Jesus Christ is a mythical invention;

 5. That the Church ought never to stand in judgment over philosophy;
 6. That every man is free to adopt whatever religion he deems in accord with reason;
 7. That in every religion men may find the way to eternal life;
 8. That Protestantism is another form of the Christian religion in which it is as possible to be pleasing to God as in the Roman Catholic Church;
 9. That the Church might not use force;
 10. That the immunity of the clergy from the military should be discontinued;
 11. That the civil power should have full control of the public schools for the education of youth in Christian states;
 12. That public schools should be free from all church authority;
 13. That the Church and state should be separated;
 14. That divorce may be pronounced by a civil authority;
 15. That marriage is not a sacrament; and
 16. That the pope should be reconciled to progress, liberalism, and modern civilization.

This work, *The Syllabus of Errors,* was a clear sign that the Church was both threatened by and desirous of being preeminent over civil and secular authorities and movements of every sort. When this document was understood in those areas where Roman Catholic missionaries were working, it made the work difficult as some saw the missionaries as agents of a foreign power. The good side was that it gave the envoys of the Church a clear line of authority. Coupled with the Vatican I's declaration of papal authority and infallibility, this papal reaction to modernism let the the priests and bishops know where they stood in relation to the world's new trends.

Most of the popes in the era covered by this chapter set themselves against modern currents. They were, however, voices "crying in the wilderness." The trends toward industrialism, civil power, personal freedom, and modern science could not be stopped by papal decree.

The missionaries in this antimodernist period were more negatively than positively affected. They came to be seen in nations seeking freedom and independence as representatives of a colonial and backward era. Yet, they were able to overcome such feelings in most cases by selfless service to the indigenous peoples they served.

Japan and Korea

James Curtis Hepburn (1815-1911) was skilled in both medicine and linguistics. He reached Japan in 1859, only a few months after the treaty with the US allowing some foreigners to have permanent residency. He soon translated most of the Bible into Japanese and compiled an English-Japanese dictionary. The emperor of Japan gave Dr. Hepburn a commendation for his work in educating young men. This Presbyterian stayed in Japan for more than three decades and was most loved by the Japanese.

A bright Dutch youth named Guido Verbeck (1830-1898) was a natural linguist who soon learned Japanese. In 1871, through his influence, an imperial contingent was sent to visit Western nations. At his death, Verbeck was given a state funeral. He received the highest of all imperial decorations, the Rising Sun.

Ivan Kasatkin entered Japan in 1861 as a chaplain to the Russian consulate. He translated the Russian Orthodox worship books into Japanese. By 1906, Kasatkin had the name Father Nicolai and was the Orthodox archbishop in Japan. When Japan and Russia were at war in 1904, he took the Japanese side. By the time of his death in 1912, Father Nicolai had seen more than thirty thousand converts. This was the largest Russian Orthodox group of churches outside of Russia.

The American missionary John L. Nevius changed Korean Christianity, especially Protestantism, by introducing

some new and radical ideas starting in 1890. These ideas
included:

1. Stewardship, including the tithe;
2. Personal neighborhood and clan evangelism through
   a "tentmaking" ministry;
3. Self-supporting churches;
4. Korean ministers supported by Koreans;
5. Korean church buildings built along Korean lines;
   and
6. Small-group Bible studies.

Nevius's suggestions were very helpful when coupled
with the pioneer work of Horace Underwood and John
Ross. John Ross had arrived in Korea in 1875 from Manchuria. He was a Scottish Presbyterian missionary who
soon translated the New Testament into Korean. The first
Korean Christians were baptized by Ross in 1884 in Manchuria. Ross's Bible translation work laid the groundwork
for Nevius's reforms. The combination of Bible-based
evangelicalism and practical church growth methods has
made Korean Protestantism one of the stablest and yet
fastest growing of the past century. Evangelicals worldwide
are enthusiastic about the church growth and spiritual
depth seen in Korea since 1975. The pioneers did their
work well.

The South Pacific

The London Missionary Society sent out missionaries to
the South Pacific Islands in 1796. Most of those who went
had gained their impressions of the islands by reading the
same journals that had spurred William Carey.

If the first missionaries to the South Seas were looking
for excitement, they soon found it. One wrote back:

> Cannibalism . . . was here elevated into a national cult and
> custom. The man who had eaten the greatest number of
> human beings was the highest in the social order. They
> used to mark these pleasant little achievements by memori-
> al stones.

The chief contingent of the Anglicans landed on Tahiti in 1796. The king was named Pomare and was a cannibal. His son later repented and was baptized. The people were won to Christ en mass during the beginning of the nineteenth century. By 1838, the whole Bible had been translated in Tahitian.

Some of the original landing party in Tahiti went on to Tonga. However, four of them were killed and the remainder fled to Australia. By 1830, the Methodist John Williams went to Tonga and left behind at least eight trained Tongan pastors. By 1834, he was able to say that no island within 2,000 miles of Tahiti had been unvisited and left without native Christian teachers.

The first missionaries landed in Hawaii in 1820. They were Congregationalists from the ABCFM. The first to arrive was a group of almost twenty. Within a score of years, the language was reduced to writing and portions of the Bible translated. A great revival broke out in 1839 and more than twenty thousand Hawaiians were baptized within the next two years, one fifth of the total population. But, the ABCFM greatly reduced its involvement in 1863 and today the percentage of Christians in Hawaii is below its 1840 peak.

Samuel Marsden reached New Zealand in 1814, leading a small party of Anglican missionaries. The first Anglican bishop, George A. Selwyn, arrived in 1842. He is remembered as stately, patient, and determined to spread the faith. In 1835, Charles Darwin visited New Zealand and wrote of the mission work there: "All this is very surprising when it is considered that five years ago nothing but the fern flourished here. . . . The lesson of the missionary is the enchanter's wand."

North America

The nineteenth century in North America was the scene of great Christian advance. There were conversions of great numbers of nonbelievers and spiritual deepening of nominal Christians by the tens of thousands.

There was an excitement in the air. Huge hunks of territory were being explored, settled, and incorporated. In 1800, the total population was just over five million in the US. By 1900, that number was seventy-six million. Cities were mushrooming literally on the edge of the wild frontier. By 1900, more than one-third of the US population was classified as urban.

American Christianity could have stood a boost as the nineteenth century dawned. In 1800, only one in fourteen Americans held church membership. Sectarian splits had people confused. Atheism and Deism were gaining popularity and status, especially in the Northeast. Yet, Christianity grew. By 1900, about three in every seven Americans were church members.

Much of this growth was helped by the Great Awakenings on the American frontier. The first Great Awakening took place in the previous century. The excitement continued as the new century dawned. The key emphasis was on conversion. Strict personal morality and deep piety followed closely.

The Great Awakening started in 1726 in New Jersey with the preaching of Theodore J. Frelinghuysen (1691-1748). He preached at many places, emphasizing daily piety. His sermons were fiery and emotional. The fervor spread.

Jonathan Edwards (1703-1758) brought the Great Awakening to Massachusetts in 1734 and again in 1739. Hundreds saw permanent changes in their lives and attitudes. Jonathan Edwards was born the son of a pastor. He was graduated from Yale in 1720. In 1746, Edwards published *A Treatise Concerning Religious Affections* in which he defended the role of emotionalism in revivalism. In 1750, Edwards resigned his pastorate in Northhampton and went to work among the Indians at Stockbridge. This gave him more time for study. In 1754, he wrote *Freedom of the Will* in which he described the inclination on man's part to turn to God as an act of grace. That helped the theology of revivalism to gain some credence among skeptics. Edwards died before he could complete a systematic theology, but his written work helped those involved in the Great Awakening in their development of a theological base.

Two samples from his treatises show the depth of Edwards's thought:

> God has endued the soul with two faculties: one is that by which it is capable of perception and speculation, or by which it discerns and views, and judges of things, which is called the understanding . . . . The will and the affections of the soul are not two faculties; the affections are not essentially distinct from the will. . . .
>
> The sense that natural men may have of the awful greatness of God may affect them various ways; it may not only terrify them, but it may elevate them, and raise their joy and praise, according to their circumstances.

In the literary world, Edwards is best remembered for his sermon, "Sinners in the Hands of an Angry God." It was read by Edwards in a low, monotone voice with little emotion. However, it was said to be terrifying and convicting by those who heard it. An excerpt reads:

> The bow of God's arrow is bent, and the arrow made ready on the string, and justice bends the arrow at your heart, and strains the bow, and it is nothing but the mere pleasure of God, and that of an angry God, without any promise or obligation at all, that keeps the arrow one moment from being made drunk with your blood. . . .
>
> The God that holds you over the pit of hell, much as one holds a spider, or some loathesome insect, over the fire, abhors you, and is dreadfully provoked: his wrath toward you burns like fire; he looks upon you as worthy of nothing else, but to be cast into the fire; he has purer eyes than to bear to have you in his sight; you are ten thousand times more abominable in his eyes, than the most hateful venomous serpent is in ours.

It is no wonder that Edwards's most famous sermon

caused consternation and brought forth repentance. Edwards was a vital link in the revival movement which was to give powerful impetus to American-based missions.

The Second Great Awakening showed its signs as early as 1792, the year of Carey's impact on missions. By 1800, revival among American Protestants was in full swing. The awakening was most influential among the Baptists and Methodists.

By 1801, the Second Great Awakening had given birth to a unique experiment in Protestant ecumenism. That year the Congregationalists and Presbyterians entered into the "Plan of Union," calling for the full cooperation of the two bodies on the American frontier. It was, however, in Kentucky and Tennessee that revivals broke out in great fervor. The "camp meeting," with hundreds of worshipers coming from miles around for two or three weeks at a time, became the order of the day. These meetings were marked by emotional outburst and physical loss of control in most cases. Some "tried the Devil" while others merely spoke in tongues.

A definite product of the Second Great Awakening was Charles G. Finney (1792-1875). He was ordained as a Presbyterian preacher although he had had no formal or theological training. He started as an itinerant evangelist in 1821. Great revivals seemed to follow his fiery and emotional preaching. Finney was also a brillant organizer and he brought some "new measures" into revivalism. These included:

1. Unusual and "unseasonable" hours for service;
2. Extended meetings;
3. The use of harsh and common language;
4. Inquirer's meetings;
5. The "mourners' bench"; and
6. The specific naming of sinners in sermons and prayers.

Finney soon invaded the Eastern cities with these methods in citywide crusades. He was highly successful in the period following the Civil War in seeing thousands of new converts to Christ.

The impact of revivalism is far from over. Its carryover into the twentieth century was aided by Dwight L. Moody (see a later section), but its methods are as current as American Evangelicalism in 1984. Holdovers include:

1. Worship formats ending in an "invitation";
2. Priority on the conversion experience;
3. Warm singing;
4. Physical signs of the Spirit's urgings; and
5. Evangelists in the tradition of Finney.

It is noteworthy here also that those American Protestant groups most closely tied to revivalism of the seventeenth and eighteenth centuries are those most productive currently, at least numerically, in the mission enterprise.

Charles Finney's lectures on systematic theology at Oberlin College included such topics as obedience, moral law, human government, and selfishness. From his lecture on sanctification comes this paragraph:

> A state of entire sanctification can never be attained by an indifferent waiting of God's time. Nor by any works of law, or works of any kind, performed in your own strength, irrespective of the grace of God. . . . The great and fundamental sin, which is at the foundation of all other sin, is unbelief. . . . A state of entire sanctification cannnot be attained by attempting to copy the experience of others.

Finney was a major activist and theologian of the Revivalism which swept the American frontier just when mission interests were being born in the US.

Samuel J. Mills

Samuel John Mills (1783-1818) was definitely a spiritual offspring of the Second Great Awakening. He heard the call to preach while following a plow on his farm in Connecticut in 1802. In 1806, he entered Williams College to study for the ministry. There he and a group of pietistic

Christians met regularly in a nearby grove of trees for prayer and discussion. They were called the Society of the Brethren. One day on their way to pray they were caught in a thunderstorm and were forced to do their praying under a haystack. This famous Haystack Prayer Meeting ended with their firm resolve to win the world for Christ. They stood to their feet and proclaimed, "We can do it if we will." They then signed a pledge to become America's first foreign missionaries. Their friends at Williams called them "The Haystack Group."

In 1808, Mills and several of the young men went to Andover Seminary, where they were joined by Adoniram Judson and Luther Rice. Under Judson's leadership, the Society on Inquiry on the Subject of Missions was formed.

In June of 1810, Mills, Judson, and two others walked to Bradford, Massachusetts, to present themselves as missionary candidates to the General Association of Congregational Ministers. As a result, nine men were appointed to direct the new American Board of Commissioners for Foreign Missions. The first five missionaries were sent out in 1812. Thus, Samuel J. Mills's dream was realized. He had wanted "to effect . . . a mission or missions to the heathen."

Adoniram Judson

Adoniram Judson (1788-1850) was a student at Andover with Samuel J. Mills and was valedictorian of their graduating class. This tall, handsome young man won the hand of lovely Ann Hasseltine in marriage. She had been the belle of Bradford, Massachusetts. The Judsons and Luther Rice (see next section) sailed together in 1812 for India. Five months later they reached Calcutta. On the way, they studied baptism in the New Testament and became convinced that immersion was the only scriptural way to baptize. The Judsons were baptized by William Ward, an English Baptist missionary shortly after their arrival in Calcutta. Judson wrote to American Baptists for help, and they organized their first foreign mission society, called the General Missionary Convention of the Baptist Denomination in the United States of America for Foreign Missions, in 1814.

Adoniram and Ann served most of their missionary years in Burma. It took Adoniram five years of study of the Burmese language before he conducted his first worship service in it. It took him until 1834 to complete the translation of the Bible into Burmese. He compiled the first English-Burmese dictionary during this time also.

A critical time came in 1826 when war broke out on the Indian-Burmese border between the Burmese and the British. The Judsons were denounced as foreigners. The king of Burma cast Adoniram into a filthy prison. There he was beaten and often tortured. Ann remained faithful, bringing her husband food daily. She also smuggled in a cushion where he kept the manuscript for his translation of the New Testament into Burmese. Adoniram was finally released from prison to be an interpreter between the British and the Burmese. Soon his beloved Ann was dead, but Adoniram worked on until his death in 1850.

Adoniram Judson marked a transition for American Protestants. While Samuel J. Mills is usually called "the father of American missions" for his vision, it was Judson who went with Mills that day to Bradford to plead the cause of missions. To complete the cycle, Judson went as part of that group which was comprised of the first foreign missionaries sent by American Protestants.

Luther Rice

Luther Rice (1783-1836) also became a Baptist after reaching the mission field with the Judsons. He had been part of the group at Andover who walked to Bradford to plead for mission appointment. He was at the Tabernacle Church in Salem, Massachusetts, when the group was commissioned. It was reported that "the entire assembly seemed moved as the trees of the world that are moved by the wind."

Luther Rice, after becoming a Baptist, labored in Burma for a short time. He returned to the US in 1813 to raise money and further the cause of missions among Baptists.

Luther Rice also had the vision of establishing a national Baptist college. In 1821, he obtained from the US Congress a charter for "the Columbian College in the District of Columbia." The endeavor did not produce a permanent institution, but it did demonstrate Rice's wide vision. He wanted a college to teach the classics, law, theology, and medicine, areas needed in missions service. Luther Rice also knew the value of Baptist publishing to arouse missionary interest. In 1816, he published *The Latter Day Luminary* in Washington, D.C. Later he published *The Columbian Star*.

Luther Rice was a driving force for Baptist missions during his lifetime. His influence is still with us.

Sheldon Jackson

Many preachers on the American frontier followed in the footsteps of the circuit-riding Francis Asbury (1745-1816). They were backed by newly created missionary organizations. In 1789, the first General Assembly of the Presbyterian Church in its first decree decided to send "missionaries to the frontier." In 1792, the General Convention of the Protestant Episcopal Church started a committee for "supporting missions to preach the gospel on the frontier of the United States." The Missionary Society of Connecticut, representing the Congregationalists in that state, was formed in 1798 "to Christianize the Heathen in North America, and to support and promote Christian knowledge in the new settlements within the United States." They meant business. By 1828, they had sent more than two hundred missionaries into territory reaching from Canada to the Gulf of Mexico.

Sheldon Jackson traveled by burro, stagecoach, snowshoes, canoe, dog team, and train to bring the gospel to the peoples of North America. Jackson (1834-1909) was inspired by the journals of David Brainerd. He was appointed by the Presbyterian Board of Domestic Missions. In 1859, he headed west to join the covered wagon trains. He made his headquarters at Denver and preached boldly to rough cowboys and miners in frontier towns. He started Sunday Schools, trained lay teachers, ordained clergy, and preached temperance. His influence, more than any other, spread the gospel of Protestantism in the new West of the last two-fifths of the nineteenth century.

In 1877, Jackson sailed north by the inland passage to Alaska. For almost thirty years, he worked there opening schools, starting churches, calling ministers, and starting little mission stations. In 1885, he persuaded the US Congress to allocate twenty-five thousand dollars for schools in Alaska. He was made Alaska's first General Agent for Education. For the next few years, he recruited hundreds of young school teachers to come to "the great white silence" to teach the Eskimos and Indians.

Jackson was upset when he saw Alaskan Eskimos starving because commerical whalers were killing off their food. He tried to help. Jackson drove across thousands of miles of frontier to bring Siberian reindeer to Alaska. In 1891, he brought the first herd there. Some say that Jackson had saved the Eskimos from extinction. Sheldon Jackson mixed practical concern with Christian piety to help those wherever he went.

James Evans

James Evans (1801-1846) was a young man when he came from England to join his parents in Canada. For four years, he worked in evangelism among the Indians of the Great Lakes. In 1825, he was approached by the Hudson's Bay Company to translate the Bible into Indian language. He answered the call and moved his wife and children thousands of miles across Canada to Lake Winnipeg. He preached to the Cree Indians. Evans made movable type from the lead lining of tea chests and printed Bible por-

tions in the Cree language. He used birch bark as paper.
These pages were sewn by the Cree women into books.
Evans was assisted in Winnipeg by Robert T. Trundle, for
whom a mountain is named.

John Mason Peck

In 1817, John Mason Peck was sent out by the Baptist
Board of Missions for the United States. He went to Missouri as a home missionary. He organized the first Baptist
church in Saint Louis the following year. This was followed
quickly by a grade school and Sunday School for slaves.

Peck was the leading spirit for the formation of schools
in the West. He called for the formation of a seminary in
Illinois or Missouri. He phrased it thusly:

> Especially . . . where ministers of the gospel, whether
> young, or farther advanced in years, could come and spend
> more or less time . . . in learning those things in which their
> deficiences were the most painfully felt.

In 1827, such a school was started in Peck's home in
Rock Spring, Illionois. It was known as the Rock Spring
Seminary until 1832, when it was moved to Upper Alton.

Peck was a pioneer educator and evangelist who proved
mostly as a pioneer missionary for the Baptists.

Dwight L. Moody

Dwight L. Moody (1837-1899), a lay preacher, almost
singlehandedly brought revival to America in the period
between the Civil War and the twentieth century. He was
known as a tireless traveler, organizer, and strong preacher. He toured both England and the US preaching against
the sins of drunkenness and sexual immorality. His sermons defended biblical innerancy and literalism.

D. L. Moody became a powerful force in American Protestantism. His revival methods cut across denominational
lines and were widely copied. His influence lives on, for
example, in the work of Billy Graham. Not only did Moody

attract large crowds for preaching but for prayer as well. At all these prayer meetings, missions was the central focal point. Everywhere he went, Moody pleaded for cooperation between denominations in world missions.

Moody was deeply concerned about education. He learned its value when it was denied him on the streets of Chicago. Even as a teenager, he started Sunday School for street orphans in that city. Later Moody was the driving force in the organization of the Northfield Seminary for girls, Mount Hermon School for boys, and the Moody Bible Institute. Each of these institutions was responsible for the training of hundreds of evangelical workers, some of whom left America for the foreign fields.

The Social Gospel

Walter Rauschenbusch (1861-1918) was a Baptist minister who broadened and deepened the concept of ministry and missions for American Christians by popularizing the Social Gospel. He was church historian and professor at Rochester Theological Seminary late in his career.

As minister at the Second German Baptist Church in the "Hell's Kitchen" area of New York City, he watched the dregs of society line up for free soup and decided that the gospel must have something to do with ministry beyond preaching. In 1917, he published his most-read book, *A Theology for the Social Gospel*, calling for an earthly realization of the kingdom of God. Yet, he did not deny the value of personal salvation.

Due to Rauschenbusch's influence, courses in ethics were added to curricula in most Protestant schools. This social emphasis was most felt on the mission fields in the early twentieth century with the popularization of agricultural, medical, and educational mission effort.

These nineteenth-century American giants wove their careers in and around the First and Second Great Awakenings and made a lasting impact on American and global

Christianity and subsequent mission effort. Together, they gave to later mission causes these and other attributes:

1. A deep concern for a spiritual piety designed to produce lives of personal and social integrity;
2. A zeal in preaching which stirred their hearers to both repentance and social concern;
3. An indefatigable zeal to take the gospel to new territory, whether it be open frontier or urban ghetto;
4. A continuing realization that the gospel is to be applied to all facets of life; and
5. A recognition of the necessity of Christian education and training for ministers and new converts.

All five of these factors influenced the doing of missions overseas, especially among Protestants, into the current century. One can see their influence wherever a daring and balanced mission program is being executed.

Four Major American Groups

Three distinctly American forms of Christianity blossomed on the new soil of America in the nineteenth century.

One of these was Christian Science, inseparable from the career of Mary Baker Eddy. She was born in Bow, New Hampshire, to Congregationalist parents in 1821. She was a victim of frequent illness and depression during her youth. Her first marriage was to George Glover, when she was twenty-one. The marriage was only seven months old when George died, leaving her pregnant with George, Jr. In 1853, Mrs. Glover married a dentist, Daniel Patterson. Their marriage ended in divorce several months after he abandoned her in 1866. Her third marriage was to Asa Gilbert Eddy in 1877, the union which gave her the name by which she is remembered today. Mr. Eddy was the first of her pupils to announce publicly that he was a Christian Science practitioner. Her third husband's death came in 1882. She charged in local newspapers that his death was cause by arsenic "mentally administered."

The turning point in Mrs. Patterson's life came in 1866 when she was healed from an injury due to a fall on an icy pavement. From that moment she vowed to spread the news of mental healing.

A major milestone in the Christian Science cause came in 1875 with the publication of *Science and Health with a Key to the Scriptures*. In 1879, a charter was obtained and the Church of Christ, Scientist, was organized in Boston, and Mrs. Eddy was called as pastor. By 1894, there were more than five thousand members of the group located in thirty-seven states.

Since Mrs. Eddy's death in 1910, no other person has served as pastor of the mother church in Boston.

The Christian Science movement was a reflection and Americanization of Hegelian idealism. Its emphasis on inner healing and positive thought had its impact on the pragmatism which characterized American-based missionaries wherever they are found.

The founder of the Jehovah's Witnesses was Charles Taze Russell, born in 1852 in Pittsburg. His parents were Presbyterians, but he gave up on Protestantism as a teenager, primarily because he thought the idea of a literal hell was repugnant to justice.

In 1879, Russell published a magazine entitled *Zion's Watchtower*. He toured the US, establishing congregations in dozens of places. In 1881, he started his organization, which would be known as Jehovah's Witnesses half a century later. World missions was part of Russell's vision from the beginning. By 1900, a branch office had been opened in London.

Russell and his followers announced the end of the world in 1914. When this did not occur, the movement's literature was not so popular. Distribution of Russell's literature went from seventy-one million pieces in 1914 to about thirty million in 1916. Russell died a disappointed man in 1916 while on a tour of West Texas. His life was characterized by the same urgency and disappointment as hundreds of millenialists who have tried to predict the Parousia's time.

The Jehovah's Witnesses have been missionary from the beginning. In spite of a deviant theology proclaiming that Jesus is not God, the Witnesses have emphasized evangelism and missions from the days of their founder.

Mormonism was founded by Joseph Smith, Jr. (1805-1844), who was born in Vermont. His family moved to Palmyra, New York, in 1816. It was a center of evangelistic fervor. Since itinerant evangelists who brought the revivals there were from various denominations, the identity of the true church was a popular topic of conversation.

Joseph Smith had a series of visions. On one occasion, an angel named Moroni appeared to Joseph and told him where he could find some golden plates and their translating devices, the Urim and Thummim. In 1828, Joseph and a well-to-do farmer named Martin Harris started translating the plates. That year Harris showed more than a hundred pages of transcription to his wife who either destroyed or hid the work. A new translation of *The Book of Mormon* came out in 1830.

On April 6, 1830, only two weeks after the publication of *The Book of Mormon*, the "Church of Jesus Christ" was started with six members in Fayette, New York. The name was changed seven years later to the Church of Jesus Christ of Latter-Day Saints (LDS).

In 1831, Joseph Smith led sixty followers to Kirtland, Ohio, where the first temple was built. There the movement picked up a new convert named Brigham Young. In 1837, in the midst of a severe banking failure, Joseph took the bulk of his followers to Far West, Missouri. In 1839, partly because of Joseph's proslavery revelations, the Mormons were forced to flee to Nauvoo, Illinois. By 1841, the city was the largest in Illinois with a private militia of more than four hundred marching men under the direction of Lieutenant General Joseph Smith, Jr. In 1844, a group of Saints became upset with their leader regarding his revelations of polygamy. Joseph Smith and his army were accused of destroying the office of the local newspaper in Nauvoo, where charges against him had been printed. The governor of Illinois ordered Joseph and his older brother, Hyrum, imprisoned in nearby Carthage. On June 27, 1844, the two were "martyred" while attempting to defend themselves from an irate mob which stormed the jail.

A controversy arose over who was to be Joseph's successor. His widow led a movement to place the leadership mantle on their teen-age son, Joseph Smith, III. This group returned to Missouri and started meeting as the "New Organization of the Church." Today it is known as the Reorganized Church of Jesus Christ of Latter-Day Saints. There were more than a quarter million members worldwide in 1984.

Brigham Young was elected by the largest group in Nauvoo and in 1847 he and others traveled to Utah. By 1867, the Salt Lake City Tabernacle was completed. Brigham Young died a decade later with more than one hundred fifty thousand followers to his credit. One of his successors, Wilford Woodruff, was one of the most famous president-prophets of the Mormons because be revoked the practice of polygamy in 1890.

There is no question that the Mormons are the most distinctly American of the religious movements to come out of the nineteenth-century frontier experience in the US. Mormon theology is a mixture of emphases on American pragmatism, hard work, progressionism, and the promise that the Saint could become god.

The LDS movement has been missionary from the beginning. In 1831, Joseph Smith sent a contingent to England. By 1984, there were more than thirty thousand Mormon missionaries throughout the world.

William Miller (1782-1849) was a Baptist farmer from Low Hampton, New York. After 1831, he preached all over the Eastern states announcing the imminent return of Christ. Based on his calculations from the Book of Daniel,

Miller announced that the end of the world was coming in 1843. He had thousands of followers. When the end did not come, it was called the "Great Disappointment." This did not deter the movement for long however. The most numerous body was the Seventh-Day Adventists, formally organized in 1863. The movement lives on in millenial and perfectionist tendencies, even among major denominations.

Ellen G. White, the founder of the Seventh-Day Adventists, had a series of visions resulting in her "Health Message." On the basis of these visions, the SDA movement has sponsored dozens of hospitals on foreign fields, including nonsmoking and nonalcohol clinics.

These four groups, sometimes referred to as the "four major cults" have missionary methods worthy of emulation by Protestant and Catholic modern missionary strategists. Despite deviant theology, they stress these actions worthy of imitation:

1. Health messages with emphasis on proper diet;
2. A negative personal ethic stressing abstention from harmful drugs and habits;
3. A fund-raising zeal for providing adequate support systems for zone supervisors, traveling missionaries, and public lecturers;
4. Family ties lending support to these actively involved in missionary service; and
5. A continuing evangelistic fervor driving their missionaries to cover most regions of the world.

Work with "Negroes"

In 1800, in the US about one in six Americans were black. By 1900, they numbered about nine million, or about one in ten. When the nineteenth century dawned, the vast majority of the blacks were slaves. They were brought from Africa and most of their cultural heritage was forcefully removed by their owners. In the early 1800s, the blacks tended to conform to the religion of their slave owners and were indirectly affected by camp meetings and revivals. The majority who became Christians became either Baptists or Methodists. The gain among blacks was due primarily to the efforts of outstanding black preachers and some white Methodist missionaries. By 1850, about 10 percent of the blacks were church members, only about half of the portion of the whites who were. After the end of the War Between States, black church membership increased rapidly. By 1900, the total number of black church members was almost four million. This was almost 40 percent, or roughly the same percentage as whites. Before emancipation, the majority of the blacks were Methodists. After 1865, the majority became Baptists. This also happened among the whites. By 1900, 90 percent of all blacks were either Baptists or Methodists.

The American Missionary Association (AMA) was formed in 1846 for work among blacks. From the beginning, it was strongly antislavery. It was transdenominational but largely dependent on Congregationalist support. The AMA was primarily concerned about founding schools, especially seminaries. Outstanding institutions started by AMA included Hampton Institute, Atlanta University, and Fisk University.

Booker T. Washington (1856-1915) was a product of Hampton Institute and later was the founder of Tuskegee Institute. Washington was born in slavery but rose to be one of the most respected men of the nineteenth century, white or black. Part of the reason, which Washington often reminded his admirers, was the influence of the white man Samuel C. Armstrong. He was appointed principal of Hampton Institute in 1876. He served for decades training bright black young people in the fields of agriculture, trade skills, and the humanities. In the process, outstanding Christian graduates were spread throughout America.

The first Baptist preacher to be a foreign missionary preceded William Carey by at least a decade and a half. He was a slave named George Lisle. During the American

Revolution, Lisle preached in Georgia as the first ordained black Baptist preacher in America. In 1777, he started the first black Baptist church in America, in Savannah. Then he went to Jamaica in 1783 where he preached and baptized five hundred new converts by 1791.

Another prominent black Baptist missionary was Lott Carey, born a slave near Richmond. In 1807, he was converted and became a member of the First Baptist Church, which had a dominantly white membership. A young white man taught Carey to read by using the New Testament, and he was soon licensed to preach. He saved and bought his freedom in 1813, after the death of his wife. In 1815, he founded the African Missionary Society of Richmond.

The American Colonization Society was organized in 1816 for the exportation of blacks to Liberia. Many Baptists contributed funds to help this cause by supporting black missionaries who wanted to go. In 1821, Lott Carey sailed and settled in Monrovia. His was a brilliant career there.

The Reverend W. W. Calley was a native of Virginia and a black missionary to Africa who served under the Foreign Mission Board of the Southern Baptist Convention (FMB, SBC). He was instrumental in starting the Baptist Foreign Missionary Convention in Montgomery in 1880.

In 1886, the American National Baptist Convention was started in an effort to coordinate all black Baptist missionary effort. The unit which accomplished that goal finally was the National Baptist Convention of America, organized in Atlanta in 1895. It set up a board of missions, an education board, and a foreign mission board. The main mission field was Africa at first. In Nigeria, the convention started the Pilgrim Baptist Mission. The Providence Industrial Mission was started in what was known in the late nineteenth century as Nyasaland. South Africa was the site of the W. W. Brown Memorial Mission and twenty sattelite missions. The Carrie Dyer Memorial Hospital was constructed in Monrovia. Since 1900, work has been conducted in the West Indies and British Guiana.

Work among blacks in the early nineteenth century paid off in the sending of missionaries by blacks themselves by the end of that period. It is fair to report, however, that that early work was done by blacks among themselves as well as white missionaries. The combined effort was fruitful.

The Triennial Convention

In 1813, two events pushed US Baptists toward the organization of a national body. News arrived of the conversion of Adoniram Judson from Congregationalist to Baptist. The other was the effort of Luther Rice to raise national support among Baptists for the cause of missions.

In 1814, a convention was called and conferees came from most of the Baptist Associations in America to Philadelphia. The avowed purpose was to start a national missionary society. The group did organize and was popularly known as the Triennial Convention because of its decision to meet every three years. The first president was Richard Furman, pastor of the First Baptist Church in Charleston.

At the first meeting, Adoniram and Ann Judson were advised to continue their work in Burma. Luther Rice was asked to continue to raise funds by traveling widely.

In 1817, at the second meeting, John Mason Peck was sent to Missouri. In 1820, at the next conference, Peck was urged to leave Missouri and move to work among the Indians in Fort Wayne. He refused and continued in Missouri on his own.

By 1826, the Triennial Convention was beginning to break up. Baptists from New England were successful in decentralizing mission efforts. The convention became mainly a foreign mission society and did not incorporate home mission, education, and publication efforts. Finally, in 1832, the American Baptist Home Mission Society was formed. After 1835, there were several complaints received that the new home mission sending agency was sending too many missionaries to the West and neglecting the South.

In 1835, there was a call for a new Baptist convention and society to meet the needs in the south. The call came from Robert Daniel, who had served as a preacher in Tennessee and Mississippi.

In 1840, the American Baptist Anti-Slavery Convention was held in New York City. Alabama Baptists responded by sending a resolution to withhold funds from the American Bible Society until they were assured that this organization had no connection with abolitionism. They threatened to form an Alabama-sponsored but Southwide agency to collect funds for Bible distribution and mission work. In 1840, the Triennial Convention's board of directors issued a statement to the effect that they as directors had no right to do or say anything about slavery.

When the Triennial Convention met in 1841 in Baltimore, the air was filled with controversy. The matter was settled with a compromise statement that pleased neither side completely.

When the Triennial Convention met in Philadelphia in 1844, only 80 of the 460 conferees were Southerners. Dr. Francis Wayland of Rhode Island was selected president, partly because he was considered a moderate on the slavery issue.

A test case settled the issue after the convention delegates had failed to agree on several compromise motions. Only a few days after adjournment, Georgia Baptists placed in nomination for home mission service one James E. Reeves as a preacher among the Cherokees. Reeves was a slave owner. The Home Mission Society board of directors finally refused to appoint Reeves.

Alabama Baptists then presented to the Foreign Mission Board a hypothetical test case, asking whether a slave owner could be appointed. They received a reply:

If any one should offer himself as a missionary, having

slaves, and should insist on retaining them as his property, we could not appoint him. One thing is certain, we can never be a party to any agreement which would imply approbation of slavery.

The Baptist Schism

In 1845, the American Baptist Home Missionary Society decided that it would be expedient if its members should carry on their work separately in the North and the South. More than three hundred delegates from Southern churches met in Augusta. Thus was the Southern Baptist Convention (SBC) formed. From the beginning, this new Convention was broader than previous ones among Baptists in America. It incorporated educational, publication, and missionary functions.

The Southern Baptist Convention immediately set up its Board of Domestic Missions in Marion, Alabama. The first missionaries appointed were the Reverend and Mrs. J. W. D. Creath, who were sent to Texas.

The orginal document issued by the SBC in 1845 clearly delineated the work of the home mission board. Missionaries were to be sent among the "Negroes," the "Indians," and to "the pagan city of New Orleans." In spite of this mandate, only two missionaries were appointed to work among blacks prior to the Civil War. Both of these worked in Georgia.

The Indian work was done in cooperation with the American Baptist Indian Mission, with headquarters in Louisville. Before 1850, Southern Baptist had contributed more than sixty thousand dollars to "Indian work."

American Baptists had organized a work in New Orleans in 1843 through the missionary work of Russell Holman, who became a Southern Baptist in 1845. By 1853, SBC mission giving was supporting four new missionaries assigned to help Holman. Fifteen thousand dollars were raised for that purpose.

The Home Mission Board's basic function in the nineteenth century became the spreading of the gospel to the poor areas of the South. Before the start of the Civil War, more than a thousand missionaries were appointed by the new home board with more than twenty thousand converts and three hundred new churches. J. Lewis Shuck, a returned missionary to China, started a new Chinese mission in San Francisco. This was done in spite of the fact that the board voted to drop California from its responsibility in 1861 for financial reasons.

M. T. Sumner saved the Home Mission Board from financial ruin. He served as its corresponding secretary from 1862 to 1875. In 1866, 125 new workers were appointed. Sumner was indefatigable in his efforts to raise money for home missions.

In 1882, the headquarters of the Southern Baptist's Home Mission Board was moved from Marion, Alabama, to Atlanta. Isaac T. Tichenor, former president of the Agricultural and Mechanical College at Auburn, Alabama, was the new corresponding secretary. Many Southern Baptist historians today agree that Tichenor may have saved the Southern Baptist Convention during his tenure which lasted until the end of the century. Tichenor's accomplished at least the following:

1. Started a work in Cuba;
2. Started a chain of mountain mission schools;
3. Started a Sunday School work;
4. Started a church building department;
5. Developed a plan of financial support for home missions through systematic giving; and
6. Gave stability to the struggling Southern Baptist Convention.

The nineteenth century was a productive time for missions causes in and from America. Revivalism, emancipation, and industrialism were movements which affected Christian missions greatly. There emerged in their midst, however, a new American mystique with emphasis on hard work, integrity, and "success."

Americans took missions seriously in the century just past. Creativity, sacrifice, persistence, and financial generosity poured into the effort. New societies, geographical conquest, and revivalistic fervor were the order of the day. America became a rival to Western Europe for the first time as a sending base for missionaries. The spirit was to continue.

In the British Isles

Industrialization greatly affected England and surrounding territory in the nineteenth century. This caused cities and their accompanying slums to grow. Labor problems surfaced, especially for women and children. The middle and lower classes grew rapidly while the aristocrats saw some of their kingdoms dwindle.

Queen Victoria ruled the last two-thirds of the nineteenth century in England. Her influence made this known as the "Victorian Era." She was a devout Christian who gave great support to the Anglicans.

The nineteenth century saw the movements of Revivalism and Evangelicalism have their great impact on the Anglican churches. Both these movements caused great numbers of Church of England members to be more concerned about prayer, personal conversion, Bible study, hymns, social reforms, and charitable giving.

The Anglicans were also affected by the Oxford Movement, or the Tractarian Movement. It was a movement which stirred interest in tradition, liturgy, scholarship, and separation of church and state.

The Oxford Movement

The Oxford Movement owed its inception to a sermon preached by John Keble (1792-1866) in 1833. It was entitled "National Apostasy," and in it Keble spoke against all attempts of Parliament to rule church affairs. Following that sermon, John Henry Newman (1801-1890) wrote *Tracts for the Times.* They were a call to return home to the

Roman Catholic tradition. The bishop of Oxford ordered their publication to cease. Newman's emphases continued. Monasticism reappeared as a sign of their popularity.

This movement was a sign of change and vigor among Anglicans. This vigor helped missions causes. In 1823, for example, the Colonial and Continental Church Society, was started to Christianize settlers and merchants who left Britain for other places. Anglican churches were planted around the globe. Just as the sun never set on the British Empire, it never went down on Anglican churches. To tie this worldwide Anglican community together, the Lambeth Conferences were started by the archbishop of Canterbury in 1867. All bishops worldwide were invited to these meetings. In effect, these became conferences on church unity and mission strategy.

Congregationalists started the nineteenth century on a revivalist upswing. Revivals brought in many former Presbyterians and Anglicans. In 1832, the Congregational Union of England and Wales was formed. The London Missionary Society came about in 1795, largely supported by Congregationalists.

Charles H. Spurgeon

Baptists were split between Particular and General in 1800. One unifying force was Charles Haddon Spurgeon (1834-1892), by far the most powerful British Baptist preacher of that era. In 1861, the Metropolitan Temple in London was completed to accommodate the great throngs who came to hear him preach. He was known as a great preacher, editor, author, and founder of schools and orphanages.

Helmut Thielicke, a renowned German preacher, said about Spurgeon:

> In the midst of a theologically discredited nineteenth century there was a preacher who had at least six thousand people in his congregation every Sunday, whose sermons

for many years were cabled to New York every Monday and reprinted in the leading newspapers of the country, and who occupied the same pulpit for forty years without any diminishment in the flowing abundance of his preaching and without ever repeating himself or preaching himself dry . . . It would be well for a time like ours to learn from this man.[5]

A sample of one of Spurgeon's sermons shows their inherent power:

> Never be content, my brethren in Christ, until all your children are saved. Lay the promise before your God. The promise is unto you and your children. . . . Look at yourselves; he that saved you can save them. . . . And, oh, Thou that dwellest in the highest heavens thou wilt never refuse thy people. Be it far from us to dream that thou wilt forget thy promise. . . . Thou hast said thy mercy is unto the children's children of them that fear thee and keep thy commandments.

Spurgeon's conversion experience came in 1850. As he put it, he was overcome with "God's majesty and my sinfulness." He was baptized in the River Lark in May of that year. He was baptized by the Baptist W. W. Cantlow, a returned missionary from Jamaica.

Spurgeon's prayer life became legendary. He advised others to be faithful in prayer. From his *Lectures to My Students* can be read:

> Live near to God . . . if your zeal grows dull, you will not pray well in the pulpit . . . worse in the family . . . worst in the study alone. When your soul becomes lean, your hearers, without knowing how or why, will find that your prayers in public have little savor in them. If true to his Master, the preacher becomes distinguished for his prayerfulness.

Spurgeon's contributions to missions came indirectly from his emphases on personal piety, social reform, and the necessity of personal conversion. He trained and inspired thousands of British and American Evangelicals to be a part of the mission enterprise.

The Plymouth Brethren

The Plymouth Brethren, or Darbyites, were also part of the Protestant movements in nineteenth-century Britain. Their founder was John Nelson Darby (1800-1882), an Anglican priest. He preached that churches should pattern their lives after the New Testament. Darby also taught that true followers of Christ should live their lives in separation from the world. The Darbyites had "meetings" but no central organization or church buildings, especially at first. For them, missions was to consist in saving persons from this world. The Brethren therefore showed little interest in social reform.

A prominent leader among the Brethren was George Muller (1805-1898). He was converted in a Pietist meeting in Halle in 1825. Four years later he was sent to England from Halle as a missionary assigned to work with Jews. He sought to follow Francke's pattern at Halle of starting an orphanages. Muller was famous for not asking publicly for financial support for his work at Bristol, relying rather on prayer and unsolicited gifts.

The Brethren eventually formed a type of mission society, called the Christian Missions in Many Lands and by 1900 had workers on all seven continents. They had a major work in Turkey in the 1860s.

The Salvation Army

The Salvation Army was started by William Booth (1829-1912). Its original purpose was to minister to those most adversely affected by the Industrial Revolution. Booth was ordained as a New Connection Methodist minister. He was a very successful preacher in Cardiff, Wales, but became more and more concerned about the poor. In 1878 in London, he started what was to be known as the

Salvation Army by 1880. Booth popularized his movement through his work, *In Darkest England and the Way Out.*

The army was organized in military style, with rank, uniforms, promotions, and Booth at the top as general. From the beginning, the movement featured open-air preaching, soup lines, and musical instruments.

The Salvation Army spread rapidly, and by Booth's death was operative in the US and India. After his death, the work spread even further, as into Seoul in 1908.

The Sunday Schools

The Sunday School movement owed its inception in England to Robert Raikes (1735-1811). He started the movement in 1780 in Gloucester. Raikes was an evangelically oriented layman in the Church of England who was concerned about the religious education of children. At first the movement's primary thrust was to teach children to read with the Bible as the textbook. By 1785, the Sunday School Union was formed in London. The movement spread quickly among Quakers, Baptists, and Methodists. It was an effective system of religious education even among adults and middle-class children who could read already. Sunday Schools were flourishing in the US and British Isles by the mid-nineteenth century. Evangelical missionaries used the method also on other fields. It has proven to be a most effective tool for instructing new converts on foreign fields.

In 1889, the first World's Sunday School Convention was held. In 1907, the World's Sunday School Association was formed. Again, it has proven to be an effective lay-led organization for both evangelism and education.

The Young Men's Christian Association

The Young Men's Christian Association (YMCA) was started in England by George Williams (1821-1905). This young Congregationalist was greatly influenced by the sermons and writing of Charles G. Finney. He was a clerk by trade and sought to win his co-workers to Christ by calling them to Bible study and prayer meetings.

In 1844, he called young Christians together to form a society for evangelism among young members of the working classes. In 1855, the World's Alliance of the Young Men's Christian Associations was formed.

The YMCAs in various parts of the world gradually added social and athletic facilities to their lists of offerings but remained based on Bible study and evangelism during the 1800s. The greatest growth has come in the US and Canada.

The Young Women's Christian Association (YWCA) was started in 1855 in England. In 1894, the World YWCA was formed.

The work of Williams was mission centered from the beginning. It was targeted at young working people who needed Christian conversion and instruction. The YMCA and YWCA continue in that tradition in 1984 but with a bit of the original evangelical thrust missing.

Florence Nightingale

The British Isles, as in the case of their former colonies in America, were the scene of great movements affecting missions during the nineteenth century. New societies and denominations produced by courageous and compassionate leaders were instrumental in calling hundreds of dedicated Christians to mission sacrifice and service. One such young woman was Florence Nightingale (1820-1910), generally regarded as the founder of the modern nursing profession. She was born in Florence, Italy, in 1820, the daughter of wealthy British parents. As a child she learned Greek, Latin, math, and philosophy.

Florence studied in a hospital in Paris against the wishes of her parents. She took further nurse's training at an institute in Germany. At age thirty-three, she became superintendent of a women's hospital in London. In 1854, during the Crimean War, the British Secretary of War asked Miss Nightingale to be in charge of caring for the wounded troops. She sailed for the Crimea with almost forty nurses.

The hospital she found at Scutari was dirty, and five hundred wounded troops had just been brought in from the Battle of Balaclava. She organized the nurses and out-patients, and soon had the place clean. Florence's job was so superb that Queen Victoria put her in charge of all the army hospitals in the Crimea.

In 1856, Nightingale started the Nightingale Home for Nurses in London. In 1858, her eight-hundred-page re-port on hospitals to the War Department caused the for-mation of the Royal Commission on the Health of the British Army. She was the first woman to receive the British Order of Merit. Whenever a mission hospital is being managed well, a debt is owed to this angel of mercy.

The British Isles produced individuals and subsequent movements which aided the flaming missionary zeal of the century just past.

Missions in Africa

Sierra Leone

In 1772, the British lord chief justice William Murray freed the slaves in the British Isles. In 1787, a party of more than four hundred freed slaves sailed for West Africa. They were joined in 1792 by about twelve hundred more who set up a colony at Freetown. By 1880, more than one hundred freed slaves had come to Sierra Leone from Great Britain.

Most of the freed slaves professed to be Christians. Most were either Baptists or Methodists. David George was a Baptist preacher who was quite influential among the first wave of settlers.

The Church Missionary Society (CMS) was very active among the freed slaves. An early preacher was William Johnson. Using Freetown as a base, the CMS sent mission-aries inland. In 1804, the team of Rlumer and Hartwig arrived for the Jaenicke Missionary Seminary in Germany. They built elementary schools in Freetown and in the bush.

The first African priest of the Anglican Church was ordained at Freetown in 1852. Twenty more followed in the next decade. In 1864, a graduate of the Fourah Bay College, a former slave, Samuel Crowther was made Bishop of Sierra Leone. The college was a major center of Christian instruction for training new converts and native clergy. Crowther was trained so well there that he later prepared a grammar for the Yoruba language and translated much of the New Testament into that language. The CMS had the Fourah Bay College affiliated with the University of Durham in 1876. This allowed the school to grant the Bachelor of Arts and Bachelor of Theology degrees. The college sent out great numbers of students who had a tremendous Christian impact on all of West Africa but did not do so well within Sierra Leone itself.

Methodists entered Sierra Leone in 1811. In 1843, the Wesleyan Educational and Theological Institution was started in Freetown. The key to the Methodist mission growth was the use of small lay-led discussion groups and Bible studies, just as John Wesley had started the movement. Circuits were set up with each pastor to visit the new Christians on a regular basis. By 1854, there were almost seven thousand such pastors in Sierra Leone.

Ghana

The Basel Evangelical Missionary Society sent four missionaries to Ghana in 1828. Johann Zimmerman came in 1850 and in 1857 started a successful evangelistic outreach among the Krobos. He had two dozen congregations and more than four thousand members by 1878. Elementary and pastor training schools were started throughout the area. Zimmerman also stressed language study and mastered the Ga language.

Thomas Birch Freeman was a pioneer for Methodists in

Ghana. He was the product of a biracial marriage between a black farmer from the West Indies and an English mother. He was educated in England. Freeman started a work among the Ashantis in 1826. Freeman founded dozens of schools and churches during his ministry. His primary gift, however, was the training of native leaders.

Nigeria

Thomas F. Buxton was an explorer who had a similar dream to that of David Livingstone in central Africa. Buxton wanted to help the people of West Africa to develop their own commerce system so they could free themselves from the slave trade. He promoted an expedition up the Niger River in 1840. A later expedition allowed Samuel Crowther to see the area for the first time. He was well-received by the Ibo.

Henry Townsend, of the Church Missionary Society, visited Abeokuta in 1842. In 1844, he returned with Samuel Crowther. There Crowther met his family after having been separated from them for a score of years. Soon his whole family were Christian converts.

Crowther made a special contribution to Christian missions in Nigeria. In 1851, he returned to England and was received by Queen Victoria and Prince Albert. He addressed a gathering at Cambridge and urged them to send help to Africa. In 1868, he received the honorary D. D. degree. Nigerian Christians lost a great friend when he died in 1891.

The CMS from the beginning saw the importance of providing native church leadership in Nigeria. In 1856, the first three native ministers were ordained.

The Southern Baptist Convention sent Thomas Bowen to Nigeria in 1849, just four years after the formation of the SBC. His work in Abeokuta was stellar. He studied the Yoruba language at the CMS station. From there he moved to Ijaye. In 1852, Bowen went on furlough but returned the next year with his new bride and two other couples. In

1854, the Bowens moved their work to Ogbomosho. He retired in 1856 after a brief career.

The Presbyterian May Slessor was called the "White Queen of Calabar" because of her work in and around that city in the interior of Nigeria. At her death in 1915, there were dozens of chiefs who had become Christians because of her strong personal witness. Her work among the Aro and Okoyong was memorable and lasting.

The Cameroons

In 1843, the Baptists of Jamaica sent their first missionaries to the Cameroons. A party of three were sent, including a medical doctor. More than forty other Jamaicans came as helpers later that year. Among that group was Joseph Merrick, who later worked in the Bimbia area as an educator, church starter, and Bible translator.

Another Baptist was Alfred Saker, who worked for a third of a century among the Duala people. He arrived in 1845 and was known as a friend to the natives. For example, he openly opposed the slave trade. It was Saker also who ordained the first two native Baptist pastors. It is estimated that he personally preached to more than eighty thousand of the Duala peoples as well as translated Bible portions into their dialect.

In 1884, the German government annexed the Cameroons. The Baptists turned their work over to the Basel Evangelical Missionary Society. The Cameroon Christians were uncomfortable with the centralized authority of the Basel missionaries. At their request, in 1891, German Baptists appointed their first missionary, August Steffens, from the US.

South Africa

Ziezenbalg and Plutschau stopped at the Cape on their way to India in 1706. They met the Hottentots and wrote back to Halle for help in evangelizing them. Georg Schmidt was finally sent in 1737 and settled in Genadendal. He was very effective among the Hottentots, setting up Sunday School, teaching agriculture, and preaching. The mission closed with his departure in 1761.

In 1792, the station at Genadendal was reopened with the arrival of three Moravian missionaries. By 1800, more than two hundred Hottentots had been baptized. Bishop Han Peter Hallbeck directed the Moravian mission for more than twenty years. His rule saw new mission stations at Mamree, Enon, Elim, and Shiloh. The Moravians were especially effective because they built small Christian villages where pietistic life-styles were exhibited.

In 1799, the London Missionary Society (LMS) sent a party of four to the Cape. The most effective was John Vanderkemp (see previous entry). Schools and churches were soon constructed. Agriculture and animal husbandry were taught. The Caledon Institution was started in 1811 at Zurubrak. It was to train a Hottentot clergy and was quite successful in that work.

In 1816, the LMS decided to try to evangelize the Zhosa people. They sent Joseph Williams. Within a year, more than one hundred had been baptized. John Brownlee succeeded Williams in 1820.

The Glasgow Missionary Society sent John Ross to Lovedale in 1821. Lovedale became an important training center for new Christians under his leadership. Instruction was given for grades 1-12 in theology and agriculture.

In 1816, the Methodists sent their first missionary to South Africa in the person of Barnabas Shaw. He was to assist British soldiers who had been holding worship services in Cape Town for a decade. Shaw stayed in Cape Town only a short while then set out for Leliefontein. There he combined teaching about Bible with that on agriculture. By 1817, almost thirty had been baptized. A decade later there were a hundred church members.

Methodists continued to send missionaries to South Africa. A chain of small mission stations were started across the northeast, such as Wesleyville in 1823 and

Mount Coke in 1825. By 1860, there were more than 130 Methodist missionaries serving in South Africa.

Zimbabwe

The Wesleyan Methodist Missionary Society started a mission in Rhodesia in 1891. Strong centers were started with numerous outlying mission posts. The Epworth Theological College was started at Salisbury and was used by five denominations to train ministers.

In 1893, the ABCFM started a work among the Ndau peoples. Schools of every level were started in the Mount Salinda area. The first congregation was started in 1897.

The Seventh-Day Adventists started a mission station in 1894 with a hospital and leprosarium. Three colleges were eventually started.

The Southern Rhodesia Missionary Conference was started in 1903 and is now called the Christian Council of Zimbabwe. It has failed largely in its purpose of unifying mission work and affecting government policy on such matters as apartheid.

Zambia

The first continuing mission in Zambia was inspired by Lesotho Christians concerned about evangelism. Their work was continued mainly by the Paris Evangelical Missionary Society.

The evangelists of the Livingstonia Mission concentrated on villages away from the cities. They founded four stations in Zambia. A station was started in 1906 in Chitambo, the place where David Livingstone died. This act was in his memory and honor.

The London Missionary Society came to Zambia in 1887 and worked among many peoples, including the Lunda and Bumba peoples. All types of schools, including medical, were opened by the LMS.

The Roman Catholics were effective in Zambia through

the work of the White Fathers, who created the Bangweulu Vicariate Apostolic. Their work was mainly among the Alundas. The Jesuits started work near Chickuni in 1905. Their work was successful in the areas of education and agriculture.

In 1905, the Baptists of South Africa sent workers to the Luangwas district in north Zambia. There they formed an alphabet, taught reading, opened schools, and gave medical aid and training in trade skills.

The Universities Mission to Central Africa was created in 1858 in response to David Livingstone's urgent appeals for help. The first mission was at Magomero. Another was started on the Rovuma River in 1875. In 1909, there was a diocese formed for Zambia.

Malawi

The Church of Scotland was stirred to action by David Livingstone's speeches about the territory now known as Malawi. It formed the Blantyre Missionary Society, and in 1875, Henry Henderson was sent. His help of six other missionaries came the next year. Among them was a medical doctor and an agrenomist. In 1877, an engineer came and constructed a sixty-mile road. In 1878, Duff Mac-Donald came and translated the first two Gospels into the Yao language.

The Dutch Reformed Church started a ministry in Malawi in 1888. Instruction in trades and agriculture were mixed with evangelism and church extension.

The Nyasa Industrial Mission came to Malawi from Zambia in 1891. It was operated by Australian Baptists. The mission concentrated on agriculture and trade guild instruction. It was given to the British Baptists in 1896.

In 1901 the White Fathers brought Roman Catholic missions to Malawi. By 1907, their first believers were baptized and four years later they had started four mission points.

Mozambique

The Roman Catholic work in Mozambique suffered a severe setback in 1759 with the expulsion of the Society of Jesus. The Jesuits returned in 1881 and opened a dozen or so new posts. Their ministry was among the few whites there. The Franciscans opened a mission in 1898 and translated the Bible and a catechetical guide into the native dialect. There were about five thousand Catholics in Mozambique in 1914.

In 1893, the Anglicans started work there by naming W. E. Smyth as the first bishop. He moved to Inhambane from where he started several other centers. In 1895, he started a ministry among the Lenges.

It is safe to say that Protestant missionaries were not largely successful in Mozambique prior to World War I.

Madagascar

Madagascar is the third largest island in the world with mostly a Malaysian population. It lies 250 miles off the coast of East Africa.

The London Missionary Society sent their first gospel agents there in 1820. Fourteen others were sent by 1828. David Griffith was one of those. He soon had most of the Bible translated for the native people. Several schools were built.

Rasoherina became Queen of Madagascar in 1863. She was very friendly to the Christian missionaries. The churches grew rapidly during this period. Church attendance by 1870 was averaging forty thousand weekly. By 1880, there were a quarter million Christians on that large island.

In 1867, the Friends Foreign Missionary Association agreed to help the LMS. A hospital and medical school were soon opened by the Quakers.

The Christian faith spread rapidly among the Hovas. Volunteer teachers were trained by the hundreds from among the people themselves. Hymn singing was used as a teaching and evangelistic tool both among and by the Hovas.

Tanzania

The Church Missionary Society started work on the south shore of Lake Victoria in 1876. The work spread to Mamboia and was still growing at the turn of the century.

The London Missionary Society sent its first representatives to Tanzania in 1878. A milestone came in 1882 when the African Lakes Company transported a steamer to Lake Tanganyika for the use of LMS missionaries. This made the gospel more accessible to the villagers around the lake.

The Benedictines started a diocese in Dar es Salaam to cover the southern part in Tanzania. They emphasized agriculture, including cattle raising.

The White Fathers started their mission work in Buganda in 1878.

Kenya

In 1873, the CMS started a settlement for freed slaves at Mombasa. By 1875, a site was bought and more than three hundred freed slaves were received late that year. The settlement was called Free Town. It signaled the beginning of a new epoch for Christian missions in West Afria. Slaves fled by the thousands to this safe harbor for protection from the slave traders. Courageous missionaries confronted the slave traders. The word was out. Christ had come to set men free in several ways. This courage still aids the work in East Africa.

In 1896, the Society of Friends from England started an industrial mission just north of Zanzibar. In 1901, the American Friends organized the Friends Africa Industrial Mission. By 1914, some forty thousand pupils were receiving instruction in the trades.

Uganda

Henry M. Stanley (see earlier entry) arrived in the Buganda territory in 1874. He made friends with the chief, Muteasa.

The Church Missionary Society sent eight missionaries to Uganda in 1876. Through their efforts, the churches became known as having powerful spiritual, legal, and moral influence. New crops were introduced to the freed slaves. Medical care was provided.

The growth of Christianity was remarkable in Uganda. By 1914, more than 120 thousand were registered as Protestants, better than one-third of the total population.

The percentage of Christians in Africa is lowest in the northern part of the continent. This is in spite of concerted and courageous effort among Christians in the nineteenth century.

Egypt

The first Protestant missionary work was started by the CMS in Egypt in 1815 when William Jowett was sent there. He was received by the archbishop of the Coptic churches and urged to cooperate with the Christianity extant there. The cooperative work continued until 1862.

In 1882, the CMS returned to Egypt to start independent work there. Medical aid was offered in Cairo. The work was proceeding slowly in 1914.

The United Presbyterian Church of America started work in Egypt in 1854. By 1875, it had some six hundred converts, mainly from the Coptics and Muslims. The Presbyterians started several colleges and a seminary.

The General Mission to Egypt, an independent British mission, came to Egypt in 1898. Seven missionaries came that year to evangelize the Muslims along the Nile. They also started a hospital and a clinic. But, their strength was in house-to-house visitation.

Tunisia

In 1843, a vicariate for Roman Catholics was formed for Tunisia. Bishop Lavigiere oversaw the coming of many Roman Catholic settlers and started churches for them. The bishop was also known for evangelization and caring for orphans.

The London Society for Promoting Christianity Among the Jews came to Tunisia in 1829. The work consisted of Bible distribution and personal witness to Jews.

Protestant work there has been difficult from the beginning, primarily because of Muslim interference from Tunisian political leaders.

Algeria

The French Lazarists worked in Algeria prior to the modern era of missions but withdrew by 1827 with little success. They reentered Algeria in 1838 when Antoine Dupuch was named bishop. By 1870, there were almost three hundred Catholic priests in Algeria. It was in Algeria that the White Fathers did their first work in Africa.

In 1881, the North Africa Mission Society sent Edward Glenny and two collegues to Algeria. They were quite successful among the Berbers. Bible translation into the Berber language was also a specialty.

The nineteenth century was a time of boom for mission effort in Africa. Both Catholics and Protestants grew rapidly in most areas. Courageous men and women worked and died to spread Christ's cause to the place called the "Dark Continent." Malaria and mosquitoes were the enemy, as well as the Muslims and malaise.

But, from Livingstone to Crowther, the gospel's spread became almost legendary as the Christians in Europe and North America geared up for mission support.

By 1914, the time since William Carey was marked by having hundreds of ethnic groups come to Christ. The credit goes to the Spirit and his soldiers.

A Word About Africa

Most American readers tend to see Africa as a vast steaming jungle filled with wild animals and poisonous insects threatening death to the white man at every turn. Further, many tend to think of Africa as a nation, such as Korea and Chile.

The facts about Africa, however, quickly dispel such impressions. One such fact is that the land mass of Africa is twelve million square miles, or a little more than a quarter of the world's land mass. Africa is an immense plateau with three large impressions: the Sahara in the North (which alone is as large as the United States), the Kalahari basin in the south, and the Congo water basin in the center.

Africa is at once the driest and wettest continent in the world. There is a belt of intense rainfall along the equator that cuts the continent in two. Along the equator it rains almost continually except in mid-June and mid-December. There the rainfall is about eighty inches per year with the humidity at a very high level. At the same time, the central Sahara is almost entirely without rain.

Africa is also a continent with a vast temperature range. At Addis Ababa at eleven thousand feet above sea level the temperature rarely rises above fifty degrees Fahrenheit. At Dakan the temperature varies only about fourteen degrees Fahrenheit during the year.

There are more than a thousand ethnic groups on the continent, each reflecting its own distinctives.

There are several startling facts about the population of Africa, each with considerable consequence for Christian missions:

1. On the land mass called Africa, there resides less than one-tenth of the world population or about 340 million;

2. Almost one-fourth of that figure lives in the nation of Nigeria;

3. The average density is only twenty-nine to the square

mile whereas it is sixty-five to the square mile in the rest of the world.

Almost 70 percent of the labor force is involved in agriculture. However, that figure is decreasing. Mining produces half of Africa's export revenue. Almost all of the world's gems and industrial diamonds are produced in Africa. Africa also produces one-quarter of the world's copper. One-third of the world's chrome production comes from Zimbabwe and South Africa alone.

In spite of these impressive figures, Africa is markedly a continent filled with persons who are economically deprived. Thirty African nations have seven-eights of the continent's population and have an annual per capita income of less than 160 dollars. Seventeen of them, with more than half of Africa's population, have only eight dollars per capita annual income. Africa is not as most American perceive it.

The religious life of Africa, as the nineteenth-century missionaries found it, was a type of animism that was extremely varied and complex. The African Traditional Religions (ATR) were profoundly influenced by their prevalent attachment to social groups. Ancestor worship was common.

Unfortunately, most of the early missionaries who ran into the ATR described them in such terms as "superstition," "tribe," "primitive," "ignorant savages," and "supernatural." These terms are more descriptive of the white man's ignorance than the actual situation in the ATR.

The ATR share certain basic tenets, beginning with that of a supreme god. This god is usually described as being creator and all-knowing. He is seen as the final disposer and judge of all things. All creation is accountable to him. This supreme god is pictured as one who does no harm to anyone. He sustains and redeems the universe with his continual presence.

Creation myths abound among the ATR. Built into these creation myths is usually found a concept of the fall of man.

Almost all of the ATR have numerous deities. The supreme god is not usually considered as a part of this pantheon but is in a class by himself. These lesser deities have an important function in this form of departmentalized religion. These deities are intermediaries who can go from people to god and back. Those faithful to the high god know that if they are unfaithful to a lesser deity, they are being unfaithful to god. In practice, the relationship to an intermediary is the same as with the supreme god.

Most ATR give much attention to certain ancestral spirits. Group festivals are often held to give homage to those who are held to be important to the clan as a whole. In the category of ancestral spirits are also the spirits of the departed members of the immediate family. This helps account for the importance given funeral rites by most ATR adherents in West Africa. It is widely believed that if a proper funeral is not held, the spirit may return to harm the responsible parties.

Evil spirits are thought to be everywhere by most participants in the ATR. These evil spirits are usually thought to be powerful and unpredictable. Any locality showing an unusual feature is supposed to be the dwelling place of evil spirits. These evil spirits are said to have the power to inflict sickness and even cause death.

Most African peoples have views of the afterlife, including explanations for how death came into the world. Death is often viewed as a direct result of sorcery. In spite of this, death is seen by most ATR as a continuation, not a complete cessation of existence. The spirit simply moves on to another level. Judgment comes after death. This is most often dreaded. Judgment is often pictured as a man kneeling before God. One must face God directly to give an account of one's life.

The dead are said to go to one of two states: potsherd heaven or good heaven. The good heaven is located above the sky and is somewhat like this world, yet without its decay and problems of a serious sort. The chief advantage of this good heaven is a reunion with relatives and ancestors.

The potsherd heaven is a hot, barren place like a pot kiln, a place full of palm kernel shells which may pierce one's feet. This "hell" is said to be "up" near heaven as a sort of celestial rubbish heap. It is a symbol of separation from god and the living members of one's clan.

The soul of animistic religion around the world is sacrifice. Sacrifice in the ATR is seldom offered to the high god but is offered to a lesser deity. The object sacrificed may be a fowl, a goat, fish, kola nuts, or yams, depending on the economic worth of the sacrifice.

In the ATR, man is seen as a complex being, as mysterious as the earth on which he lives. He is created by the high god and must respond to him through lesser dieties.

The ATR are much involved in rites of passage, as a means of dealing with life's critical changes. Each stage of life is marked by a religious rite. These create a bond between temporal processes and heavenly forces. The first such rite is at birth. Typically, in the ATR, the process begins with the announcement of pregnancy in which the woman tells her husband and parents. Diviners are consulted to safeguard the pregancy. The ATR rites of passage are also quite evident at puberty. This ceremony symbolizes the entry into the adult world and its responsibilities. Mythological origins of the clan are communicated and clear delineation of one's new adult responsibility is taught. This rite also provides an opportunity for the society to accept the child ritually. Almost always, this process involves circumcision. Marriage in the ATR is sometimes a sequel to the puberty rite. One becomes eligible for marriage only after going through the puberty rites. Marriage is very important because the bearing of children is central to the gaining of security. The ATR rites of passage are also effective at funerals. Funerals are seen as the initiation into the world of ancestral spirits. The deceased may become of the "living dead" only if proper funeral rites are conducted and the person has led a good moral life.

The persons involved in the ATR have a mind-set that sees the world as a potentially evil place with each person being thwarted by evil forces. The high god has made provisions for dealing with such problems. Ordinarily one would not approach him directly until he had exhausted the ordained provisions for handling such problems.

Divination is one of these provisions. Diviners are regarded as extrasensitive persons open to spiritual reality and are subjected to years of training. Their main function is to uncover human and spiritual causes of events. They are consulted about every part of life. Many methods of divination are employed in ATR societies. They include stargazing, watergazing, trances, and reading kola nuts on a string or chain.

Another provision for coping among ATR peoples is the use of protective charms. One often sees finger rings, arm bands, and pieces of metal and wool buried under thresholds and hung at entrances to villages and homes. One has to be prepared and protected at all times. The goal is survival in an unfriendly world.

The morality of the ATR people is indicated by the taboos with which their lives are surrounded. If a person breaks a taboo, he expects a supernatural penalty to follow and his friends may either desert or punish him. There is no such thing as an accident. The whole world is said to be divinely or justly governed. Therefore, penalties and rewards follow as surely as the effects of specific causes. Taboos fill the life of the ordinary person, including one's words, eating habits, names, oaths, and clothing.

Here are the ATR, a formidable challenge to nineteenth-century Christian missionaries who were opening Africa up to the white civilizations. These complex expressions demanded that those missionaries know their doctrine and how it related to other forms of revelation. Those who mixed compassion with courage and creativity were successful in penetrating the advance world of the animist in Africa. The challenge continues in 1984.

Latin America

James Thomson

James Thomson was born in Galloway, Scotland, in 1781 and was a product of the revival in that nation. He became copastor in Edinburgh with James Haldane. He later moved to London and became interested in the British and Foreign Bible Society. He became an ardent supporter of Bible distribution.

As early as 1817, Thomson began to feel the call to Latin America. He arrived in Buenos Aires in 1818 and received an unusually cordial welcome from the Argentines as "a melancholy sea of illiterates." By 1819, Thomson was operating a primary school in Buenos Aires. He devised lesson materials from the Bible, and the government introduced them into other schools. By 1820, Thomson was made director of all schools in the capital city. Thomson also won the respect of the Franciscans who cooperated with him on his education work. He was later awarded honorary citizenship in the United Provinces of the Rio de la Plata, the highest recognition that Argentines grant.

In 1820, Thomson visited Montevideo, Uruguay. He set up a school there in which learning to read a Bible chapter a day was the norm. In 1821, Thomson went to Santiago, Chile, where he opened a primary school with 200 pupils. In 1822, he was declared to be an honorary citizen of Chile.

In 1822, Thomson went to Lima, Peru. San Martin set him up as director of public education and assigned a priest to assist him. Thomson taught and established primary schools without a regular salary. When Thomson left late in 1824, he had reached his objectives; the establishment of a central school in Lima with the daily use of the

New Testament as the text and the regular training of new teachers.

Thomson got to Bogota, Colombia, in 1825. There he found a school of his style already going, so he gave his energy to the formation of a Bible society. He was remarkably successful in getting government and Roman Catholic leaders to aid him in this project. By late 1825, a thousand Bibles and two thousand New Testaments had made their way into the nation.

Thomson's early efforts in education and Bible distribution made the work of Evangelicals much easier in the last half of the nineteenth century in such nations as Argentina, Chile, Uruguay, and Peru.

Brazil

The first Protestant church building in Latin America was erected by Anglicans in 1819 in Rio de Janeiro.

The British and Foreign Bible Society sent thousands of testaments to Brazil from 1800 to 1810, many of these were sent to British merchants living along the coastal areas.

In 1857, a Scottish medical doctor, Robert Reid Kelley, achieved huge success as an evangelist in the Madeira region. In 1858, he formed the new converts into a congregation, the forerunner of the Congregational Union of Churches, closely akin to the Baptists in polity.

In 1859, Ashbel G. Simonton arrived in Brazil as a missionary of the Presbyterian Church in the USA. He started a new congregation in Rio de Janeiro in 1862. A presbytery was formed three years later. One of the converts was Jose da Coneicao, who came from the Roman Catholic priesthood and became a very effective Presbyterian evangelist. On one occasion, he was stoned and left for dead. When he stood up, the people spread the rumor that he had risen from the dead.

General A. T. Hawthorne, of the Confederate Army of America, came to Brazil in 1866 and visited the leader of that nation. He encouraged Southerners to move to Brazil, most of whom settled in Campinas. Texas sent about a dozen evangelists and pastors to care for the immigrants.

American Methodists worked in Rio de Janeiro between 1836 and 1842. They were joined by Methodists who came to Brazil after the Civil War. Several missionaries came in 1867.

All the Protestant denominations were successful in starting schools. The most famous was Mackenzie Institute, which is now called Mackenzie University. It was said that these schools "helped to change the didactic process, influenced by the imported ideas of North America pedagogical technique, and for a long time they were to be among the few innovating forces in education . . . in Brazil."

By 1890, the Brazilian census showed more than sixty churches and three thousand members among Presbyterians; twenty churches and almost four hundred Methodists; five churches and almost three hundred Baptists; and three churches and about three hundred Congregationalists. In all, there were about four thousand evangelicals in Brazil in 1890.

William and Anne Bagby were the first Southern Baptist missionaries to Brazil. They went to Rio in 1881. They had nine children. Four died in infancy and the other five became missionaries. The Bagbys started the first Baptist church in 1882 in Bahia. By 1884, they returned to Rio de Janeiro, which became the center of Baptist work. In 1897, Erik Nelson came to assist (see next entry).

The Brazilian Baptist Convention was formed in 1907 with a home and foreign mission society. Missionaries since then have been sent to Argentina, Chile, Portugal, Bolivia, and Paraguay.

Erik Alfred Nelson was born in Orebro, Sweden, in 1862. His mother was a Lutheran, but his father was not. He was baptized as an infant into the state church. Erik's schoolteacher was a Baptist, and Baptist doctrines became known to Erik and his father. It was illegal to belong to any church except the Lutheran. They were baptized at night. The man who baptized them, a traveling salesman, was caught, whipped, had his legs broken, and was thrown into a river to drown. He escaped and Erik saw him later in Kansas.

In 1869, Erik and his family set sail for Britain where they could find religious freedom. From Liverpool, after only a few weeks, they set sail for America. From New York, they went overland to Ottawa, Kansas. There they tended cattle. At age twenty-two, Erik left Kansas to become a roving cowboy. Later he worked for the Santa Fe Railroad. In 1890, Erik was called to preach and preached his first sermon. While in a Swedish Baptist Association meeting back in Kansas, he read of missionary W. B. Bagby in Brazil. This greatly impressed him, and he felt called to go.

Although unordained, Erik set sail on his own for Brazil in 1892. Once there, he wrote back for Ida Lundburg to join him as his wife in 1893. They started ministering to the sailors who came off the ships at Belém.

From the beginning, Nelson made Bible distribution a part of his ministry, securing copies from the American Bible Society. He wrote:

> It was a godsend, for there is nothing so necessary on a new field as the Word of God. And for a man who doesn't know the language of the country, a splendid way to learn it is to get acquainted with the Bible language.

Nelson found Bible distribution helpful in relating to the Catholic people. His notes read:

> It is a difficult matter to enter into the the thinking of the Catholic people. They have heard, all of their lives, that the Protestants are heretics and haters of God, that they do not believe in the saints or in the virgin Mary. The people confound the worship of the images with the true worship that is due the Master. Therefore, it is most natural for them to despise us even if they do not hate us.

Nelson soon moved into the Amazon Valley. After a

year, he returned to the US and asked for support among both Northern and Southern Baptist conventions. In a letter he said,

> November 19 will make fourteen years since I first saw the Amazon and, with the exception of one year and a half, I have been steadily at work. The result is small, only eight churches, but it is a beginning and a glorious beginning. The valley is a Baptist valley. Now is the time to come and help us.

Nelson soon had mission outposts along all the rivers tributaries into the Amazon. In 1906, the Nelsons decided to move to Santarem and build up Baptist work there. A strong church was going there within a year.

In 1907, all of the churches in Brazil sent representatives to Bahia for the organization of the Brazilian Baptist Convention. Nelson attended. That same meeting saw the organization of the Brazilian Home Mission Board.

Nelson immediately approached the new board for assistance in securing help in the Acre area. The man was appointed as the first worker of the board. In a reciprocal agreement, the new home board asked the Nelsons to go to the town of Sao Luiz on the Atlantic early in 1908. From Sao Luiz, Erik Nelson went on several trips up the Maderia River to found churches. Everywhere he went, he gave away copies of Bible portions. He wrote about his journeys: "For forty-five years on the Amazon God has kept us so that we have never been wrecked or had to call for help to get back home, although canoes and lauches are going into these whirlpools constantly."

The Nelsons left Brazil in 1936 and planned to return. Because he was well past the retirement age, however, the board retired him. He was heartbroken.

He returned in 1939 without official board appointment, only to die there with malaria. A native of Brazil spoke for all when he said at the funeral: "He is my spiritual father. If it had not been for him, I would still be in the darkness and ignorance of a mistaken religion. . . . Who will care for the people of the Amazon Valley now that Nelson has gone?"

The answer has come in the hundreds of Christian missionaries who have come to the Amazon region in the past generation. But few have duplicated the spirit and enthusiasm of the Swede who stopped in the US only long enough to get help for Brazil. He is remembered by the people he loved and served and the "apostle to the Amazon."

Mexico

The first Protestant communion was shared in Mexico in 1859. James Hickey came in 1860 to start a congregation in Monterrey.

During the 1880s, persecutions of Protestants raged in Mexico. Despite persecution, converts were won from among the mestizo masses. By 1890, there were about thirteen thousand evangelical Christians in Mexico with about five hundred congregations.

The ABCFM entered Mexico in 1872. One of their pioneers was J. C. Stephens who started a church in Guadalajara. The Congregationalists built the *Colegio el Pacifico* in Mazatlan.

Southern Baptists entered Mexico in 1880 when John Westrup, who was already in that nation, was hired. The National Baptist Convention of Mexico was organized in 1903, and the Baptist Seminary in Torreon opened two years earlier. The seminary has since been moved to Mexico City.

Uruguay

The American Methodists were the first Protestants to enter Uruguay, arriving in 1839. Their permanent mission was signaled by the arrival of James Thomson in 1870. A school for young women was started in 1878.

Southern Baptists sent two missionaries from Argentina to Uruguay in 1911. Work there has been quite small from the beginning.

A Waldensian, Pastor Armond-Hugon, came to Uruguay in 1877. He served there more than forty years. He was known as a builder of schools and establisher of churches. By 1905, the Moravians became a district of the world church. By 1900, there were about six thousand Waldensians in Uruguay with nine churches and six pastors. Laymen have taken the lead from the beginning.

The Salvation Army came to Uruguay in 1890 and was recognized officially there in 1917. At that time, it had about four hundred members there.

Chile

The Reverend William Taylor came to Chile in 1877, sent by American Methodists. He started self-supporting schools in English-speaking settlements. In 1905, Chilean Methodists started their own annual conference, having been a part of the South American Annual Conference since 1893.

The Christian and Missionary Alliance came to Chile in 1898. Four others went two years later, the same year the chapel at Valdivia was dedicated.

German Baptists started the first Baptist church in Chile in 1892. The Chilean Baptist Convention was organized in 1908. The first Southern Baptist missionaries arrived in 1917.

The Pentecostal movement in Chile goes back in 1910 when a Methodist minister, W. C. Hoover, received the baptism of the Holy Spirit. The movement grew rapidly. The Methodist leaders in Chile condemned Hoover and the movement as "anti-Methodist, contrary to the Scriptures and irrational." Three churches withdrew and started the Methodist Pentecostal Church.

Colombia

It is often said that Colombia is and has been the most Catholic dominated nation in Latin America. An 1887 Concordiat with the Vatican declared Roman Catholicism to be the official religion. Nonetheless, Protestant work has gone on with much zeal and some success.

Henry B. Pratt was sent by the United Presbyterian Church, USA, into Colombia in 1856. By 1893, he had the whole Bible translated into modern Spanish. He also started a chain of schools.

The Gospel Missionary Union came from Ecuador in 1912 and started a monthly publication, *El Mensaje Evangelico.*

Venezuela

The United Presbyterian Church, USA, started permanent work in Venezuela in 1897 in Caracas. The previous year the Presbyterians had started the *Colegio Americano.*

The Plymouth Brethren came to Caracas in 1910 with two missionaries.

The Evangelical Alliance Mission came to Maracaibo in 1906 with four missionaries, including the Bachs. By 1907, the publication of *The Morning Star* was begun.

Caracas was the scene for the establishment of the first Evangelical Lutheran church in 1893.

Costa Rica

The Reverend Joshua Sobey was sent by Jamaican Baptists to Costa Rica in 1887. The sponsoring group was the Jamaica Baptist Missionary Society. He started the First Baptist Church in Limon the next year.

The pioneer Methodist missionary was a layman named Sydney Stewart who came in 1894, also from Jamaica.

The Society for the Propagation of the Gospel (SPG) started their work in Costa Rica in 1896. A decade later the

Anglicans had a dozen mission stations organized between Limon and San Jose.

The Central American Mission was the first one from North America. The McConnells arrived in San Jose in 1891. They had been joined by eight others by 1895. The emphasis was almost solely on personal evangelism.

Panama

Southern Baptists came to Panama in 1905 under the sponsorship of the Home Mission Board. The work was an assimilation of the work done by the Jamaica Baptist Missionary Society. Southern Baptists have built a seminary, several school, a camp, and numerous churches. A unique work is among the people on the San Blas Islands. The work was transferred to the Foreign Mission Board in 1974.

American Episcopalians entered Panama in 1906 and took over the work started by the SPG.

The South Seas

The nineteenth century saw Oceania opened up to the industrialized world. Traders and missionaries came almost simultaneously. The world of the people would never be the same.

Australia

In 1771, James Cook sailed into Botany Bay and Australia became a British possession. In 1789, Britian sent a shipload of convicts to start a colony there. The great social reformer William Wilberforce urged the British government to send out missionary chaplains to the new colony. By 1793, Samuel Marsden (1764-1838), an Anglican, went to Botany Bay as a chaplain. He worked there and in New Zealand for almost half a century. Marsden became known as an industrious starter of schools and churches. His sharp tongue railed against drunkenness and moral laxity of other sorts. Marsden was especially harsh with the new white settlers who treated the Austrialian aborigines as subhumans. Marsden is credited with saving the entire race from extinction by British cruelties to them.

A flood of revivals swept across the churches of Australia in 1859. The chief human agent was Henry Baker, who later was ordained as a Methodist minister. The movement started in Brighton and soon spread to Melbourne.

The revival swept through the churches of all denominations. Many new Baptist churches were started in the decade of the 1860s as a result of the awakening.

Methodists reported that their number of chapels in 1860 grew from 142 to 171. Average church attendance nationally was near forty thousand per week.

All Protestant denominations reaped the fruit of the movement in the Victoria area as the chart demonstrates:

Group	1859	1864	% Growth
Anglican	173,000	212,000	22
Presbyterian	65,000	87,000	25
Methodist	27,000	47,000	72
Congregational	11,000	13,000	20
Baptist	6,000	9,000	50
Lutheran	6,000	10,000	60

The retention of the 1859 revival fervor in Australia was largely the work of one man, William Taylor (b. 1821). He was a Methodist evangelist who came to Australia in 1863. He was known as an unemotional preacher. More than six thousand new converts were added to Methodist churches as a result of his ministry. Others were added to other evangelical churches as his was a transdenominational ministry.

Taylor's greatest impact was in Victoria, where more than two thousand new Methodists were added to the rolls. Taylor is remembered as one at home on the revival circuit and in intellectual discussion of the faith.

Another revival swept across Australia in the early twentieth century. Its roots go back to 1889 when the evangelist

John MacNeil enlisted a group of ministers to pray for revival in Australia.

R. A. Torrey arrived in 1902 to preach. He was at that time president of Moody Bible Institute in Chicago. The crusade opened in the Sydney town hall with a full house of four thousand people. Three hundred visitors attended special meetings during the daytime to study and discuss evangelism. The revivals spread to New Zealand. "Gracious spiritual influences" were noted by Methodist leaders. R. A. Torrey reported on the major factors in the New Zealand meetings later that year in London.

First came the power of believing and united prayer undergirding their enterprise; second, the power of the inspired Word of God providing the messages; third, the power of the atoning blood of Christ upholding the thousands of inquirers; and finally, though not least, the power of the Holy Spirit ensuring great success.

New Zealand

At the age of fifty, Samuel Marsden came to New Zealand in 1814. By 1839, the Maoris had made peace among themselves, largely through the influence of the gospel. By 1840, there were almost two thousand whites living in New Zealand. By 1860, there were one hundred thousand. The Maoris were taught to read and write (especially Bible translations), plant new crops, and raise new domestic animals. By 1900, more than 90 percent of the Maoris were members of Christian churches, mainly Anglican.

Melanesia

John C. Patterson (1827-1871) became the first Anglican Bishop of Melanesia in 1861. He was known as an excellent navigator and brilliant linguist. Patterson started a college on Norfolk Island to train young island boys in the rudiments of being missionaries to their own people. He was viciously murdered by white men. His death had a profound effect in England and dozens followed his footsteps.

Australian Methodists began missionary work in the Solomon Islands in 1902. They were accompanied by islanders from Fiji and Samoa. By 1914, more than thirty churches had been started with more than seven thousand in average weekly attendance.

New Guinea

The first Protestant missionaries to arrive in New Guinea came with the LMS in 1870. The Anglicans came in 1891, and their first bishop was consecrated in 1898. That new bishop wrote to the few courageous missionaries of that new generation:

> We must endeavor to carry out our work in all circumstances, no matter what the cost may ultimately be to any of us individually. God expects this of us.[6]

The Anglicans, inspired by the bishop's letter, did meritorious work in that first generation.

New Guinea was the first mission field entered by Australian Methodists. The first missionary they sent was George Brown. By 1886, the mission was able to report five hundred members and another two hundred receiving catechetical instruction.

The Neuendettelsau Mission Society of Germany sent the first Lutherans to New Guinea in 1866. Johann Flierle was the pioneer. He started a mission station at Finschafen. He stayed for more than forty years. The Germans were joined by Australian Lutherans. The two groups produced outstanding pioneer work. It is reflected in the almost half million Lutherans in New Guinea in 1984.

Indonesia

The outstanding Protestant missionary of the nineteenth century in Indonesia was Ludwig Nommensen (1834-1918), who came to Sumatra in 1862. He wrote of his dreams on his arrival: "Where now stand only uncultivated hills, I see fair gardens and flourishing woods, and countless well-ordered villages of Christians. I see Batak teachers and pastors standing at the desk and in the pulpit to teach and preach."

Nommensen worked for a half century in Sumatra to make his dreams come true. By his death in 1918, there were a leper colony and numerous schools. Also, he had translated the entire Bible into the Batak language.

The growth rate of Christians among the Bataks is remarkable:

Year	Number
1866	50
1876	2,000
1881	7,500
1914	105,000

That growth rate was made possible by Nommenson's methods. The key concept was to build a Batak, not a European church. By 1883, the training of native pastors had begun. It was evidence of the rapid indigenization of the Batak Christian churches.

Indonesia was a difficult field in the nineteenth century but one made easier by the work of Nommensen.

Philippines

In 1984, almost three-fourths of the people in the Philippines are Roman Catholics. This is largely due to extensive mission work of a day long gone by. Philip II of Spain deserves much of the credit for this as he encouraged the opening of schools, churches, and hospitals. The first Filipino bishop was named in 1905, Jorge Barlin.

The Philippine Independent Church was started in 1902 by Gregorio Aglipay. His was an attempt to start a national Catholic church. Hundreds of thousands flocked to the new church. The movement was dealt a severe blow when the supreme court ruled that the church buildings had to be returned to the Roman Catholic Church.

The Presbyterian Church in the USA sent Dr. James

Rodgers to the islands in 1899. Silliman University was started in 1901.

The Methodist Episcopal Church sent missionaries in 1900. Homer C. Stuntz came in 1901 to supervise the work. A Bible school for women was started in 1903. The first mission conference was held in 1905 and the first Filipino bishop elected in 1945.

American Baptists came in 1900 with the arrival of Eric Lund. He completed a translation of the Bible in 1912.

In 1905, Anna Johnson started the Baptist Missionary Training School. The Convention of the Philippine Baptist Churches was started in 1935.

The Disciples of Christ first appeared in the Philippines in 1901. By 1946, more than sixty of their missionaries had served mainly in northern Luzon.

In 1902, the ABCFM sent agents to the island of Mindanao, where about a third of the population was Muslim.

The Protestant Episcopal Church came in 1902 and has specialized in work among the Chinese and Igoruts.

The Christian era to follow was to see rapid growth in spite of turmoil.

Hawaii

Damien de Venster (1840-1889) was a Roman Catholic priest who gave his life to the lepers isolated on Molokai, Hawaii. He was born in Belgium, the son of dairy farmers. He was sent out by the Fathers of the Sacred Hearts of Jesus and Mary. Serving first on Oahu, Father Damien requested service among the lepers. He gave spiritual and medical aid to them.

De Venster was a strong advocate for leper's rights to the governor of Hawaii and got for them such basic benefits as proper food. He was happy to announce to his flock in 1885 that he, too, was a leper. Father Damien is remembered as an example of complete identification with his parishioners. When he died in 1889, he was honored by the poor lepers; he was buried on Molokai. There is a statue in Washington, DC, put there by the citizens of Hawaii in appreciation of his sacrifical life.

Christianity About AD 1914: Beginnings

The time from 1792 to 1914 was one of rapid and wide geographical expansion for Christianity. Never has a world religion spread so far before, especially within a century and a quarter. Hundreds of languages were given written form. New forms and quality of Christian literature appeared. Orphanges and primary schools provided services to children as never before. Improvements in agriculture and animal husbandry were widely introduced and lives were saved. Hospitals and clinics were started around the world by the hundreds. Women and their status were uplifted by the social reforms brought about by missionaries following in the pattern of William Carey's protest. "Colored" races was fought by the missionaries in Africa, Asia, and Central America.

Back in Europe and America, home missionaries were having their effect. Prison reform and improved labor conditions were affected by Wesley and others. New colleges and universities sprang up, usually under Christian sponsorship.

The mission societies grew in numbers and popular support during this time. This allowed a proxy participation in missions by thousands who would never see a rain forest in Brazil or an Indian village in Peru.

Parachurch movements started which would aid Christian growth even more in the twentieth century. These included Sunday School, the YMCA and YWCA and the Salvation Army (now considered a denomination).

The nineteenth century was a period of immense triumph for the churches who sent missionaries. That reality was to continue until World War I.

Case Study: Washington Gladden and the Social Gospel

Washington Gladden (1836-1918) was a Methodist minister who drew on progressive social thought and the kingdom as taught by Jesus to be an instigator of the Social Gospel. He called for the achievement of social justice as legitimate work of the churches. Gladden called for reform in the spheres of politics and business in the name of Christ.

Questions

1. Is working for changes in the political realm a legitimate part of the work of churches?
2. Does social justice effort take away from soul winning?
3. Should a foreign missionary spend any time trying to change the government of the nation where he serves?
4. Did Jesus teach anything regarding the kingdom on earth?
5. Do protest against social abuses have any part in the work of a preacher?

Time Line: AD 1792-1914

1792	William Carey's speech
1800	
1810	
1811	John Vanderkemp died
1814	Jesuit status restored
1820	
1830	
1834	Robert Morrison died
1836	Luther Rice died
1840	
1845	Home Mission Board of the Souther Baptist Convention formed
1850	Adoniram Judson died
1856	Johann Krapf died
1860	
1870	Timothy Richard arrives
1873	David Livingstone died
1880	
1883	Robert Moffat died
1888	Woman's Missionary Union of the Southern Baptist Convention formed
1890	
1899	D. L. Moody died
1900	
1905	Hudson Taylor
1910	
1912	Lottie Moon died
1914	

7
Triumph Amid Turmoil:
AD 1914-1946

Christian missions came to the year 1914 on a rising tide. With few exceptions, it was a time of triumph over ignorance, poverty, and resistance. This was particularly true of Protestant missions. There was a strength and vitality that has been rarely duplicated since.

But, world war, the "War to End All Wars," was on the horizon. However, in the decades since 1914 and the beginning of World War I, almost all the world has been engaged in military combat. Ancient monarchies have been swept away, as in Russia. Some of these monarchies, such as in Italy, were in Western Europe. Western Europe, with competition in the latter half of the nineteenth century coming from the US, was the base of most mission operations prior to World War I. After WWI, the scene shifted more and more to America. In Europe, the portion of those who claimed even nominal connection with the church was declining. In the US, church participation was increasing. Between 1925 and 1946, Protestant participation increased by 64 percent and Catholic by 54 percent.

This shift has been less critical, however, because the Third-World churches have become less dependent on the sending bases for their strength. Native leaders were taking over vast areas of responsibility from the missionaries. The clergy was more and more of native stock. The era was one of triumph amid the turmoil of wars and depression.

All of Asia was to be affected by the militarism of Japan.

In spite of this upheaval, such Christian missionaries as Bill Wallace of China were triumphant through perseverance amid persecution. Even within Japan, the consistent witness of Toyohiko Kagawa gave some credence to the gospel message in the midst of militarism.

Africa was a continent entering the twentieth century, almost reluctantly, with a quest for independence and a quizzical look at Europeans and Asians fighting among themselves. Yet, valiant peacemakers came in Christ's name to bring stability and serenity to a situation in which most Africans could have turned their back on Christianity. These ambassadors included the famous Albert Schweitzer and the lesser-known people on commission sent through such agencies as the Sudan Interior Mission (SIM) and the Salvation Army.

Both Catholic and Protestants continued energetic mission activity in Latin America from 1914-1946. These efforts were occasionally marred by hatred between these two factions but both grew.

Europe was in violent upheaval during most of this period, but Christianity managed to survive. This era of warfare produced such giants of the faith as Karl Barth and William Temple. Russian Orthodoxy was struggling for its very existence in the period just after 1917 but the underground church was flourishing by 1946.

The US was the scene of rapid social change prior to 1946. The "military effort" gave rise to economic impetus and helped rid the nation of a crippling depression. The churches grew as well in both percentage and total numbers involved in church membership.

Meanwhile, Protestant Christians worldwide were becoming involved in the growing ecumenical movement. Charles H. Brent, John R. Mott, and Nathan Soderblom, among others, were giving steady leadership. The ecumenical movement was to have positive impact on the doing of missions because it reduced the bewildering fragmentation of denominations. Would-be believers in un-

derdeveloped nations could now see some helpful groupings of missionaries.

By 1946, the cause of Christian missions was enmeshed
in the aftermath of two world wars, but ecumenical consoli-
dation and numerical growth were causes for optimism.

Asia

Asia in the period inclusive of the two world wars was the
scene of tumultuous political upheaval. Against this backdrop, visionary mission leaders and pioneers struggled
bravely. Yet, in spite of their efforts, less than 4 percent of
the people of Asia were Christians by 1946.

China

The first three decades of the twentieth century saw
three major revolutions in China. The Boxer Uprising in
1900 was a protest against the partitioning of China. The
Russo-Japanese War in 1905 showed China's powerless-
ness in the midst of a war on her own soil. In 1911, the
common people in China rose up against the Ching dynas-
ty which had ruled China since 1644. Revolution in another form took place in 1927 and was against foreign
missionary effort primarily because it was seen to be an
outreach of foreign political powers.

In 1931, Japan started an undeclared war against China.
This led to Japan's creation of the Free State of Manchuria
the following year. In 1937, a large portion of China came
under Japanese occupation.

The fact that China was abandoning agelong traditions
during this period gave Christian missions an inroad into
the field of education. From 1900 to 1910, almost forty
new mission organizations started their work in China. By
1912, the YMCA and YWCA occupied a dozen Chinese
cities with more than fifty secretaries. The new republic
proclaimed in 1912 helped missions because it put all
churches and religions on equal footing. In 1913, a day of

prayer for the republic was proclaimed by President Yuan Shi Kai.

The antiforeign revolution of 1927, as stated earlier, was a major blow to Chinese missions. But, with the triumph of Chiang Kai-shek, in 1930, the tide turned. He was a baptized Christian. The war involving Japan in 1937 brought great hardships on the Chinese and the missionaries serving. The missionaries served so well that they were cited by Dr. Hsu Shih, China's ambassador to Washington. He said, "I want to pay my respects to all the Christian mission workers, Protestant or Catholic, who have aided China during those years of China's war of resistance to aggression."

In 1927, the churches in China launched their five-year forward movement. The theme and prayer was "Revive thy church, Lord, beginning with me." Christian schools were started and adult literacy improved. When it was over in 1934, a minister wrote:

> The movement has already made a marked contribution to the enrichment of the spiritual life of many persons, to a growing desire to share with others the blessings of the Christian Gospel, which desire is manifesting itself in a wider evangelistic outlook and to the strengthening of many churches.

In 1932, the Medical Missionary Association and the Chinese Society united to form the Chinese Medical Association. A chart shows the growth of its ministry:

	1927	1940
Doctors	800	863
Nurses	1360	1600
Hospitals	231	274

Bible distribution increased during these trying times. A typical year was 1939, in which 240,000 New Testaments were distributed and calls were coming for more.

By 1946, there were about 750 thousand Protestants in China with 60 thousand awaiting baptism. This compared to 3 million Catholics. That year Protestants had more than 6 thousand congregations with more than 2 thousand Chinese pastors. There were about 5 thousand Protestant missionaries at that time including 2 thousand single women.

Ecumenism was a mark of Christian work during this time. The first Great Chinese missions conference took place in Shanghai in 1877. The National Christian Council was formed in 1922. A home mission society was formed and supported by the Chinese churches. It gave way to the Three Self Patriotic Movement in 1950.

China was the scene of Protestant and Catholic growth prior to 1946. Few would have predicted the Communist takeover just three years later.

In 1935, William L. Wallace[7]was appointed by the FMB, SBC, to serve in Wuchow, South China. When he arrived, he was the only missionary there. Bill was soon thanking God for the surgical training he had as a resident at Knoxville General Hospital. He had to perform operations of every sort.

In 1937, the Japanese attacked and overran part of China. Bombs were soon falling all around the hospital. The hospital was moved, under Bill's supervision, to the old city of Wertlum. That refuge did not last long. The Japanese conquered that city in 1938. Bill returned to Wuchow where he cared for the flood of refugees. All along, he managed to mix his medical help with a verbal witness for Christ.

In 1940, Bill Wallace wrote to friends to tell of his work at Wuchow: "Everything is going along peacefully in Wuchow. . . Perhaps in light of some inquires, I should also say I have never felt happier in my whole life than I am right now."

That year he returned to his beloved Knoxville for a furlough. He spent a few weeks there and then enrolled in the University of Pennsylvania's graduate school in surgery. He also did further study at Harvard.

Bill returned to China late in 1940 and found the problems of carrying on mission work were great because the supply lines were cut off from the free world. The difficulties were affecting Bill's health in 1943. By early in 1944, he had recovered and was running the hospital compound by himself.

The Japanese started an all-out offensive in the spring of 1944. Bill was ordered to evacuate. The American consul urged him to close the hospital. By September, he received word that the whole city of Wuchow was to be evacuated. His diary of September 16 reads:

> We left Wuchow on September 16 just ahead of Japanese. We included our hospital equipment and staff and nurses, a total of fifty-five people. . . . We are doing our best to keep the Stout Memorial Hospital intact. . . . I do not know if we can survive or not, but we're going to try. And if we fail, we will have the assurance that we failed trying.

In 1945, after V-J Day, the hospital staff was able to return to Wuchow. They found a badly battered and filthy hospital compound. Bill led the task of cleaning up with a positive attitude and dogged determination. In 1946, Dr. Bill Wallace came back to the US on furlough. He studied at the Cooke County School of Medicine in Chicago. He also studied tropical medicines in New Orleans at Tulane University.

Early in 1947, Bill wrote this succinct summary of the beginning of his third term of service in Wuchow:

> Every effort has been put forth to fulfill the mission of the hospital. . . . It is our high hope and prayer that the medical service of this institution shall be on the high plane befitting the glorious gospel which is preached daily within its walls.

Late in 1948, the Communists were about to conquer all of China. When 1949 dawned, the hospital staff was wary. Their fears were well-founded. By July, the Communist forces were just outside Wuchow. They took the city in

August and put pressure on the hospital staff to leave. Christmas that year was a subdued one.

The final crisis came in mid 1950. Wallace was accused of being "President Truman's chief spy in Wuchow." He was arrested as a "counter-revolutionary." The Communists framed a confession. While Bill was in prison, his friends asked how he was. Bill replied, "All right, trusting in the Lord."

Bill Wallace was killed in prison by the Communists. They said it was suicide. Bill's friends knew better. His body was placed in a small wooden box. No service was allowed. A grave marker went up months later. It read: "For me to live is Christ."

One of the 1951 editions of the *Journal of the International College of Surgeons* paid tribute to Dr. William Wallace. One of the pages read:

> The Chinese Communist Party, in its valiant attempts to remake the world, found Bill Wallace's presence in China an inconvenience. He was a living example of all they abhorred. . . . No selfless life is devoid of effect upon others.

In Pusan, Korea, today stands the Wallace Memorial Baptist Hospital. It is a fitting but inadequate memorial to the one who lived in Christ's spirit of healing and teaching.

Japan

In 1931, Japan invaded and annexed Manchuria. In 1937, the Sino-Japanese war started. In 1941, the Japanese bombed Pearl Harbor. V-J Day came in 1945, only after atomic bombs were dropped on Nagasaki and Hiroshima. Douglas MacArthur entered Japan in 1946. The emperor declared he was not a god. This, to say the least, was a time of great turmoil for Japan; but missionaries worked with some limited success.

Christianity made some progress in Japan from 1913 to 1926. The political climate was favorable to the spread of Western ideas. John R. Mott visited in 1913 and conducted five conferences. He set up the "Cooperative Campaign of Evangelism." Three-quarters of a million Japanese heard the gospel preached late that year. More than thirty thousand "inquirers" moved forward in evangelistic crusades in major cities. Millions of pieces of Christian literature were distributed.

The churches of Japan, led by American and European missionaries, took a strong stand against the Shinto worship of the emperor they saw developing in the 1920s. In 1930, the National Christian Council issued this statement:

> To treat the Shinto shrines . . . as unreligious has been unreasonable. The shrines of Shrine Shinto are actually engaged in religious functions. This has given rise to much confusion. Furthermore, recently the Government in its effort to foster religious faith has promoted worship at the shrines of Shrine Shinto and even made it compulsive.

Hard times came in 1939. Salvation Army missionaries were arrested as spies, as were envoys of the Seventh-Day Adventists (SDA). Almost three hundred Pentecostal preachers were taken to jail. In 1942, the Japanese government outlawed Sunday as a day of rest and worship. Compulsory emperor worship was introduced into the churches. The churches were affected negatively, and most missionaries were forced to leave.

During this time, a saint among saints, Toyohiko Kagawa (1888-1960) rose to prominence among Protestants. He received a theological training in Japan and in America. He returned to live in one of the worst slums in Japan, often sleeping in the doorway of his hostel at night to ward off robbers and welcome transients. He argued for the rights of organized laborers and encouraged cooperatives. In his later years, Kagawa was a traveling preacher who spoke to almost a million persons. Toyohiko was a prolific writer. A most popular book was *Before the Dawn* in which he called for spiritual renewal in Japan. Kagawa also started the

Kingdom of God movement which was an expression of the Social Gospel. So Japan was not without its Christian heroes during this time of turmoil.

Korea

Korea was a part of the Japanese empire from 1910 to 1945. In spite of this, the period under discussion opened with Korea undergoing a spiritual renewal. Christian literature was being distributed widely. By 1914, there were almost two hundred thousand Christians in Korea with more than three hundred missionaries giving leadership.

But, all schools were soon brought under Japanese control. In 1915, a Japanese educational system was imposed on the nation which forbade religious instruction in all types of schools.

In spite of all these injunctions against Christianity, the work continued. By 1925, there were six hundred Protestant missionaries. By 1941, there were more than one thousand ordained Korean pastors and about one-third million Protestant Christians.

This sustained growth was due primarily to a method of church growth introduced to Korea by the Presbyterian John L. Nevius. The Reverend Nevius came to Korea in 1898. He met with Korean pastors and lay leaders and explained the "Nevius Method" of church growth, based of four principles:

1. Let each new convert continue in his own trade and witness in his own neighborhood;
2. Develop church methods only so far as the natives can care for them;
3. Set aside the better qualified from among the natives to do evangelistic work among their neighbors;
4. Let the natives provide for their own church buildings. This method aided particularly the Presbyterians in rapid church growth prior to World War II.

Philippines

The Christians in the Philippines in the twenty-five years after 1914 saw a time of great progress. The number of Christians doubled.

The American Episcopal Church, under its mission-minded bishop, Charles H. Brent, in the years following 1914 confined itself to work only among non-Catholics. This principle was soon abandoned, under the ecumenical leader's protest. A united seminary was started in Manila, the United Theological College. By 1941, there were eight high schools and middle schools and five colleges supported by Protestant missions. This was in addition to more than a dozen hospitals, two dozen dispensaries, and forty mobile clinics. There were about thirteen hundred Protestant churches with a membership of one-third million.

The Christian and Missionary Alliance (CMA) came to the Philippines in significant numbers in 1923. By 1941, there were thirty CMA workers in the area. In 1947, the CMA churches in the Philippines became independent.

The Seventh-Day Adventists came to the islands in 1910 and immediately set about to start schools, hospitals, and churches.

The Association of Baptists for World Evangelism started work in the Philippines in 1928. During the work of Dr. and Mrs. R. C. Thomas and Ellen W. Martin, the growth was good, especially in Luzon, Mindanao, and Palawan. This group always coordinates medical work with evangelism and church starting.

The Assemblies of God (AG) work in the Philippines was started in 1935 by Filipinos who were converted and trained in the US. From the beginning, the emphasis has been on evangelism and church planting.

In 1905, the American Baptists started an industrial school for boys at Iloilo. In 1923, it received the designation as Central Philippine College.

The witness in the Philippines suffered greatly during World War II.

India

About 1925, steps were taken to use a charter given to Carey's work at Serampore for its original purpose of training missionaries and preachers. The college had been authorized by the Danish government to offer degrees in theology. Today colleges all over India can be identified with it to offer the Bachelor of Divinity degree. At the same time, the Bishop's College in Calcutta was restored to its role as a theological training center.

Sundar Singh, a former Sikh, was baptized in 1905. He was most effective in spreading the gospel because he lived the life of a Hindu teacher. He died in 1929 but had inspired the Christian Ashram movement in which potential converts are invited to sit at the feet of a wise teacher and consider Christianity.

Mahatma Ghandi returned to India from South Africa in 1915. His known interest in the New Testament and teachings of Christ spurred hundreds of young Hindus to study those precepts.

The population of India grew rapidly during this period, as this chart shows:

Year	Number
1914	300,000
1931	340,000
1941	389,000
1946	415,000

The work of the missionaries stayed strong but could not keep up with the population growth. Christian education was one order of outstanding achievement however. There were more than thirty Christian colleges by 1946 with about fourteen thousand students, 10 percent of whom were women. There were three medical schools open in

India that year with more than fifty centers for treating lepers.

There were almost eleven hundred foreign missionaries in India in 1946, with twenty-six hundred native pastors. The number of baptized Protestants was more than two and a half million.

William Carey had written letters in 1806 calling for a worldwide missions conference to meet in South Africa in 1810. That ecumenical fervor has stayed on in India. In 1901, the South India United Church came into being. The National Missionary Society came into being in 1905 and is a major factor in helping Indians assume church leadership roles.

Iran

The revolution that put Riza Khan on the throne in 1926 had far-reaching consequences. The status of Muslim women was raised. In 1937, the removal of their veil was made compulsory by a special decree.

The Lutheran Orient Mission work was started among the Nestorian Christians and the Muslim Kurds in 1911. The work closed in 1917. The German Christian Mission for the Blind was started in 1911 as well. Seventh-Day Adventists came that same year. The CMA has been in Iran since 1930.

In 1932, all Christian mission schools were closed in Iran. In 1936, the schools were permitted to reopen, but no religious instruction could legally be given in them.

In 1912, the Episcopal diocese of Persia was inaugurated. There were about a thousand members in 1946. Medical and educational work was established.

In 1909, a group of Assyrian Pentecostal Christians came from Chicago to northwest Iran. Many of them were martyred during World War I. John Warton was assigned to Iran in 1924 and served in Reziah, his birthplace.

Saudi Arabia

Samuel Zwemer arrived on the Arabian peninsula in 1890, sponsored by the American Arabian Mission. The sponsorship was taken over four years later by the Reformed Church in America. Zwemer gave the better part of sixty years of missionary service to Arabia. He is remembered as "the apostle to Islam." He set the pattern for the modern Christian approach to the Muslim. Zwemer was an excellent scholar, prolific writer, and skilled preacher. He founded *The Muslim World,* a scholarly journal given to the pursuit of Christian missions among the followers of the Koran.

The work of the Independent Board for Presbyterian Foreign Missions in Arabia came to Saudi Arabia in 1941 in the presence of Sarah L. Hosmon, M.D. She started a small hospital in Sharjah.

Africa

Liberia

The Assemblies of God came to Newaka, Liberia, in 1908. A school was opened in 1931 at Feloka. Bible schools to train native pastors was a part of the strategy from the beginning, with two schools established before 1946.

In 1931, Baptist Mid-Missions came to the central part of Liberia. From the beginning, the work has stressed medical aid and a leprosarium.

The Worldwide Evangelization Crusade (WEC) came to Liberia in 1938. As the name implies, there was much emphasis on church planting and personal evangelism. Protestant work in Liberia has made rapid strides since World War II.

Ivory Coast

William Wade Harris was an Episcopal Christian from Liberia who, in 1913, became the center of a mighty movement of the Holy Spirit. He began the next year to preach to those involved in the African traditional religions. One of his peers described Harris as:

> An impressive figure, adorned with a white beard, of tall stature, clothed in white, his head enturbaned with a cloth of the same color, wearing a black stole; in his hand a high cross and on his belt a calabash.

Harris was already sixty years old when he started his ministry. He was a powerful preacher. It is estimated that as many as one hundred thousand persons gave up their tribal gods to follow Christ because of his preaching. Whenever he preached, churches were begun. A preacher was installed for each new congregation. Harris sent evangelists, whom he called "minor prophets" to go into the bush to make converts.

The English Methodist Society came about a decade later to follow up on Harris work. They found some fifty thousand Christians who were still faithful.

Harris was an early example of the move of Africans to form their own churches. The trend toward indigenization but containing African traditional religions elements is worthy of analyis so long as the Christian missionary is able to dissect adequately those various elements.

The Paris Tabernacle Mission came to the Ivory Coast in 1927. It is now known as the *Mission Biblique* and is at work chiefly in the southwest corner of that nation.

In 1930, the Christian and Missionary Alliance entered Ivory Coast and opened its work in Bewako. Between 1930 and 1946, four other centers were opened.

The Worldwide Evangelization Crusade first came to this West African nation in 1934. Work was started in Abidjan, the capitol, and in four other centers by 1946. Student work and Bible translation have been specializations for the WEC.

Upper Volta

The American branch of the Assemblies of God came to the capital city of Ouagadou, Upper Volta, in 1921. They started a Bible school in 1933. By 1946, more than a hundred students were graduated from it. The church became autonomous in 1949 and was recognized by the dominantly Muslim government.

The CMA missionaries have worked chiefly around Bobo-Dioulasso, in the western part of Upper Volta. They have been there since 1923. By 1946, they had opened four centers, mainly in the western part of the country.

The Sudan Interior Mission came to Fada N'gourma in 1930 and soon started a Bible school for training native clergy.

The WEC started in Upper Volta in 1937 with an international group of missionaries. They have worked mainly with the Lobi and Birifor peoples.

Nigeria

The Sudan Interior Mission started evangelism among the Tangales in 1917. In 1925, the SIM started work in Kano, among the Muslim Hausas. Jos was entered in 1923 and became the headquarters of their mission effort. The SIM was a pioneer in radio on station ELWA and the magazine called *African Challenge*. SIM sent out more than a thousand missionaries to Africa between 1914 and 1946.

The Sudan United Mission (SUM) was started in London in 1904. The branches are self-supporting and autonomous. The Christian Reformed Church has sent out more than a hundred missionaries in cooperation with the SUM. The largest field is northern Nigeria which had almost fifty stations by 1946.

The Synodical Conference of Lutheran Churches started mission work in Calabar in 1936 with a Bible school, seminary, and teacher training college.

The Assemblies of God started work in eastern Nigeria

at Port Harcourt in 1939. The quality of the work has been excellent, with emphasis on Bible schools and church extension with native workers.

Gabon

The Christian and Missionary Alliance came to Gabon in 1934. The main station has been at Bongolo, where the Central Bible School is located.

The outstanding missionary in Gabon's history came out under the Paris Evangelical Missionary Society. His name was Albert Schweitzer.

Albert Schweitzer (1875-1965) was a brilliant philosopher, theologian, musician, and missionary. He won the Nobel Peace Prize in 1952. Schweitzer built his missionary career on the philosophy of "reverence for life."

He was born in Alsace and educated in both France and Germany. By age thirty, he had won an international reputation as an organ builder, musician, and expert on Bach. In 1902, Schweitzer became principal of Saint Thomas Theological College at the University of Stasbourg. He studied medicine there from 1903 to 1912, after receiving a call to missionary service. He raised money for a hospital at Lambarene in French Equatorial Africa, now called Gabon. He started serving there himself in 1913. There he built a larger hospital and medical station. Thousands of Africans were treated annually. The thirty-three thousand dollars he received from the Nobel Peace Prize went into the expenses of the hospital.

Schweitzer continued to write while doing missionary service. In 1923, he published *The Philosophy of Civilization*. Other works included *Out of My Life and Thought* in 1931 and *From My African Notebook* in 1939.

Schweitzer was buried at Lambarene at his request, symbolic that he had chosen mission service above all the possibilities open to his brilliant mind and caring heart.

The Africa of the nineteenth century was seen by most

Europeans as one giant steaming jungle covered with mosquitoes and crocodiles. The continent was referred to frequently as the "white man's grave." It was a place to be feared, and one to be fought over for its raw materials. In the midst of that warped view of Africa, there were a few European Christians who could see the persons of Africa as in need of ministry. Albert Scweitzer was one.

Latin America

Latin American Christianity between 1914 and 1946, as it was before and after, was dominated by Roman Catholicism.

Yet, Protestant Christianity was not dormant. By 1946, there were about four million Evangelicals in South America and an equal number expressing an interest. Protestantism between 1914 and 1946 found some growth possibilities in the middle classes. In 1912, the Britisher Lord Bryce noted the possibilities in *South America, Observations and Impressions:*

> Men of the upper or educated class appear wholly indifferent to theology and to Christian worship. It has no interest for them. They are seldom actively hostile to Christianity, much less are they offensive when they speak of it; but they think it does not concern them.

The Protestants had good years between the wars, in spite of liberal governments which persecuted Evangelicals.

Paraguay

The United Christian Missionary Society, representing the Disciples of Christ, started work in Paraguay in 1917. Soon after, the International Academy and Friendship Mission were started.

Mennonites have done good work in Paraguay, dating back to 1935. The group also sponsors a work called the Light to the Indians.

Baptist work started in Paraguay in 1919 when the Argentine Baptist Convention sent a couple named Fernandez to Ascuncion. Southern Baptists first entered this nation in 1945.

Bolivia

The largest non-Catholic church in Bolivia is the Seventh-Day Adventist one. By 1946, they had five thousand members. The SDA's witnessed a revival in 1915 and again in 1934 among the Indians. Their most lasting contribution, however, has been in the establishment of schools.

Joseph A. Davis started the South America Indian Mission in 1922 in Bolivia. It was originally designed to work among the Ayoreo and Chiquitano Indians but has spread out since.

The Evangelical Union of South America started work in Bolivia in 1937. In 1944, work was begun among the peoples of the eastern lowlands. In 1945, the union merged with the Eastern Bolivian Fellowship.

The World Mission Prayer League came to LaPaz in 1938. It is a Lutheran mission. The group sponsors a book store in LaPaz.

The New Tribes Mission (NTM) came to Bolivia in 1942. It has grown to be a large mission.

The World Gospel Mission came to the Bolivian people in 1943. The United World Mission came the following year.

Foursquare Gospel missionaries came to Bolivia in 1929, when they came to the "Green Hell" area and started a Christian commune for the Indians.

Peru

Nazarene missionaries entered northern Peru in 1917. A Bible school was started.

The Assemblies of God have had missionaries in Peru since 1919. There were almost a hundred churches in 1946.

The South American Indian Mission first came to Peru in 1921. The area of concentration has been the jungle lowlands. Much of the work has been among the Conibo, Campa, and Shipibo Indians.

In 1922, the Peru Inland Mission started a hospital and Bible school in Lamas.

The Christian and Missionary Alliance first started work in Huanuco in 1926. The group started the Peruvian Bible Institute in 1933.

The Association of Baptists for World Evangelism entered Peru in 1939 and established centers later on the Amazon River. Another Baptist group, the Baptist Mid-Missions, has been in Peru since 1937.

Colombia

Resident work in Colombia for the Evangelical Alliance Mission was begun in Cucuta in 1922. The John Christiansens were the first arrivals, coming from Venezuela.

Seventh-Day Adventists faced tough times when they first came to Colombia in 1930 but had almost six thousand members by 1946.

The Worldwide Evangelization Crusade entered Colombia in 1932 when Bogota was the site of the initial station.

The South America Mission came to Colombia in 1934. The work was primarily in the northeast part of the nation.

Two single female missionaries pioneered the work of the Latin American Mission (LAM) in Colombia starting in 1937. A Bible school opened in 1942. The LAM is best known for its work in evangelism training.

The Southern Baptists came to Colombia in 1941 and helped to form the Colombia Baptist Convention. There were almost a dozen SBC missionaries there by 1946.

The Wesleyan Church came to Colombia in 1941 into the city of Medellin. They soon had a publishing house and church going.

The area in northeast Colombia called Magdalena was

entered by the Evangelical Union of South America in 1942.

The Pearsons and Gilbanis entered Medellin in 1943 as representatives of the Inter-American Missionary Crusade. Early in 1944, they started a seminary in that city.

Mennonites have been in Colombia since 1945, starting first near the Cauca and San Juan River.

Venezuela

The Orinoco River Mission (ORM) was started in 1920 by Van Eddings in Carupano. They opened a primary school each of the first four years they were there. The ORM started a Bible institute in Las Delisians in 1939.

The Venezuela Interior Mission started work in 1925 in the Guarico region. The work continues in north Venezuela.

Southern Baptists started work in Venezuela in 1945 through native Christians. The first church was started that year in Caracas. It was followed by one in Maracaibo in 1946. American missionaries representing Southern Baptists did not arrive until 1949.

Mexico

The Mexican Indian Mission started its work in 1931 with the coming to Mexico of James C. Dale. The heart of the mission from the beginning was in Tamazunchale. By 1946, there were almost two dozen missionaries engaged in the work.

The Wesleyan Church sent the Solteros to Mexico to start a Bible school and printing plant. They did so in San Luis Potosi in spite of intense persecution.

One small plane and a dedicated pilot were the raw material for the start of the Missionary Aviation Fellowship (MAF) in Mexico in 1946.

Three denominations—the Congregationalists, Methodists, and Disciples—got together to start the Union Theological Seminary in Mexico City in 1919.

Guatemala

Thomas A. Pullin and others started The Church of God (Cleveland) work in Guatemala when they came to Totonicipan in 1916. The work was moved four years later to be of assistance to the Quiche Indians.

The John L. Franklins were the pioneer Assembly of God missionaries in Guatemala. They came to Jutiapa in 1937. They moved to Guatemala City in 1941 where there were four churches by 1946.

The Guatemalan Baptist Convention was started in 1946 with the assistance of staff personnel from the HMB, SBC. This was two years before the first Southern Baptist missionaries came.

Nicaragua

In 1922, the American Baptist Home Mission Society started the Baptist Academy in Managua. Five years later, the women's society for American Baptists opened the Evelyn Briggs Cranska Memorial Hospital. The Nicaragua Baptist Convention was formed in 1937. By 1946, the membership was about two thousand.

The Assemblies of God entered Nicaragua by starting the Nicaragua Bible Institute in Matagalpa.

Haiti

The West Indies Mission came to Haiti on the Tiburon Peninsula in 1936. A Bible school was started that year in Aux Cayes.

The Unevangelized Fields Mission came to the northwest part of Haiti in 1943. The work has centered on education.

The Church of God (Cleveland) entered Haiti in 1934 with the start of a Bible school.

Except for occasional German intrusion during World War II, Latin America remained virtually untouched by that global conflict. This left the area open for active Christian missions. The major conflict was between Catholics and Protestants with increasing Protestant incursions.

Europe

Catholicism

World War I dealt a crushing blow to the Roman Catholic establishment of Europe. France, Germany, Belgium, and Italy were dealt staggering blows, including the loss of precious human life.

The quality of the popes after World War I was, however, very high. That factor aided the recovery. They were Benedict XV (1914-1922), Pius XI (1922-1939), Pius XII (1939-1951).

This was a time of theological refreshing for the Church, as seen in the writings of Jacques Maritain (1882-1973). He was a French philosopher and educator who helped to revive the study of Thomist theology. He taught at the University of Chicago and at Notre Dame, among other schools. His books include *An Introduction to Philosophy* in 1937 and *Degrees of Knowledge* in 1938. He was awarded the French Grand Prize for Letters in 1963. His philosophy was an attempt to build a foundation for a Europe he saw crumbling about him.

Mission interest among European Roman Catholics increased in the period between the wars. In 1922, the Society for the Propagation of the Faith was moved to Rome and put under the direct control of the pope. The popes emphasized the training of native clergy and increased the number of bishoprics in foreign lands. Roman Catholic growth was remarkable in Sub-Sahara Africa, but especially in the Belgian Congo.

Protestantism

Protestantism in Europe underwent radical theological struggles between the wars. A leading example was Karl

Barth (1886-1968), the son of a lecturer in theology at Basel. He started a theological revolution with his *Commentary on the Epistle to the Romans* in 1918. In it he attacked liberal theology and the Social Gospel. One of his major themes was sin. Barth maintained that people must listen to and heed the Word of God.

Another major personality was Nathan Soderblom (1866-1931), a primate in the Church of Sweden. He was known for his part in the ecumenical movement and for helping to form the Universal Christian Council for Life and Work.

Another major contribution to the changing world of European Protestantism was William Temple (1881-1944). He was an Anglican bishop who led the Life and Liberty Movement. An ecumenical visionary, when Temple was named Archbishop of Canterbury, he used the occasion to call forth a Christian fellowship marked by "true unity and mutual love."

Russian Orthodoxy

Russian Orthodoxy was dealt a severe blow by the Communist takeover in October 1917. The USSR declared all land to be national property late that same year. All schools were ordered turned over to the state. In 1918, religious vows and oaths were dissolved, all religious instruction was forbidden in all schools, and no religious rites were to be allowed at state functions. Priests and bishops were disfranchised. At least a thousand priests were murdered between 1917 and 1922. In 1922, all church articles were confiscated.

By 1946, more than 92 percent of the churches operating in 1917 had been confiscated for use by the state. The number of priests had been reduced by a similar percentage.

The underground church movement in Russia grew stronger between the wars. Secret training of priests continued and baptisms were done in Christian homes.

In 1946, there were about twenty thousand Orthodox churches, thirty thousand priests, ten theological seminaries, and almost ninety monasteries still in operation in the USSR.

Russian Orthodoxy was finding centers of life outside Russia in the 1920s. One such center was in Paris where Nikolai Berdayev (1874-1948) was a popular figure. His wife was an active Roman Catholic. He was deported in 1921 by the Soviet authorities while teaching at the University of Moscow. He was soon associated with the YMCA and World's Student Christian Federation in France and Germany. Berdayev was read widely. He maintained that all theology and philosophy must begin with Christ, who is the only way God is to be known. It was Berdayev who gave hope to those Russian Orthodox Christians exiled from their homeland.

Christianity was never to be the same in Europe after the two world wars. In most nations, the states tie with the Catholic Church was either loosened or severed completely.

But European Christianity in 1946 was far from dead. New life was coming partially through the effort to rebuild after the wars. Missions were dealt a temporary setback but were ready to swing into full gear.

The United States of America

By 1946, the USA was generally regarded as the most powerful nation on earth. This was partly due to the decline of Western Europe but mainly due to the respect the rest of the world had for the military and economic might of the US. The US was, by all measurements, much more powerful than it had been in 1914.

America's rise in strength was due to more than militarism and economics however. The years between and including the great wars saw an increase in population, mainly from emigration. Church membership and involvement increased as well. In 1914, the percentage of Americans in someone's church was 44 percent. By 1946, it had risen to 53 percent.

The churches of the nation had to learn to minister in urban settings. New words appeared in American vocabularies, such as *shopping center, suburbs, housing projects,* and *trailer parks.*

In 1914, the Roman Catholics were by far the largest Christian group in the nation, with about fifteen million communicants. By 1946, that number was twenty-seven million. Home mission agencies included the Paulists, the National Converts League, and the League of Prayer for the Conversion of America. By 1946, the annual increase rate was better than one hundred thousand per year.

American Catholics sent out foreign missionaries by the thousands during this period. Among those dispatched were those sent by the Franciscans, the Society of Jesus, and the Society of the Divine Word. The Maryknolls got started in 1911 in conjunction with the Foreign Mission Sisters of Saint Dominic. In 1918, the Catholic Students' Mission Crusade was started. The mission effort was in full swing between the wars.

Individuals

The most colorful character in American Catholicism during this period was *Charles E. Coughlin* (1891-1979). He was a Roman Catholic priest who favored inflationism and isolationism. Coughlin rose to prominence while directing the Church of the Little Flower in Royal Oak, Michigan. He had a nationwide radio audience and called Franklin D. Roosevelt a "liar" and a "scab president." He declared that Jewish bankers were the cause of Russian Communism. He was reprimanded by his bishop.

Another user of the media was the radio and television personality *Bishop Fulton J. Sheen* (1895-1980). He was a member of the faculty at the Catholic University of America and a popular writer of more than fifty books. In 1950, he became director of the Society for the Propagation of the Faith in the US. Pope Paul VI made him bishop of the diocese of Rochester, New York, in 1966.

He appeared on the radio show entitled "The Catholic Hour" and was known as an eloquent foe of Communism. His first book was *God and Intelligence in Modern Philosophy* in 1946. Sheen was best known for his appearances on the "Life Is Worth Living" television show. Sheen showed the power of the broadcast media in popularizing Catholicism.

Protestantism showed tremendous growth between 1914 and 1946. The growth of that branch of Christianity was about 30 percent from 1914 to 1926. It grew by a similar percentage in the next score of years. This growth was most seen in Baptist groups. By 1946, the combined membership of the Southern Baptist Convention and the three black Baptist groups was about thirteen million.

A Baptist *Charles E. Fuller* (1887-1968) appealed to the masses through his radio program, the "Old-Fashioned Revival Hour." He started broadcasting in 1925 and by 1942 had a worldwide audience. His influence gave rise to the Fuller Seminary, a large evangelical training center in California.

In the years immediately following World War I, a labor movement grew up around *Frank Buchman* (1878-1968). He started Moral Re-Armament, which was designed to strengthen democracy and capitalism by stressing moral and spiritual values. Buchman started "Oxford Groups" in the 1920s, based on the style popularized by John Wesley. A motto was "a race in time to remake men and nations."

US Protestantism between the wars was racked by a Liberal-Fundamentalist Controversy. The former movement stressed the ability of human reason to discern religious truth. The most popular spokesman for this position was *Harry Emerson Fosdick* (1878-1969). Fosdick stressed the right of science to find its place in the world of religious thought. He was pastor of the Riverside Church in New

York City and professor of preaching at Union Theological Seminary.

The Fundamentalists fought Liberalism by maintaining the inerrancy of the Word of God. There were certain "fundamentals" listed which this conservative group was willing to defend. They included: the virgin birth of Christ, an eternal hell, and the inspiration of the Bible. By 1919, the World's Christian Fundamentals Association was formed. The outstanding spokesman for Fundamentalism was *J. Gresham Maechen* (1881-1937).

Fundamentalists were down on "evolutionism" because it seemed to deny the uniqueness of humanity and the Bible's authority. The famous test case was the Scopes Trial, held in Dayton, Tennessee, in 1925. William Jennings Bryan defended the traditional view and Clarence Darrow, the evolutionists. It received international publicity.

The era between the wars was one of controversy plus rapid growth for American Protestants.

The founder of the Jehovah's Witnesses, *Charles Taze Russell* (1859-1916) died during World War I. The movement suffered a temporary setback but picked up steam quickly under the leadership of "Judge" *Joseph F. Rutherford* (b. 1869), who ruled the movement from 1916 to 1942. Rutherford wrote twenty-two books and dozens of pamphlets, circulating more than 450 million pieces of literature. It was the judge who initiated the idea of involving the members in door-to-door visitation. He used billboards in 1933 to announce the end of the age with the declaration, "Millions Now Living Will Never Die."

Rutherford had an effective radio ministry which popularized the Witness theology and castigated Christians, especially Catholics, for being the "great whore of Babylon" mentioned in the Revelation. Rutherford gave the movement its modern name, Jehovah's Witnesses, in 1931. The period was one of mushrooming growth under his leadership.

The Ecumenical Vision

In 1806, William Carey wrote letters to mission societies and leaders to try to convene a conference on ecumenical cooperation in mission effort. This letter, from a Baptist, called for a council to meet in South Africa in 1810. The meeting never occurred, but the dream and problems never died. The dream was that all the followers of Christ "may be one" and the problem was that of fragmentation on the field.

Each denominational group and interdenominational group pressed forward with its own ambitions and goals in the nineteenth century. The result was that the indigenous peoples were often confused by conflicting claims and emphases. Each mission station was a virtually watertight compartment.

John R. Mott

The American visionary who brought the ecumenical movement to fruition in the twentieth century was John R. Mott (1865-1955). In 1888, he became the secretary for the International Committee of the YMCA. Mott was chairman of the Student Volunteer Missions Movement from 1888 to 1920 and later started the World's Student Christian Federation. Mott received the Nobel Peace Prize in 1946 and the Distinguised Service Medal for his work during World War I.

Mott was a layman who traveled worldwide as an evangelist and student organizer. His was a worldwide vision, and he had little time for parochialism. He knew that missionary service could be broadened and deepened by cooperation. Mott often reminded critics of the ecumenical movement that it began out of missionary and evangelistic concern.

The Ecumenical Missionary Conference was held in New York City in 1900. The participants were from the US and

Western Europe. Almost two hundred mission boards were represented.

Edinburgh, 1910

The turning point came in 1910 with the World Missionary Conference Meeting in Edinburgh. At that meeting, Mott reminded the messengers that well-planned cooperation between mission leaders would be equivalent to doubling the missionary forces without adding a single new missionary. Mott stunned the meeting with his memorable phrase, "If he is Lord at all, he must be Lord of all."

The Edinburgh Conference was a milestone for four reasons:

1. It was a delegated body, made up of official representatives of mission agencies;
2. It was a deliberative body, asking serious questions about the future of mission policy;
3. It gave assignment for further study of missions; and
4. It was a comprehensive gathering, including almost all Protestant mission societies.

From the 1910 meeting came the *International Review of Missions,* a scholarly periodical. It is noteworthy that by deliberate choice, Latin America was not considered a mission field because of the large presence of Roman Catholic work there.

The International Missionary Council remained separate from, but gave impetus to, the World Council of Churches.

In the meantime, ecumenical concern in the US was taking concrete form. Josiah Strong (1847-1916) and Elias B. Sanford (1843-1932) made the Federal Council of Churches a reality in 1908, with more than thirty American Protestant denominations subscribing to its initial charter. By 1946, it represented about 130 thousand local congregations and almost 30 million members. By 1946, similar national federations had developed in France, Germany,

Switzerland, New Zealand, Australia, Canada, and Great Britain.

Charles H. Brent

Charles H. Brent (1862-1929), an American Episcopal bishop, caught a vision at Edinburgh. He wanted a world-wide discussion of doctrinal issues which had not been introduced at Edinburgh. He called on the Anglicans to take the lead in discussing the faith and order in the churches. The first World Conference on Faith and Order met at Lausanne in 1927. More than four hundred delegates came to represent more than one hundred communions. The next meeting was called for Edinburgh in 1937. At that meeting, a statement on Christ's grace was prefaced with the statement, "There is in connection with this subject no grounds for divisions among the churches."

Ecumenical Conferences

The first Universal Christian Conference on Life and Work came in 1925. The conference's purpose was three-fold:

1. To unite the churches in common practical work;
2. To furnish the Christian conscience with an organ of expression in the midst of the spiritual movements of the time; and
3. To insist that the principle of the gospel be applied to the solution of contemporary social and international problems.

The conference was largely due to the efforts of Nathan Soderblom (1866-1931), a Swedish Lutheran pastor who later became Archbishop of Uppsala. The Reverend Solderblom gave such leadership to the movement that the continuation committee named at the 1925 meeting grew into the Universal Christian Council for Life and Work in 1930.

In 1938, a provisional structure for the World Council of Churches was drawn up. The basis for the union was this sentence: "The World Council of Churches is a fellowship of Churches which accept our Lord Jesus Christ as God and Saviour." Finally, in 1948, in Amsterdam, almost 150 communions from 44 nations participated in the formation of the World Council of Churches. Most of the newer churches in Africa and Asia joined with most of the major Protestant bodies of Europe and America.

Meanwhile, the International Missionary Council (IMC) was continuing to meet, this time at Jerusalem in 1928.

A meeting of the IMC was also held in 1938 at Madras, with half of the delegates representing the newer churches. This was a signal of the indigenization and ecumenical cooperation within mission causes just prior to World War II.

The Baptist World Alliance

The Baptist World Alliance (BWA) was started in 1905, to show, according to its constitution, "the essential oneness of Baptist people in the Lord Jesus Christ, to impart inspiration to the brotherhood, and to promote the spirit of fellowship, service and cooperation among its members."

The BWA serves as an agent of communication between Baptists. In 1984, it represented almost thirty million in more than two dozen nations. A Baptist World Congress and a World Conference for Baptist Youth is held every five years. The women's division sponsor an annual Baptist Women's Day of Prayer. The BWA sponsors study commisions on evangelism and missions as well as Christian teaching and training.

Christianity About AD 1946: The Aftermath and Advance

The period between the wars was a time of trial for Christian churches. By and large, the churches responded with vigor to a situation that had every possibility of being depressing. Ecumenism, faith missions, theological renewal, and disputing and controversy over evolution kept the movement from stagnation. There was a note of realism about the era. The "War to End All Wars" had been fought. Then another worldwide holocaust burst upon the scene. With rare exception, the churches behaved with valor in trying and dangerous times. Wherever German Christians were run from an area, Christian missionaries of other nationalities stepped in, and vice versa. The missions movement plowed on, even when the missionaries were filled with sorrow and indignation at the needless loss of human life in World War II. The spectre of Communism robbed the Russian Orthodox churches of their vitality and holdings, but such writers as Berdyaev kept the hopes alive. He was the Jeremiah to the saints in exile.

Hope was springing up for the future of Christian missions in the development of Third-World churches and leaders. The faithfulness of nineteen centuries of missionary effort was to pay off. As World War II ended, the aftermath was evident. Burned out Christians and bombed out buildings were evidence that there was a horrible experience just behind those brave mission leaders who were looking now to the future. It was a time for picking up the pieces and reassessing values and priorities.

Advance was a possibility then in 1946 when the times demanded creativity and flexibility in mission effort. The postwar world was waiting to see if the gospel could restore dashed hopes.

Case Study: Miguel de Unamuno, Irritator of People

Miguel de Unamuno (1864-1937) was a Spanish scholar and writer. He was exiled to the Canary Islands in 1924 for his criticisms of the Spanish government. He said: "My painful duty is to irritate people. We must sow in men the seeds of doubt, of distrust, even of despair."

Miguel de Unamuno wrote and spoke against complacency, traditionalism, and hypocrisy in society. He was, in his own eyes, a devoted Roman Catholic but was regarded with alarm by the Church, and two of his books were placed on the Index. Among his works was *The Agony of Christianity* (1928). In it he reminded Christian believers that Christ did not come to bring peace but a sword.

Questions

1. Amos and Jeremiah were "people irritators." Is there room for that spirit on mission fields in the late twentieth century?
2. To what degree do hypocrisy, complacency, and traditionalism hinder mission service today? What can mission leaders do about them?
3. Can sowing seeds of disquiet and despair be a preparation for the gospel in some cases? Why or why not?
4. Does one risk ostracism from his own church when criticizing it? What should be his response?
5. Do you agree with the statement, "It is those who love the church the most who are most critical of it"? Why?

Time Line: AD 1914-1946

1914	
1915	
1918	Barth's *Commentary on the Epistle to the Romans* published
1919	Union Theological Seminary founded in Mexico City
1920	
1922	Society for the Propagation of the Faith placed under papal control
1925	"Old Fashioned Revival Hour" goes on the air
1929	Charles Brent died
1930	
1931	Japan enters war against China
1932	Chinese Medical Association formed
1935	
1937	Miguel de Unamuno; Peru Bible Institute formed
1940	
1941	Colombian Baptist Convention formed
1942	New Tribes Mission comes to Bolivia
1945	V-J Day
1946	Guatemalan Baptist Convention formed

8
The World Changes:
AD 1946-1984

The aftermath of World War II brought new labels to the same set of problems Christian missionaries have always faced.

Persecution was now evident in the Soviet Union and Eastern Europe. The Communists were flexing their muscles early in the process of testing the strength of international Communism. But the churches could reflect on the Roman persecutions of a few centuries earlier. The task of rebuilding after a war could psychologically not be much worse than starting Christian missions after the fall of Jerusalem in AD 70. The immense challenge of taking the gospel to the whole planet with the aid of airplanes and radio could be no worse than the apostle Paul on small ships tossed about in the Mediterranean. Intellectual opposition in the forms of the "death of God" school and the "new morality" could hardly be the threat that Paul felt in the public markets at Athens. Political advocacy could be no more important than at the Areopagus. Jewish persons who were hesitant about commitment to Christ could hardly be as retiscent as the rabbis at the synagogue at Athens. The problems of the postwar era were great but history-minded missionaries could draw strength from knowing that the Lord of Jerusalem is the Lord of Jos and Jakarta.

At the start, the prognosis for Christian growth seemed negative. There were a few resources but none in comparison to those of the Romans and Mongols and Turks. Yet, the early mission pioneers brought the gospel to most persons in the Roman Empire within a generation. Then came the Muslim hordes to take such geographical centers of Christian strength as Alexandria and Jerusalem. This proved to be only a temporary setback, however, as visionaries for Christ invented ways of making their Lord attractive to the readers of the Koran.

The Reformation brought fragmentation and diversity to the churches. Pietism spread throughout Europe and America, emphasizing the necessity of the new birth. The stress on Bible study, prayer, and the priesthood of the individual believer gave sustenance on a daily basis to those willing to risk their lives for the gospel.

The Industrial Revolution ushered in the modern era with its accompanying secularism and materialism. The challenge to Christian missions was to maintain vitality in the midst of distractions. The churches proved able as they moved into new territory.

Now two world wars had been fought and won only by the process of survival. It was time to look forward. The Berlin Wall and Bamboo Curtain were about to be constructed either with mortar or in the minds of humanity. As in the first century, those of God's commissioning were challenged to cross barriers.

The key resourses of the years 1946-1984 would prove to be the same as in the beginning; that is, the love and power of God coupled with the faith of a minority who could see beyond their small frames of references to a world without Christ. The resources proved more than adequate in the years following World War II.

Interfaith Collisions

Islam

The specter of Islam did not die out after the death of Muhammad, the "seal" of the prophets. In fact, the movement spread rapidly in the last two-thirds of the seventh century. A new revival of Islam has come to pass in the past decade. Today Islam is once again on the march toward the West. This is so obvious that it has been called a "Muslim Crusade," a religious and cultural jihad, or holy war. Teachers from Cairo's Al Azhar University mosque, whose walls carry the inscription, "A thousand million Muslims," are spreading the Muslim faith through Africa and Asia. One-fourth of the total population in the USSR may be Muslim by the year AD 2000. In the British Isles, Muslim leaders estimate that more than a million Muslims worship at more than three hundred mosques.

In London, the elegant Regent's Park mosque is one of the most beautiful worship centers to be built in England in recent years. In Brent, England, Muslims pray in what was once a Reformed Church building. In the East end of London, Muslims have bought an old synagogue. In Stuttgart, Germany, Mercedes Benz has built a company mosque for its Turkish employees. There are at least two million Muslims in France today. A new mosque was completed in Rome in 1980. Its call to prayer is within hearing of the Vatican itself.

In 1975, on the sands of the Moroccan desert, an important movement came in the worldwide Islamic revival. A beleagured army, eventually numbering three hundred thousand crossed the Sahara desert and took from the Spanish a barren strip of North African territory. Shouting "Allah is great" and clutching copies of the Koran, the marchers surged across that rocky desert convinced that their faith would triumph over the might of Spain. It did. The territory was gained by faith without a shot being fired.

On November 21, 1979, Islam reached another milestone. A new century started with the dawning of the Islamic year 1400. There is today great optimism among Muslims for the future of Islam, including Muslim spread through missionaries. One Muslim sect in Saudi Arabia alone has set aside one million dollars weekly for missionary effort in the US, a total of fifty million dollars for 1984 alone, with a higher goal set for 1985. New mosques have been built in Los Angeles and Dallas. The Muslim revival is here.

The present Muslim resurgence into the Christian world is being helped along by three factors:

1. The rising power and involvement of the Muslim layperson. Muslim laypersons are working to establish orphanages, educational journals, job training programs, etc., all in the name of Allah. The self-help movement is now widespread.

2. Newly discovered economic power, based on oil revenue. This new power has helped to remove defensive attitudes from the Muslims. Muslim nations can now feel at ease in the world community of nations. This has produced in Muslim's a spirit of optimism that has not been present for centuries.

3. The rise of modern education. This has led to a more rational explanation of the faith. It is now seen that modern knowledge does not contradict, but confirms, truth in the Koran.

Islam today is in a state of revival. Christians of this era will be forced into involvement in missions and to forge life-styles while surrounded by persons of Muslim background. These two great religious competitions will be propelled toward each other even faster.

Modern Christian missions among Muslims will be forced increasingly to be articulate in presenting the gospel. Those who know best are advising the following effective Christian apologetic:

1. Remember that the name of Jesus (Isa in the Arabic) is found ninety-seven times in the Koran;

2. Remember that the Muslim is commanded to read the gospel (Injil in the Arabic) in one section of the Koran; and

3. Remember that misinformation may have to be corrected before witness can continue. For example,

some Muslims believe that the Christian concept of the Trinity includes God, Jesus and Mary.

The faith collision between Muslims and Christians is occuring. It is but one of the challenges of the modern missions era.

"New Religions"

The "New Religions" in Japan and their development is another area creating an interfaith collision with Christian missionaries.

In 1946, when the US army and American political rulers arrived in postwar Japan, a state of martial law was declared and the emperor was forced to deny that he was Divine. The state religion of Shinto was officially declared nonexistent. The people of Japan found themselves in a severe identity crisis. Almost overnight the "New Religions" sprang up, giving new forms of religious expression to afford the Japanese people a new form of identity with the Divine and with each other.

All of the "New Religions" in Japan have some common elements, including:

1. Belief in a strong, charismatic person who demands allegiance in an authoritarian fashion and receives it from loyal sect members;
2. Such shamanistic elements as promises of physical healing and other physical benefits;
3. The promise of immediate material benefits;
4. The sociological and psychological needs for belonging are reinforced and demonstrated;
5. Youthful vigor is given a channel of release;
6. Little or no demand for a radical, inner change through repentance; and
7. A sense of continuity with family and national heritage.

The classic example of the "New Religions" in Japan is Sokagakkai. From the postwar period to the present, Sokagakkai has averaged winning about ten thousand converts per month worldwide. In the western nations, it is usually known as the Nichiren Shoshu Association.

Nichiren (1221-1282) was without doubt the most controversial figure in the history of Japanese Buddhism. He was a man of great intensity whose mind would not permit sidetracks. He appeared frequently at the Japanese military capital of Kamakura to admonish government officials with his "memorials," flaming speeches or pantomimes on behalf of the common folk. The first of these occured in 1261 when Nichiren prophesied a foreign invasion. He was banished to the Izu peninsula for two years.

A summary of Nichiren's teachings is as follows:
1. Through knowledge of the Lotus Sutra, all persons can attain Buddhahood;
2. Buddha is eternal, without beginning or end;
3. The salvation of the original Buddha, Gautama, guarantees the possible salvation of all;
4. Gautama made a secret prophecy that, after his death, all his teaching except the Lotus Sutra will lose their power;
5. All bodhisattvas, or embodiments of the Buddha ideal, are committed to proclaim the wonderful Lotus Sutra;
6. Nichiren will receive harsh persecution but eternal comfort and protection shall be given to all who keep the sacred chant, Nam Myoho Rengekyo, "Hail to the Glorious Lotus Sutra."

The most powerful figure in the modern Sokagakkai was Josei Toda (1900-1959). It was Toda who gave the society a serious drive to win converts. He authored a book entitled *The Manual of Forced Conversion* and by 1958 announced that his goal of three-quarters of a million households in Japan following Nichiren had been reached.

In 1965, Sokagakkai began to make serious inroads in the US, with the establishment of headquarters in San Francisco and the start of a newspaper entitled the *World Tribune.* Because the Nichiren Shoshu Association is growing so rapidly in the US in the 1980s, an official stance is articulated toward the dominant religion here, Christianity. The official statement is, "In America we are not taking an anti-Christian stance, but a non-Christian one."

The current world leader of Sokagakkai, a Mr. Ikeda, set out a more militant stance in his inaugural address in 1960:

> Sokagakkai is the greatest ally of the people. The enemy of man is false religion and will cast him into hell; the upright Dharma makes of them Buddha. Such is the golden saying of the great holy one, Nichiren. Taking up his banner, let us his followers pursue after the extermination of all false religion.[8]

This militant stance can be traced back to the thirteenth century prophet Nichiren, who said: "The whole world in in rebellion against the right. Men have universally become the slaves of evil. Evil spirits and demons have come to take their places, and calamaties and sorrows have befallen us."

In modern practice, Shinto practitioners are ridiculed by such statements as, "Praying at a Shinto shrine is like praying to a fishmonger." It is Christianity that is singled out as the basic non-Buddhist religion for vicious attack. For example, the Christian idea of a personal creator is considered to be nonscientific. Christianity is also presented as a religious system without the power to change anyone's present condition. The Christian beliefs about the incarnation and resurrection of Jesus are said to be beyond rational thought. It is further contended that not one of Christ's prophecies was ever fulfilled.

Sokagakkai is a strange wedding of Western militarism and Oriental mysticism. It is a clever amalgamentation of politics and religion. As such, it is representative of the vital "New Religions" in Japan since 1946. It presents a challenge to those in Japan, the USA, and Europe to know to mix compassion with confrontation to present the exalted Christ. One challenge is to an apologetic which can demonstrate that Christ's dreams have been fulfilled, partly through the expanse of Christian missions.

Roman Catholic Renewal

A few months prior to the release of the movie, *Shoes of the Fisherman,* the following story was released from Rome:

> From the "Bells of St Mary's" to "The Cardinal," the Catholic Church has always fascinated movie-makers, and the Church has frequently cooperated. But the people making the "Shoes of the Fisherman" are learning that there have been some changes made; the Church no longer sits still for the camera.
>
> But since production started on the "Shoes of the Fisherman," the film has been hit with one delay after another—while it catches up with the latest change announced by the Vatican or nervously awaits the next change.
>
> "So much has happened in the Catholic Church since the book was published five years ago," said producer George Englund, "that a good portion of the futuristic vision the author originally created reads like yesterday's news."
>
> The film . . . deals with such subjects as papal infallibility, divorce, celibacy and birth control.[9]

The 1960s brought sweeping and radical changes in the Church which so strongly influences the lives of the more than eight hundred million Roman Catholics in the world and the fifty-three million in the US.

The Second Vatican Council met from October, 1962 to December, 1965. It was called by Pope John XXIII, a man who is regarded and remembered as one of the best-liked religious leaders of the twentieth century.

John XXIII

The man who became the twentieth century's most beloved and effective pope was born in a little town called "Under the Mountain." The year was 1881 and the parents were the Roncallis. The family was poor but joyous in their

Christian faith. Looking back, the pope was to say that his childhood was spent in "blessed poverty."

Angelo went three years in the little primary school in his hometown. Then he went to Celano for secondary school. There he made poor grades. Despite that, he was accepted into the seminary at Bergamo at age eleven. In 1895, he received his first tonsure and in 1900 he was graduated with honors. In 1901, he went to Rome for further study. He was such a scholar by that time that he was made an assistant lecturer in canon law. (Roncalli was serving in that capacity when World War I started.) He volunteered for duty as a chaplain with the 73rd Infantry Regiment of Belarmo in 1903. In 1904, Angelo become the secretary the bishop of Belarmo. In 1906, he taught church history at the seminary at Belarmo.

In 1914, the bishop died. In 1915, Angelo served again as a military chaplain. He was discharged from the army late in 1918. He served as a chaplain and professor at the Belarmo seminary for the next three years. In 1921, Angelo Roncalli went to Rome to serve as an assistant to the director of the Society for the Propagation of the Faith (SPF). In 1921, he was named director of the Italian branch of the SPF.

Pope Pius XI declared 1925 to be a holy year. As Roncalli called it at the time, it was a "Holy year, missionary year." That same year Roncalli was named Archbishop of Areopolis and moved to Sophia, Bulgaria. It was in Orthodox territory. Roncalli developed an ecumenical spirit which was to manifest itself in his rule as pontiff.

Vatican Council II

Vatican Council II, called by Pope John XXIII, evolved into an experience of openness and change which affected Roman Catholics around the world in at least seven ways, all of which enhanced the cause of missions.

1. The clergy is changing. Nuns are experiencing a new sense of freedom and versatility in their vocation.

Many priests, also, are in a state of reflection on their role in the modern world and Church. A Gallup Poll in 1978 indicated that more than 40 percent of all US Catholics feel that priests should be free to marry. More importantly, more than half the Catholic seminary students felt that they should be free to marry.

2. The laity in the Catholic Church are becoming more aware of themselves as a valuable person in the mind and purpose of God and the Church. The document on the laity from Vatican II emphasizes the responsibility and freedom of the Catholic layperson. It reads in part:

Bishops, pastors of parishes, and other priests of both branches of the clergy should keep in mind that the right and duty to exercise the apostolate in common to all the faithful, both clergy and laity, and that the laity also have their own proper roles in building up the Church. . . . Through continuing dialogue with the laity, these priests should carefully search for the forms which make apostolic activity more fruitful.

After Vatican II, the Catholic laity realized for the first time that they were full members of the Church and called to an active role in performing its mission.

3. The matter of birth control has been called the "Pope's Vietnam" of this century. Many Catholic observors maintain that July 29, 1968, may prove to be a turning point in their history. On that date, Pope Paul VI released the papal encyclical entitled *Humanae Vitae* ("of Human Life") which condemned all methods of artificial contraception as opposed to God's law. This ran against popular emphasis on lay freedom in the Church. It is as yet an unresolved matter in practice, despite the encyclical.

4. Documents calling for Christian unity came from Vatican II. A portion of one reads:

Let all Christ's faithful remember that the more purely

they strive to live according to the gospel, the more they are fostering and even practicing Christian unity. For they can achieve depth and ease in strengthening mutual brotherhood to the degree that they enjoy profound communion with the Father, the Word and the Spirit. . . . Before the whole world, let all Christians profess their faith in God, one and three, in the incarnate Son of God, our Redeemer and Lord. United in their efforts, and with mutual respect, let them bear witness to our common hope, which does not play us false. . . . Cooperation among Christians vividly expresses that bond which already unites them, and it sets in clearer relief the features of Christ the Servant.

After Vatican II, non-Catholics are referred to as "separated brethren" rather than the formerly used harsh term, *heretics.*

5. Catholic youth are caught in the revolution going on inside their Church. The only Church they have known is characterized by chaos, change, collapse and openness. They are trapped between what-once-was and what-will-be, with no memory of the Church before Vatican II. For example, the past president of the teenage section of the Catholic Youth Organization summed up the feelings of most of his peers when he said:

Today's young people desire to participate in the Church. In the past, most people thought that if youngsters were altar boys, they were participating. But this was not enough. We want the Church to know that when we are mature enough to make responsible decisions, we should be allowed to do so.

Catholic youth are now more assertive in their faith, both inside and outside the Church. This constitutes a vast reservoir of talent for Christian missions.

6. New worship forms have shocked more traditionalists in the Church in the past score of years. A Catholic layman reflected on the changes.

Take the liturgical renewal in the wars, for example. For a long time, attendance at mass was mechanical for some people. Now the liturgy has been changed, and it fits the circumstances of the contemporary Church society. The folk mass is an asset. This certainly helps young people identify with the Church. The songs we sing in folk masses have so much significance if we sing them our way instead of in the way of the fifteenth century.

The new worship forms include a sermon in the place of the homily. The service is in the vernacular, or language of the people, instead of in Latin. The Bible is given a central place in worship. The priests now face the congregation during "the elevation of the host," the highest moment in the Mass.

7. Beliefs are changing somewhat among Catholics as a result of Vatican II. On June 30, 1968, Pope Paul VI issued a statement commonly referred to as the "Credo" or "I Believe." It reads, in part:

Above all, we place our unshakeable confidence in the Holy Spirit, the soul of the church, and in theological faith. . . . We believe in the one only God, Father, Son and Holy Spirit. . . . We believe in our Lord Jesus Christ, who is the Son of God. . . . He was incarnate of the Virgin Mary by the power of the Holy Spirit, and was made man. He died for us on the cross, saving us by His redeeming blood. He was buried, and by His own power, rose the third day . . . He ascended to Heaven, and He will come again, this time in glory, to judge the living and the dead.

Protestants were stricken by the similarities and commonalities for all Christians in the statement. It is reflective of an openness among Catholics for those called "separated brethren."

Vatican Council II shook the world of Catholicism a score of years ago. It remains the high moment in this century for the Church. The council's decrees have aided Catholic mission efforts by encouraging an openness toward dialogue with and evangelization among the non-

Christian world religions. Christians missions through the eight hundred million people called Roman Catholic will never be the same.

The Catholic world was shaken again early in 1983 when Pope John Paul II promulgated a revised code of canon law that now affects the life of every Roman Catholic worldwide from birth to death and beyond. The document was the first overall revision of Catholicism's legal code since 1917. It reduced the holy days of obligation, when Catholics are required to attend mass, from ten to only two: Christmas and a Marian holiday to be decided by each national conference of bishops. This change proved to be so radical that the pope reinstated the ten holy days but more discretion was given to national bishops to determine those ten.

The 1983 code also reduced from thirty-seven to only six the grounds for automatic excommunication, the church's most serious penalty. The six are now:
1. Involvement with an abortion;
2. Desecration of the Eucharist;
3. Physical violence against the pope;
4. Abuse by a priest of the power of absolution;
5. Consecration of a bishop without papal mandate; and
6. Violation by a priest of the secrecy of the confessional.

This streamlining of the rules of the Church should facilitate Catholic mission effort because the Church's rules will be easier to interpret and enforce.

Evangelical Efforts

Wycliffe Bible Translators

The Wycliffe Bible Translators (WBT) entered Mexico in 1935 as their first field of service. Since then the WBT have started work in more than a hundred languages and published the Scriptures in more than eighty dialects. There are new Christians in more than eighty tribes worldwide through the work of the WBT. Today the WBT have some 350 translators, including a score of short-term assistants in Mexico alone. Mexico is also the site of the WBT's Jungle Training Camp at which all their Latin American recruits receive their basic training. WBT is the fastest growing evangelical mission in the world. In half a century, it has grown from zero to more than twenty-five hundred missionaries in more than twenty nations of the world. The goal of the WBT is to give every tribe in the world a translation of the New Testament by AD 2000. There are almost two thousand tongues to go, but the WBT are determined in Christ's name.

The Elliots were the most famous of those serving with the WBT since its inception. Their story was told through the popular book *Through Gates of Splendor*. In 1956, the world was shocked to hear of the killing of five missionaries by the Auca Indians. The tragedy did not stop the relatives of those brutally slain from reentering the area. Rachel Saint and Betty Elliot, sister and wife of two of the five martyrs, moved in and worked among the Aucas. Rachel Saint worked hard on a Bible translation. She presented the Gospel of Mark in the Auca language to the people in 1965. More than three dozen Aucas have now been baptized including the five men responsible for the murders. Two of the Aucas attended the Berlin Congress on Evangelism in 1966. The courage shown by Betty Elliot and Rachel Saint continues to be a source of inspiration to missionaries everywhere.

American Bible Society

The American Bible Society (ABS) continues the tradition of the movements inaugurated a century and a half ago. With headquarters in New York City, this society was founded in 1816 with one purpose, "To promote the distribution of Holy Scriptures without doctrinal note or comment and without profit." The society is a member of the United Bible Societies, a partnership of Bible societies throughout the world cooperating to make Scriptures available to people everywhere in their own languages at prices they can easily afford. The ABS awards annually their Gutenberg Award, established in 1952, on a person who has made a distinctive contribution in Bible distribution. Recipients have included Billy Graham and Fulton J. Sheen. The 1982 award went to Norman Vincent Peale.

The projects of the ABS are varied. For example, in 1982 the ABS provided a thousand New Testaments for use by the Salvation Army in Indiana. Another was fifteen hundred Scripture portions donated for use in Sunday School at the Scottish Rite Hospital of Atlanta, a fifty-bed institution for treatment of children.

United Bible Societies

The United Bible Societies is doing a similar work. For example, in 1982 three thousand Bibles were sent to Paraguay for sharing with people in prisons, hospitals, and nursing homes. In Thailand, twenty thousand Scripture portions were distributed on National Children's Day in Bangkok. Five thousand New Testaments were distributed to prisoners in Brazil.

Missionary Aviation Fellowship

The Missionary Aviation Fellowship (MAF) is a group dedicated to the transportation of evangelical missionaries and their needed supplies from one spot to another in their chosen fields. The first operation of MAF was in Mexico in 1946, beginning with one pilot and one small airplane. In 1984, it had six planes serving eight evangelical groups in Mexico alone. It has more than seventy planes serving almost a hundred missions and churches in more than a score of nations worldwide. The new home bases are in Australia and Great Britain. MAF, for example, helped Southern Baptist missionaries leave Ethiopia.

Christian and Missionary Alliance

The Christian and Missionary Alliance (CMA) is an American-based denomination with missionary enterprise as a high priority. It has one missionary overseas for every eighty church members at home, a ratio without peer or precedent in the modern Christian movement. The CMA now sponsors more than a thousand missionaries serving in thirty nations and using more than two hundred languages and dialects. The CMA can now point to more than five thousand self-supporting overseas churches and six thousand students in thirty-five Bible schools and seminaries.

The Salvation Army

The Salvation Army commanded more than eighty mission stations a century ago manned by 130 fulltime evangelists with another one thousand speakers holding seventy-five thousand services a year.

The USA was entered in 1880, Canada in 1882, and India in 1883. By 1900, the Salvation Army had expanded into impressive social action, including cheap food depositories, employment exchanges, a missing persons bureau, night shelters, a farm colony, soup kitchens, leper colonies, hospitals, and schools.

In 1984, the Army is at work in seventy-five nations with two million members worldwide. There are almost twenty-four thousand officers. In 1983, the Salvation Army served twenty-five million low-cost meals provided eleven million hostel beds, eight thousand missing persons traced, and twenty thousand unwed mothers care for. The Army is running more than forty hospitals with more than 150 thousand patients annually.

African Inland Mission

The African Inland Mission (AIM) was started by Peter Cameron Scott in 1895. The first field entered by the AIM was Kenya that same year. The group now has more than six hundred missionaries in half a dozen African nations. One of the outstanding mission fields for AIM remains Kenya, where the African Inland Church was formed in 1970 with a membership today of almost two hundred thousand. AIM maintains both an ecumenical and evangelical base to its cooperative effort between missionaries and African nationals.

Youth for Christ

Youth for Christ, International (YFC) was started in the US in 1945 to engage in teenage evangelism, high school Bible clubs, and prevention of juvenille delinquency. The first president was Torrey Johnson. The motto from the beginning has been, "Geared to the times and anchored to the Rock." "Teen Teams" are sent overseas to do evangelism. Organizations sponsored by Youth for Christ both home and abroad include Youth Guidance, *Campus Life* magazine, and high school Campus Life chapters. The national headquarters of YFC is in Wheaton, Illinois, but world conferences on evangelism have been held elsewhere frequently since the first one in Switzerland in 1948.

Navigators

The Navigators started informally in 1933 when the founder, Dawson Trotman, discipled a born-again sailor with 2 Timothy 2:2 as his guiding principle. It was officially organized a decade later. Work was started in Europe in 1950. The specialty of the group is systematic Bible memorization and study. The headquarters are in Colorado Springs.

InterVarsity Fellowship

The InterVarsity Fellowship (IVF) was started in 1927 to further the cooperation between Evangelicals in the centers of higher education in Great Britain. In 1919, the first annual intervarsity conference was organized to promote missionary activity in the colleges.

The aim of IVF is to: "Present the claims of the Lord Jesus Christ to the members of the university; to unite those who desire to serve him; and to promote the work of home and foreign missions."

From the beginning, the IVF has held international missionary conferences and promoted work overseas through such groupings as the Christian Medical Fellowship and in the production of quality Christian literature.

New Tribes Mission

The New Tribes Mission (NTM) is a group in half a dozen nations in South America. The last of these entered was Brazil in 1949. Today Brazil has more than 160 missionaries, making it the largest of all the fields in which the NTM works. By definition, the work is confined to primitive Indian tribes. The NTM specializes in evangelism, church growth, Bible translation, and primary education.

Home Mission Board, Southern Baptist Convention

The Home Mission Board, Southern Baptist Convention (HMB, SBC) was started in 1845 and has been growing ever since. Report on work done in 1983 showed more than 850 career missionaries, more than 650 associate missionaries, more than 50 US-2ers (young adult, two-year missionaries), more than 700 pastors receiving Church Pastoral Aid, more than 150 receiving Pastoral Assistance for language churches and more than 80 on the state staff level.

More than a hundred home missionaries serve in these states: Arizona, California, Florida, Louisiana, New Mexico, New York, Ohio and Texas.

The 1983 expenditures for the HMB, SBC showed more than fifty million dollars spent. This was administered by more than a hundred professional staff persons under the leadership of Dr. William G. Tanner.

Work in 1983 included:

1. Two dozen "Growing an Evangelistic Church" Seminars;
2. Involving more than seventy thousand persons in personal evangelism;
3. Starting more than twelve hundred church-type missions with more than five hundred new churches constituted;
4. Appointing more than sixty bivocational pastors;
5. Endorsing more than three hundred chaplaincy candidates;
6. Conducting dialogues with Jews, Catholics, Lutherans and Episcopalians;
7. Starting more than three hundred new units of ethnic work;
8. Helping more than thirty hundred adults serve as mission volunteers; and
9. Processing more than seven hundred applicants for home mission service and appointing more than six hundred persons.

Foreign Mission Board, Southern Baptist Convention

The annual report of the Foreign Mission Board, Southern Baptist Convention (FMB, SBC) for 1983 showed the following figures:

1. Work in 100 nations
2. 2700 career missionaries
3. 210 missionary Journeyman
4. 240 missionary associates
5. 11,500 SBC-related churches
6. 14,500 missions
7. 145,000 baptisms
8. 9,700 national pastors
9. 21 hospitals
10. 114 clinics
11. 24 publication centers
12. 6 million pieces literature distributed

13. 1,000 TV broadcasts
14. 370,000 enrolled in correspondence courses
15. 87 theological seminaries and institutes
16. 22 children's homes
17. 26 agricultural missionaries
18. 4700 served in short-term projects overseas

These sparkling figures show that Southern Baptists are still very much in the missions business with a bright future ahead.

Sectarian Missionary Efforts

(Note: the term *sectarian* is used here to describe religious groups which are smaller than major denominations and which have doctrines which deviate radically from those of mainline Christian groups.)

Jehovah's Witnesses

Nathan Knorr took over the movement called Jehovah's Witnesses in 1942, following Charles T. Russell and Joseph F. Rutherford. Until his death in 1977, Knorr gave brilliant leadership to the missionary growth of the group. He was succeeded in 1977 by Frederick Franz, who has retained that emphasis.

This is very obvious by looking at the fact that the Jehovah's Witnesses is the only American-born movement that can say it has a 1:3 ratio to foreign membership. There is only one Witness in the US for every three elsewhere in the world. The figures in 1983 were .56 million in the US and 2.4 million in the world.

Around the world the Jehovah's Witnesses are very active in door-to-door witnessing and literature distribution. The phenomenal number of people reached worldwide annually is due to their effective organization for witnessing. Each member of the group is considered a minister of the gospel and is given impetus, resources, and encouragement for this endeavor by three corporations: the Watch Tower Bible and Tract Society of Pennsylvania, which is the worldwide supervisory agency for the Witnesses; the International Bible Students' Association, which is the foreign missionary agency; and the Watch Tower Bible and Tract Society of New York, publisher of most of the Witness literature for the US.

The mission outreach of the Witnesses is aided greatly by the voluminous amount of literature produced by the group. Almost two million copies of *Awake!* magazine are distributed twice a month. *Awake!* is second in circulation among the world's religious journals only because the Witnesses also publish *The Watch Tower,* with a circulation of almost 2.5 million copies every two weeks. These two journals are published in almost forty languages.

The Jehovah's Witnesses also have over one million active members who are known as "publishers" (of the good news of the coming kingdom). This is in addition to full-time "pioneers" spread worldwide. Of these "publishers," about 30 percent are found in the US, 8 percent in West Germany, and 5 percent in England.

The faithful lay witnesses and vast literature distribution will cause future growth for the movement in spite of its deviant theology.

Mormons

The Church of Jesus Christ of Latter-Day Saints (LDS), also known as the Mormons, have a remarkable record in worldwide missions.

There is a Mormon Sunday School song which goes: "I hope they call me on a mission when I have grown a foot or two. I hope by then I will be ready to teach and preach and work as missionaries do."[10]

From the time Mormon children, especially boys, are four or five years old, they are conditioned to anticipate two years of missionary service during their late teen years. This leads to the fact that Mormons field more missionaries than any other church in the US, about thirty-five thousand. These young men are called upon to labor sixteen hours a day six days a week for two years.

The young Mormon men who "go on mission" have a severe regimen: no movies, no dates, no phone calls to parents or girl friends, and no going anywhere alone. Thirty percent of eligible Mormon males in North America actually volunteer for mission. This costs their parents an average of three hundred dollars per month. Almost all LDS missionaries are male because baptizing converts is a privilege reserved for the church's male-only clergy. Female volunteers are called "ladies" and are welcomed as missionaries but are not allowed to serve until they reach age twenty-one. Most young men go out at age nineteen. It is the official stance of the Mormons that the first duty of a woman is to be a wife and mother.

Mormon doctrine teaches that human beings are born for eternal self-improvement. A common belief is, "As God is, man may become." The training center for future missionaries, located near Brigham Young University, is built on the self-improvement philosophy. Self-confidence is a central talent which the young missionaries are expected to develop during their one-month training period.

The training method is by rote. All students memorize the standard set of eight "discussions"; that is, questions and answers about the Mormon Church which must be presented to outsiders verbatim.

Every LDS missionary must file a weekly report accounting for each hour of each day. This is in spite of the fact that the conversion rate per household visit is very low. Only about nine doors out of a thousand open to missionaries. Yet, the LDS church in 1983 won almost a quarter million converts worldwide. This was a result of almost two hundred million missionary hours.

In a strange belief, Mormons contend that missionary work will go even beyond this earthly existence. It is maintained that, in eternity, companions from the celestial kingdom will call on non-Mormons in the lower realms of heaven, offering them just one more chance to accept prophet Joseph Smith, Jr.

The mission work of Mormonism was made easier in the early 1980s with the completion of new temples in Atlanta and Dallas and four others under construction worldwide.

The Reverend Moon

Few religious groups have caused such a furor in the past twenty years as the followers of the Reverend Sun Myung Moon. His followers may appear as representing any one of more than two dozen separate foundations, including the D.C. Strider's Club and the Holy Spirit Association for the Unification of World Christianity (the official name of the movement).

The "Moonies" were first seen and heard in the US in the late 1960s when the Reverend Moon began to gather disciples by the thousands.

The financial empire built by the Reverend Moon is phenomenal. The Unification Church now takes in more than sixty million dollars a year from fund-raising and contributions. As of the fall of 1983, the Unification Church was operating more than one hundred fifty communal recruiting and fund-raising centers in cities across the nation, with recruiting teams covering almost two hundred college campuses.

Being a "Moonie" is not easy. Members are not allowed to smoke, drink alcoholic beverages, or engage in premarital or extramarital sex. Even marriage between believers is a difficult proposition since new converts are expected to be in the movement for three years and achieve a high state of spiritual perfection before they are allowed to wed. This is partly because of the promise the Reverend Moon makes to his followers that they can potentially bear perfect children.

It is noteworthy here that the Faith and Order Commission of the National Council of Churches, USA, denied entrance to that body for the Unification Church in 1978.

The denial was done on theological grounds. Reverend Moon's teachings that Jesus was a failure and that God is part evil were two examples of what the commission deemed to be heresy.

On any given day in the US, there are more than eight thousand "Moonies" out in the public trying to sell trinkets or flowers for a dollar each. Each of the young missionaries is given a daily quota. The result is a weekly income in the US alone of more than a million dollars. A similar amount is added weekly worldwide. The "Moonie" missionaries are especially effective in Western Europe, Japan, Korea, and the US.

Seventh-Day Adventists

Seventh-Day Adventists (SDA) launched the most ambitious mission program in the history of the movement on September 18, 1982. It is entitled "One Thousand Days of Reaping" and will extend through 1985. It is designed to bring an average of a thousand persons a day into the movement for a thousand days. The year 1982 also saw the Adventists enter Mali, making a total of 185 nations in which they are now operating. World membership at the end of 1983 stood at 3.9 million. It is apparent that the Seventh-Day Adventists have a bright future in Christian mission endeavor, especially in medical missions.

Seventh-Day Adventists have been mission-minded from the beginning. The group was officially organized in 1863, and eleven years later their first foreign missionary, J. N. Andrews, was sent out.

SDA missions have been helped by the "missionary movement" for all ages in sabbath school and by being one of the highest in American churches in per capita giving.

SDAs stress a total mission program. They operate schools from kindergarten through the university level. They conduct an extensive medical program with hospitals and clinics centered in Loma Linda University in California, from which more than fifteen thousand medical missionaries have been sent abroad.

Billy Graham Evangelistic Association

The Billy Graham Evangelistic Association has had a worldwide evangelistic impact. It has headquarters in Minneapolis and is built around the ministry of Billy Graham (1918-   ), the first evangelist of the newly formed Youth for Christ, International, in 1943. Graham acquired national fame through his Los Angeles Crusade in 1948 and international exposure through his London Crusade of 1954.

The crusades sponsored by the association have always been in cooperation with local churches. The emphasis is always on personal decision for Christ.

The weekly "Hour of Decision" radio broadcast was started in 1950. Graham has a weekly syndicated newspaper column entitled, "My Answer." The monthly magazine, *Decision,* has been published since 1960.

In 1966, Graham inspired the World Congress on Evangelism and a similar one in Mexico City in 1980. Billy Graham is the most recognizable twentieth-century evangelical worldwide and has aided the mission effort immeasurably.

Oral Roberts

The evangelist Oral Roberts was healed as a child. His career in the 1940s and 1950s was composed of "faith healing" in tent meetings. In 1967, at a meeting of the World Council of Churches, Roberts decided to become a part of the Methodist Church.

Oral Roberts University in Tulsa, Oklahoma, is now a well-respected institution awarding degrees in medicine, theology, business, nursing, and other fields. The "City of Faith" medical center was completed in 1983 and treats hundreds of patients daily in addition to a center of medical research.

The Reverend Oral Roberts reaches millions in the US through his television program. But, just as important for missions, Mr. Roberts sends mission groups from ORU annually. Each year dozens of his students graduate and begin careers in mission service. His contributions to missions are major.

National Association of Evangelicals

The National Association of Evangelicals (NAE) is but one example of evangelical alliances. It was organized in 1942 with a conservative creedal statement. The first national convention was held in 1943.

The NAE supports the Evangelical Foreign Missions Association with more than 7 thousand missionaries in 125 fields. It was formed in Chicago in 1945, "to provide a medium for voluntary united action among the evangelical foreign mission agencies." It cosponsored the Wheaton Congress of 1966 and the Summer Missions Institute at Wheaton. The group publishes the *Evangelical Missions* quarterly and sponsors the committee to assist missionary education overseas.

World Evangelical Fellowship

The World Evangelical Fellowship was formed in the Netherlands in 1951 to provide a base of cooperation for evangelical missions worldwide. The group is administered from London and has three programs:
1. Theological education assistance;
2. International relief assistance; and
3. Evangelistic and Bible study ministries.

The World Congress on Evangelism was held in West Berlin in 1966, as a paraecumenical effort to consider Christ's Great Commission to evangelize the whole earth. Delegates from more than one hundred nations came and were identified with seventy-six different church groups. The Berlin Congress achieved a significant correlation of theological and evangelistic concerns. Targets of evangelism were singled out, including; cities, college students, the media, computers, lay involvement, and social ministries. The Berlin Congress was a significant meeting in that Evangelicals could see their vast potential for missions if cooperation were increased.

World Council of Churches

The World Council of Churches (WCC) was formed in 1948 and is the main international agency for agreement among churches.

The basis of WCC membership is, "The World Council of Churches is a fellowship of churches which confess the Lord Jesus Christ as God and Saviour according to the Scriptures and therefore seek to fulfil together their common calling to the glory of the one God, Father, Son and Holy Spirit." The council is of assistance in the doing of missions because it coordinates the work of more than two hundred member bodies.

The World Council of Churches became involved in controversy early in 1983 when a *Reader's Digest* article appeared. The journalistic piece was written by sociologist Rael Jean Issac. He charged that the World Council supports "revolution instead of religion" by favoring Marxist-backed liberation groups in Third-World nations over moderate democracies.

The CBS news program, "60 Minutes" aired a segment on January 23, 1983, charging that the World Council of Churches supports leftist groups and has helped to finance violent revolutions. It was also reported that the Southeastern Jurisdiction of the United Methodist Church (in the US) had voted to set up a blue-ribbon panel of bishops to look into the activities of the World Council of Churches.

Most of the pressure came from the Institute for Religion and Democracy, formed late in 1982 to counteract leftist leanings in mainstream Protestant churches.

Leaders of the World Council responded that less than

10 percent of the council's expenditures were going to leftist-governed nations and that the charges were grossly out of proportion. The controversy is still raging in 1984, slightly impeding the work of the council.

The Missions Advanced Research and Communication Center

The International Congress on World Evangelization was held in Lausanne, Switzerland, in 1974. At that time a Strategy Working Group was set up. This committee asked the Missions Advanced Research and Communications Center, or MARC, to prepare a picture of the current status of world missions. The first report of MARC made it clear that the world is filled with unreached peoples. These have been placed in such major categories as Muslims, refugees, and the poor.

MARC is now producing an annual book reporting on one specific aspect of reaching unreached peoples. The book series began in 1979. *The Refugees Among Us* was the title for the book in the series for 1983. The book for 1984 features a status report on the involvement of mission agencies to reach the unreached peoples.

Evangelical mission effort in 1984 is in full swing. The various agencies are operating at full speed with increased cooperative effort, especially in the area of reading previously hidden people groups. This increasing cooperation is alongside and often in spite of similar efforts by sectarian groups. The future of evangelical efforts is partially dependent on finding ways of cooperation and coexistence with the active mission work of Roman Catholics and ecumenical Protestants. In spite of somewhat fragmented effort, Christian mission work is bearing much numerical fruit in the present.

In 1984, there are almost a quarter million Christian missionaries at work in the world. Protestant Christians in underdeveloped nations are sending out 15,000 missionaries of their own, including more than a thousand to Europe and North America. This is in spite of the fact the Protestant denominations which are members of the National Council of Churches, USA, now support fewer than three thousand career missionaries overseas, compared with almost ten thousand three decades ago. By contrast, American Evangelicals have tripled since 1954 the number of career missionaries sent out from the US. That number is now more than thirty thousand.

This vast number of missionaries from every theological perspective are being effective numerically, as is made clear in the next section.

Comparative Numbers

Christianity is doing well in 1984 in comparison to other world religions as the following chart indicates:

Christianity	1.4 Billion
Roman Catholic	800 Million
Eastern Orthodox	80 Million
Protestants	500 Million
Judaism	15 Million
Islam	800 Million
Zorostrianism	280 Thousand
Shinto	58 Million
Taoism	32 Million
Confucianism	160 Million
Buddhism	300 Million
Hinduism	500 Million

If Communism is included as a religion, the total would be 1.6 billion currently under Communist domination, although not all those are Communist.

Christianity is gaining percentage-wise in relation to population growth, however, in very few places. The challenge is to spread the gospel in a favorable relation to population growth. To do so will take all the resources of the churches in the latter sixth of this century.

Africa

Senegambia

The two nations of Senegal and Gambia combined their political, economic, and religious resources in 1981 to form the new country of Senegambia.

The Assemblies of God (AG) came to Senegal in 1956. By 1960, there were three stations operating. Dakar was the site of the *Temple Evangelique,* opening in 1963. A Bible institute was opened the following year in the same city. More than a dozen AG missionaries are currently under appointment in Senegambia.

The Conservative Baptists sent their first missionaries to Senegal in 1961 by starting work in Thies. Today the CBFMS force in Senegambia is small.

The Southern Baptists entered this area in 1970 by sending one couple to work in Dakar. There are now three couples there, operating a Baptist center and book store. Due to the strong Muslim influence, there are only a few converts.

Anglicans have done work in this area through the United Society for the Propagation of the Gospel. The first native Gambian bishop for the Anglicans was consecrated in 1965. The Anglicans still operate two schools, but the enrollment is 95 percent Muslim and the rate of conversion from Islam is almost nil.

Liberia

The Southern Baptists came to Liberia in 1961, with the main center being in Monrovia. By 1984, there were more than three hundred churches with almost thirty thousand members.

Chris and Gwen Wilkinson serve with valor for Southern Baptists in Liberia. In 1980, they were responsible for the baptism of twenty members of a tribe in which none had been a Christian before. Margaret Fairburn serves in church extension in northern Liberia and is already responsible for the starting and sustaining of several churches.

There are only three specifically Christian radio stations on the whole continent of Africa. One of these is located in Monrovia. It is the voice of the Sudan Interior Mission (SIM). It is now broadcasting with one thousand watts and can reach much of west Africa. It is known as Station ELWA, and its staff is composed of more than fifty missionaries from eight nations. It now has television programs as well. ELWA broadcasts the gospel in more than forty languages to west Africa and much of the Middle East. More than eleven thousand students have been enrolled in its Bible correspondence courses. The SIM personnel also operate a hospital.

Ivory Coast

The Free Will Baptist (FWB) Mission in Ivory Coast was started in 1957 by the Reverend and Mrs. Lonnie Sparks. There are now more than two dozen FWB missionaries in Ivory Coast with more than six hundred indigenous church members.

The Southern Baptists first came to Ivory Coast in 1966. There are now a dozen missionaries, mostly in Abidjan. The SBC-related churches now number more than twenty with a total membership of more than fifteen hundred.

An interesting work is being done in publication by the Sudan Interior Mission. Abidjan is now the site of the magazine *Champion* and the Intermission Evangelical Publishing Center. *Champion* is a popular news-magazine that is interspersed with articles with a strong evangelical appeal.

Liberia was shaken by a revolution in 1980. Evangelicals first went underground but the work is progressing well today. The progress made by the churches in West Africa in the past forty years has been remarkable. The Scriptures have been translated into many languages. Numerous independent churches have come into existence. An African theology and liturgical system is emerging. It is a time of excitement for Christian missions in West Africa.

Cameroon

In 1953, the Cameroon Baptist Convention was formed. There are now more than five hundred congregations with a membership of more than thirty-five thousand. The group also sponsors more than eighty foreign missionaries. Two colleges are maintained along with more than a hundred primary schools.

The Presbyterian Church of Cameroon (PCC) was organized in 1957 with three synods and ten presbyteries. American missionary doctors still operate the half dozen Presbyterian hospitals in the Cameroon. There were more than seventy thousand members of the PCC in 1984 with more than three hundred churches. The group also operates the United School of Theology at Yaounde.

Somalia

This predominantly Muslim land was entered by the Eastern Mennonite Board of Missions and Charities in 1953. The mission is focusing on education and a nonverbal witness therein. There is also a clinic and a hospital. A book store is reportedly doing much business.

The Sudan Interior Mission entered Somalia in 1954 and now runs night schools in English and typing. The translation of the New Testament into Somali was completed in 1966 and the Old Testament in 1973. There are more than thirty SIM missionaries now serving in Somalia. Part of them operate two hospitals and three clinics.

Uganda

The Salvation Army has a church membership in Uganda of almost ten thousand and operates a half-dozen dispensaries.

The Conservative Baptists came to Uganda in 1963. There are now more than thirty organized churches with two dozen preaching points. There are almost four thousand members.

The Southern Baptists entered Uganda in 1962 and now have more than thirty missionaries in a half dozen centers, including Kampala. The SBC mission operates a Bible school at Mbale. There are more than two thousand members of the more than forty churches.

Wimpy Harper[11] went as a pioneer Southern Baptist missionary to East Africa in 1956. He had a heavy administrative load as he supervised the work of Southern Baptists all over East Africa.

Harper meant almost as much to the people back home as he did to those in East Africa. He made a speech which made many examine their racial attitudes:

> The prejudices of your churches are affecting the lives of your young people who may someday be called to serve on a mission field. I have decided in light of my own youngsters' experience on the mission field that all children are color blind until we teach them otherwise. How do you think we feel when we have to tell African young people that they would not be welcomed in the churches that send the missionaries to them?

Wimpy Harper drowned in 1958 when his work was but beginning in East Africa. Indians, Pakistanis, Americans, Britons, and East Africans were at the funeral. His tombstone reads: W. O. Harper, Missionary Statesman. The work of Wimpy Harper lives on. By 1965, there were more than a hundred SBC missionaries in East Africa, more than two hundred churches, a hospital, a seminary, a publishing house, and three community centers.

Mozambique

The first missionary couple to serve the Church of the Nazarene came to Mozambique in 1954. There are now more than three dozen serving that communion there.

There are now more than nine thousand Nazarenes in Mozambique with more than 350 preaching stations.

The Pentecostal Assemblies of Canada came to Mozambique in 1950 when the Chawners entered. There are now some eleven thousand believers with four hundred assemblies.

South Africa

The table below shows the relative strength of Christian groups by church membership in South Africa in 1984:

Dutch Reformed	2,000,000
Evangelical Lutherans	500,000
Methodists	1,350,000
Full Gospel	150,000
Reformed	135,000
Presbyterian	110,000
Moravians	70,000
Pentecostal	65,000
Salvation Army	35,000
Seventh-Day Adventists	45,000

Africa since 1946 has been in a state of flux. Thirty-eight new nations on that continent have gained their independence since 1956. This has caused most missionaries to avoid political criticism. Those who have not practiced such avoidance have sometimes found themselves deported with only twenty-four hours notice. New African nations are often quite sensitive to criticism.

Modern missionaries in Africa must also work with new emerging African Christian denominations. These new denominations now number about seven thousand with a total membership of thirty million. These new African-based Christian groups are also sending out missionaries of their own to neighboring African nations or to England and the US.

In the midst of this flux, Christian missionaries to Africa from the West are working hard, with the knowledge that

Christianity may well be the dominant religion of Africa by the year AD 2000.

Latin America

Brazil

Southern Baptists are currently working in all twenty-two states of Brazil and in the four federal territories. The SBC missionaries operate more than thirty Bible schools and four regional seminaries. The SBC-maintained Carroll Memorial Publishing House in Rio produces great quantities of Scriptures and other types of Christian literature. There are more than 3 hundred missionaries assigned to more than 50 centers all over the nation. There are now more than 25 hundred churches served by almost 2 thousand pastors. The church membership is now about 350 thousand.

The New Tribes Mission entered Brazil in 1949 and today has almost two hundred missionaries. This makes Brazil the largest field in which the NTM works.

The Wycliffe Bible Translators entered Brazil in 1956. There are now almost two hundred linguists working from five centers. Bible translation is now taking place in more than forty tribes.

The Missionary Aviation Fellowship helps to cover the vast territory of Brazil. They operate five planes in five centers and provide help for more than a dozen missions operating in the jungles of Brazil.

Paraguay

The Paraguay Assemblies of God was formed in 1958, and a Bible institute opened the following year. There are more than five hundred local churches in the movement served by a dozen missionaries.

The Church of God (Cleveland) now has more than eleven hundred believers in Paraguay, being served by some forty churches and seventy missions.

The SBC opened a fifty-bed hospital in 1953 in Paraguay, the first opened by SBC missionaries in all of Latin America. The Paraguay Baptist Theological Institute was opened in 1956. That same year the Paraguay Baptist Convention (PBC) was formed. There are now, in the PBC, some twenty churches and more than sixteen hundred members.

Today there are more than sixty New Tribes Mission workers in Paraguay, working in a half-dozen tribes, including the Moros and Makas.

Bolivia

The Assemblies of God came to Bolivia in 1946. Soon there was work going in three centers: La Paz, Santa Cruz, and Cochabamba. Church membership is now well above three thousand with a dozen missionaries assisting a hundred national pastors.

The Wycliffe Bible Translators entered Bolivia in 1955. They now have almost a hundred linguists working in twenty tribes.

The George Allan Theological Seminary was begun in 1909. It is distinctive in that it has an extension department which takes theological education to national pastors in the small villages and towns.

Peru

Southern Baptists entered Peru in 1950. There are now some three dozen missionaries there and several book stores along with a seminary. The Peruvian Baptist Convention was formed in 1966 and today has a membership of more than fifteen hundred.

The Wycliffe Bible Translators came to Peru in 1946 and today has almost three hundred missionaries. The WBT agents are working in some forty tribes.

World Presbyterian Missions came to Peru in 1947. A National Presbyterian Church was formed with more than twenty congregations served by more than a dozen missionaries.

Ecuador

The National Evangelical Church of Ecuador was organized in 1952. Today there are a dozen churches with three hundred members.

The Evangelical Convenant Church of America opened its work in Ecuador in 1947, primarily to do evangelism. There are churches now in half a dozen cities, including Quito. In 1961, a nationalized Covenant Church was organized. There are a dozen missionaries there running a medical clinic and several elementary schools.

Southern Baptists entered Ecuador in 1950 with a center in Quito. A book store and primary school were soon founded. There are now more than thirty missionaries serving in ten centers. A small Bible institute has been operating in Guayaquil since 1961. There are more than thirty churches today serving more than thirteen hundred members.

The first team of Wycliffe Bible Translators arrived in Ecuador in 1953. Translators are now working in more than a half-dozen tribes, including the Aucas. There are more than eighty WBT agents now working in Ecuador.

The International Church of the Foursquare Gospel sent their first missionaries, the Gadberrys, to Guayaquil in 1956. There are now more than twenty churches and almost three thousand converts.

The largest evangelical-operated radio station in Ecuador by far is HCJB in Quito. It is owned by the World Radio Missionary Fellowship. HCJB is the oldest of all missionary radio stations in the world. It has been broadcasting since 1931. There are almost four hundred persons on the staff today. HCJB broadcasts on five hundred thousand watts. An equally important ministry comes through short-wave radio, making HCJB receivable throughout the world.

Colombia

Southern Baptists entered Colombia in 1941 and helped to organize the Colombia Baptist Convention just six years later. There are now more then seventy missionaries located in the eight major cities. There has been a Baptist hospital in Barranquilla since 1953. That same year the SBC opened an international seminary in Cali. There now are more than six thousand members of the Colombia Baptist Convention.

The Wycliffe Bible Translators now have almost two hundred missionaries in Colombia working among three dozen tribes.

Colombia was the scene of a black epoch in mission history in the decade following 1948. Protestants suffered severe persecution at the hands of Roman Catholics. Many churches were destroyed and almost a hundred others closed by force. More than two hundred elementary schools were closed. Four score Protestants were executed because of their faith. In spite of the persecution, Protestant church growth increased fourfold during that decade of persecution. By 1970, there were more than ninety thousand Protestants in Colombia.

Venezuela

The New Tribes Mission started work in Venezuela in 1946. The work has been mainly in Amazon Territory where the NTM representatives operate three schools.

The first American representatives of the Southern Baptist Convention came in 1949. The Venezuelan Baptist Convention (VBC) was started in 1951. There are now three dozen SBC missionaries in ten cities. The VBC has more than forty churches with more than two thousand members.

The Worldwide Evangelization Crusade (WEC) has been in Venezuela since 1953. There are now a dozen missionaries, mainly in the eastern part of the nation. The

WEC operates a book store, a bookmobile, and correspondence courses.

Honduras

The Eastern Mennonite Board of Missions and Charities has more than forty missionaries in Honduras. The work was started in 1950. Today there is medical and dental work along with Pine Grove Academy, a Bible institute. There are more than three hundred church members in two dozen congregations.

The Conservative Baptist Home Mission Society (CBHMS) came to Honduras in 1951. In 1960, the CBHMS started radio station HRVC in Gautemala City. There are now more than eight hundred church members with the work being supervised by a dozen missionaries.

The first resident Southern Baptist missionaries arrived in Honduras in 1954 with the Association of Honduras Baptist Churches started in 1958. There are now more than a dozen churches and twelve hundred members. There is a book store and theological institute in the capital city. There are more than a dozen missionaries in six major centers.

Costa Rica

Southern Baptists transferred the work in Costa Rica to the Foreign Mission Board in 1949. This was two years after the start of the Baptist Convention of Costa Rica. The SBC missionaries have run a seminary in San Jose since 1950. There are now two dozen churches and a dozen SBC representatives in Costa Rica.

Southern Baptists and others train at the Spanish Language Institute. There is now an annual enrollment of about 400. The institute has been in San Jose since 1950 and has helped to train more than 5 thousand new missionaries representing more than 140 mission agencies.

In 1984, Latin America received more American missionaries than any other part of the world. This includes more than nine thousand Protestants, two thousand Catholics, and one thousand sectarians. This has created tension. As recently as the 1950s, more than a hundred Protestants were killed in Colombia alone. Pope John XXIII stopped this persecution when he took office. Meanwhile, missionaries work on with good results in the Hispanic nations. This is partially due to a greater tolerance level for the other respective missionaries there.

Europe

The continent of Europe was not generally regarded as a mission field until after World War II. Even today the only large denomination with extensive missionary work in Europe is the Southern Baptist Convention with more than a hundred missionaries in a dozen nations. Sizable contingents of SBC missionaries are in Spain and Italy.

However, there are almost a hundred mission agencies with almost two thousand missionaries at work in Europe. These agencies include Youth for Christ, International, and the Navigators.

Trans World Radio was set up in Monaco in 1960. Today it broadcasts in more than thirty languages even into Russia and the Middle East. There is now a German branch with effective work in West Germany.

Asia

The Soviet Union

The Christian churches are not dead today in the Soviet Union by any means. The Russian Orthodox churches have more than forty million members. The All Union Council of Evangelical Christians-Baptists represents a membership of more than five million. There are more than one million Lutherans in the USSR and almost four million Roman Catholics.

Afghanistan

The most effective missionary in Afghanistan since World War II by far was Dr. J. Christy Wilson, often called "the apostle to the Muslims." Wilson was the son of Presbyterian missionaries to Iran. He first went to Afghanistan in 1951 to be a teacher at the invitation of the government. He was made principal of a boys' school with more than two thousand students. By 1954, Dr. Wilson was certainly the most respected foreigner in Kabul.

Wilson started a small church which at first met in his home. In 1956, Dr. Wilson became pastor of the Community Christian Church in Kabul. Two years later Wilson opened Ahlman Academy, a Christian school, strictly for the children of the international community. In the 1960s, a few Afghans enrolled in the school.

The Soviet takeover of Afghanistan in 1980 has made Christian missions there virtually nonexistent.

Thailand

Southern Baptists came to Thailand in 1949 when some of their missionaries were forced out of China. Today more than two dozen national pastors aid in the work of pastoring over fifteen hundred church members. There are today upwards of eighty SBC missionaries in Thailand operating a seminary and a hospital and helping in evangelism and church extension.

In 1952, the Overseas Missionary Fellowship (OMF) also arrived with former missionaries to China. Today it has almost three hundred missionaries in Thailand. The OMF also operates a hospital at Manorom.

American Baptists returned to Thailand in 1952. In 1965, the Karen Baptist Convention was brought into being. The name has now been changed to the Thailand Baptist Convention.

It is significant that Thai Christians held their own Congress on Evangelism in 1970. As a result, spontaneous prayer groups sprang up around the nation and a nation-wide youth conference was held a year later.

Indonesia

Southern Baptists started work in Indonesia in 1951 with the arrival in Djakarta of several former missionaries to China. By the next year, there were more than a dozen missionaries, and a Baptist church had been formed in Bandung. By 1956, a seminary was opened. A hospital was started the following year. There are now more than 120 SBC missionaries in Indonesia. There are more than eleven thousand church members with more than thirty self-supporting churches.

The Overseas Missionary Fellowship came to Indonesia in 1965, primarily to work with the Chinese. There are today more than thirty Chinese churches in Indonesia sponsored by the OMF with more than three thousand persons baptized in the past twenty years. The OMF workers today are involved in education, medical aid and student work.

The Evangelical Alliance Mission (EAM) started work in 1952 in Indonesia by sending workers to West Iran. Today the EAM workers number more than forty in more than a dozen centers doing evangelism, Bible translation and medical work.

The Regions Beyond Missionary Union (RBMU) entered Indonesia in 1957 with their first four workers. Today there are more than seventy churches with more than nine thousand baptized members. Since 1969, the local Christians have supported five of their own missionary couples. The RBMU has also started a hospital and Bible institute.

Philippines

In 1948, the United Church of Christ in the Philippines (UCCP) was formed with a union of large Methodist, Disciples, Brethren, Presbyterian, and Congregational groups.

Today there are more than fifteen hundred congregations affiliated with the UCCP with more than five hundred ordained ministers. The combined membership is more than one hundred seventy thousand, making the UCCP by far the largest Protestant group there. The UCCP has also sent its own missionaries to such places as Thailand, Okinawa, Taiwan, and Canada. Two seminaries and Silliman University are operated by the group.

Southern Baptists started work in the Philippines in 1948 when missionaries expelled from Communist China came to Manila to work with the Chinese. There are now more than a hundred SBC missionaries in the Philippines, helping to serve the more than fourteen thousand members in just over one hundred fifty churches.

The first Wycliffe Bible Translator who came to the Philippines was Richard Pittman, who arrived in 1953. Portions of Scripture has been produced by WBT workers in almost thirty Filipino dialects.

The Far East Broadcasting Station (FEBS) was organized in 1948 by ex-G.I.'s who had served in the Philippines during World War II. Station DXAS is known as the "Voice of the Orient" and is located in Manila. More than 1.5 million students have now been enrolled in the Bible correspondence courses offered by the FEBS. An average of 14 thousand letters a month come in from more than 60 nations. The FEBS also broadcasts daily into Red China and the 900 million people there. There are more than 300 persons on the FEBS staff.

Iran

In 1954, International Missions, Inc., (IMI) came into Iran from India and absorbed the Iran Interior Mission. During the 1960s, some thirty thousand persons enrolled in the IMI Bible correspondence courses.

In 1968, the George Braswells went to Teheran as envoys for the Southern Baptist Convention. They taught

English to the Muslim theological students at the University of Teheran.

The coming of the Ayatollah Khomeini to power in 1980 has made missions impossible. The power of the Ayatollah Khomeini became evident in a war with Iraq in 1982. Khomeini stated, as his troops invaded Iraq, "This is a war between Islam and blasphemy." Khomeini (b. 1900-) sees himself as guardian of the faith of Shiite Islam. He calls for and gets from his loyal followers a radical obedience, making them willing to die for him.

Israel

The war which brought independence to Israel in 1948 caused great damage to the cause of Christian missions.

The Arbishopric of the Anglican Church in the Middle East has its headquarters in Jerusalem. The area of influence now includes Iran, Eygpt, Libya, Sudan, Jordan, Lebanon, and Syria. The combined membership of the Anglican churches in the Middle East is more than 170 million.

Southern Baptists went to work in Nazareth following the 1948 war. Now there are centers in Haifa, Jerusalem, and Ashkelon. There are now than thirty missionaries representing the SBC in Israel. There are a dozen churches with a membership of more than three hundred. The churches are organized into the Associations of Baptist Churches in Israel.

Japan

The United Church of Christ in Japan, called the Kyodan by the Japanese, is by far the largest Christian denomination in that nation. Its membership is about a quarter million or almost half of the total number of Protestants in Japan. There are more than two thousand churches in the Kyodan. The group sponsors half a dozen seminaries with an enrollment of more than seven hundred. The Kyodan sponsors more than thirty missionaries in more than half a dozen nations.

Today the churches in Japan number:

Protestants	600,000
Catholics	400,000
Eastern Orthodox	30,000
	1,030,000

This number represents less than 1 percent of the total Japanese population.

Korea

Korea is the only non-Christian nation with a strong network of Christian radio stations. The largest is HLKY which started broadcasting in 1954 from Seoul.

The total Protestant community is now over three million. About two-thirds of the Protestant community is Presbyterian. There are about one million Roman Catholics in Korea.

The Christian churches of Korea are now known worldwide as riding the tide of a great spiritual revival. In some evangelical churches, a new convert is required to lead another person to Christ before he can be baptized. Presbyterians in Korea are now sending more than fifty missionaries to more than a dozen nations.

The largest church in the world today is located in Seoul, Korea, with an average Sunday School attendance of more than 120 thousand. There is a Baptist church there which averages more than 20 thousand every Sunday. The church growth methods introduced by John L. Nevius almost a century ago have worked. The evangelical churches worldwide are looking to their Christian friends in Korea for inspiration and church growth patterns.

China

When World War II ended, missionaries returned to China, optimistic over the possibility of resuming their work. In 1946, four hundred missionaries, the most ever to sail on one ship, left San Fransisco for Shanghai. A total of almost four thousand missionaries went to China that year.

But, the optimism faded quickly. The People's Republic of China was started in 1949. The next year the missionaries left in China published the "Christian Manifesto" listing the reasons that Christians ought to be allowed to remain in China. It was signed by more than fifteen hundred church leaders. It read, in part:

> Christianity was first introduced into China more than 140 years ago. During that time it had made considerable contribution to Chinese society. Unfortunately, however, shortly after the coming of Christianity, imperialism also commenced activities. . . . Christian churches, must wipe out all traces of imperialism influence in the Church.

More than 400 thousand Christians representing 8 churches signed the statement by 1952. Meanwhile, Chou En-lai declared in 1951 that the churches must expel all missionaries and severe all ties with the West. Most missionaries left that year. This removal was the greatest mass defeat ever suffered by Protestant missionaries.

The instrument used by the Communists to purge the churches of Western influence was the Three Self Movement. It was headed by Y. T. Wu, who had experience in YMCA work. Every local church and Christian group in China was forced to attend an annual mutual accusation meeting. Often shouters from the audience would say, "Drive out the running dogs. Kick them out of the church."

The churches which survived these accusation meetings were never given the religious freedom they had been promised. Finally, in 1964, the Chinese Communists made it an offense to teach religion to children under eighteen years of age. The Sunday Schools ceased to function.

But, even today, Christianity is far from dead in Communist China. Clusters of Christians are being found mainly in rural areas. Christians worldwide are gaining confidence that there are millions of believers behind the Bamboo Curtain. As contacts increase, this is becoming evident.

Part of the modern life in the churches behind the Bamboo Curtain is due to the witness by radio of the Evangelical Alliance Mission in Taiwan. There are an estimated seven million shortwave radios in China today. The message is obviously getting through.

Baker James Cauthen

A former missionary to China who became the foremost leader and spokesman for foreign missions among Southern Baptists in the twentieth century is Baker James Cauthen.

Cauthen was born in 1909 in Huntsville, Texas. The family soon moved to Lufkin. Baker James had a personal conversion experience with Christ at age seven in the First Baptist Church there.

Cauthen started pastoring his first church in 1926 and was ordained to the gospel ministry. He was enrolled at Stephen F. Austin College. He was graduated from there in 1929 with a Bachelor of Arts degree. Cauthen had majored in English and minored in both history and education. He enrolled in graduate school at Baylor University that fall. There he met Eloise Glass, the daughter of missionaries to China.

After a year at Baylor in which he received a Master of Arts degree, Baker James Cauthen enrolled at Southwestern Baptist Theological Seminary (SWBTS) at Fort Worth in the fall of 1930. He received the Master of Theology degree in 1933 and was called to pastor the Polytechnic Baptist Church in Fort Worth. He married Eloise in May of 1934.

Baker James taught part time as a graduate student at SWBTS beginning in the fall of 1934. During that time, he began to feel God's call to China. He received the Doctor of Theology degree in 1936. There was trouble in China.

The Japanese invaded in 1938. But, the Cauthens were still feeling the call to go.

The Cauthens were appointed by the FMB, SBC and assigned to the language school at Peking in 1939. He was involved in pastoring and evangelism after language school.

In 1941, relations between the US and Japan deteriorated rapidly. The Cauthens, now with small children, decided to stay in China but were forced to sail to Manila. The family stayed in Manila, and Baker James went to work in Hong Kong. Soon they were on their way back to their beloved China. They were there on December 7, 1941. But, they stayed on in Kweilin even into 1943. In 1944, they were forced to leave amid severe persecution from the Japanese.

Cauthen was named Secretary for the Orient in 1946 for the FMB, SBC. He went to China that year to assess the situation. While there, he presided over the opening of the All-China Seminary in Shanghai.

By 1948, it was evident that the Communists meant business about conquering China. He wrote a letter to the director of the FMB, in which he said, "Whatever the future holds, we are grateful for the work which has been accomplished in the past three years." By the end of 1951, Cauthen had supervised the removal of the last Southern Baptist missionary from China.

In 1954, Cauthen was made Executive Director of the FMB, SBC. At that time, there were just more than 900 foreign missionaries in 32 nations. The budget was $6.5 million. At Cauthen's retirement in 1980, the FMB had almost 3 thousand missionaries in almost 100 nations with a budget of more than $70 million. His leadership was simply spectacular. Southern Baptists are in debt to him.

Christianity About AD 1984: The Prospects

As one stands with his feet firmly planted in 1984, looking forward and backward, an appropriate statement would be that the status of missions has been better and has been worse. Days of persecution marred the church in the beginning, almost causing Christian missions to be stillborn. There are spots of persecution today in the USSR, Poland, and Iran for example.

The year 1984 does not hold the remarkable possibilities of 1792, but there are some bright spots. One of those is the rapid development of the younger churches. In 1914, it was evident that Western missionaries were slow to recognize and develop the gifts of native Christians.

The problem was not unique to Protestantism in that era. Pope Benedict XV issued a statement in 1919 in which he complained that "it is to be deplored that there are regions in which the Catholic faith has been introduced for centuries, without any indigenous clergy as yet to be found there except of a lower order."

1984 is a year in which Christian missionaries are opening up to the possibility of indigenous church leadership. It is now obvious that many insights into mission strategy are coming from the Third-World churches.

This year may be seen as the beginning of a new age. The reservoir of strength for Christians involved in missions includes the churches themselves. The church today is the only truly worldwide religious community. It is now apparent that the understanding of a missionary as a white man, with a special calling, in a distant uncivilized land, saving souls, comes down to our day but must be dropped soon. The task of the church must be thought of in terms outside the category of geography. This comes at a time when there are more Christian missionaries than at anytime in history.

The key to missions in the future will be the servant role. This includes the willingness to risk the possibility that natives may take over the work. The servant stance will allow for a brother-brother relationships with the indigenous church members, not in a father-brother relationship.

This is a time beset with alternative religions. Communism and Islam are major factors in Christian missions, closing doors and opening opportunities for creative mission effort, such as Bible smuggling and short wave radio broadcasts. The call is for an adequate apologetic to match missionary zeal.

The year 1984, as always in missions, is a time for removal of apathy and ignorance. There is no time for the luxury of a parochialism which limits the gospel's growth because of geography or race or economics or politics. The time is to face the future with the assurance that "God so loved the world . . ."

Case Study: Mr. Smith's Black Parish

In mid-1982, the Reverend Nico J. Smith, a Dutch Reformed minister, resigned his professionship to become the pastor of a black church in Mamelodi, South Africa. In 1972, Smith published *Storm-Kompas,* a booklet in which two dozen Afrikaner clergy and writers attacked racial separation on religous and moral grounds.

As Smith went to his new one-thousand member black church where members set on crude benches, he said, "I feel I am starting my life all over again. I have a great opportunity to get to know the black people, their hopes and their fears. There must be change."

Questions

1. Is it ever wrong to go with the majority feeling of a Christian group?
2. Is it legitimate to vote on ethical issues in a Christian church?
3. Is there a time for social protest in the name of Christ?
4. Did Mr. Smith do the "Christian" thing?
5. What groups of people do you know who are being separated by social pressure from others?

Time Line: AD 1946-1984

1946	Missionary Aviation Fellowship entered Mexico
1950	
1951	World Evangelical Fellowship formed
1953	Cameroon Baptist Convention formed
1954	SIM entered Somalia
1955	
1960	
1962	SBC entered Uganda
1965	Close of Vatican II
1966	World Congress on Evangelism
1970	
1975	
1977	Nathan Knorr died
1979	Islamic year 1400
1980	
1984	The future awaits

9
The Future of Missions

Futurists abound in the fields of energy, computer technology, food production, psychology, and sociology. Alarmists in 1984 speak loudly on such matters as soil erosion, extinction of species, population control, and air pollution; all with good reason.

A Mission Moratorium?

In the area of Christian missions, futurists and alarmists are getting great attention as well. Brilliant and able analysts of missions in the past are calling for a moratorium on missions. They say that mission effort is a holdover from Western colonialism and imperialism. Charges fly that all missionaries, consciously or subconsciously, are merely perpetuating a nineteenth-century model of behavior in which the helper comes to impart etiquette and information to a helpless, ignorant, primitive savage. The critics can point to plenty of evidence, citing photographs of indigenous peoples—made in 1984—all neatly lined up in their starched blue with their headmaster smiling nervously in the center of the picture.

In 1953, an Indian historian, K. M. Panikkar, in his work *Asia and Western Dominance*, argued that all Christian missionary work in Asia is merely an epiphenomenon of Western political and economic expansion. He is not alone in those charges in 1984. Leaders in Iran argue that American missionaries are part of the "Great Satan" whose primary wish is overthrow the "messiah" Ayatollah Khomeini. Chinese Communist leaders identify missionaries as agents of Western imperialism. Soviet agents keep American tourists in the USSR under constant surveliance, afraid the tourists could be smuggling Bibles or hymnals into that nation. These criticisms are to be expected, considering their political backgrounds.

But, there are Christian critics crying "triumphalism" as well as imperialism. They contend that American and European mission leaders still think in terms of an over-under relationship to the national Christian leaders and the results are tragic. Generations go by without significant additions being made to indigenous clergy and lay leadership. The critics proclaim that even missionary terminology speaks of triumphalism and militarism. Missionaries live on compounds and take furloughs. Only military personnel and missionaries speak in those terms. The century-old motto, "Christ for the World in Our Generation" smacks of triumphalism, say the critics. The call is for all missionaries to return to their home bases and leave the peoples of the world alone with their given world religious, politics, and philosophies. In that manner, say the advocates of a missionary moratorium, the peoples of such a missionized territory as Nigeria can develop in their own cultural ways whatever Christianity they may have learned in the past.

Those calling for a missionary moratorium in the last sixth of the twentieth century also contend that the Western world is not universally identified with militarism. The vast sale of war materials by the US, for example, to Israel constitutes an image in the minds of Third-World leaders as to American worship of the dollar. Missionaries going out from the US are, therefore, unwittingly a part of that monster turned loose in the world.

But, 1984 is not filled solely with the voices of crying for the cessation of mission effort. Credible scholars still make their case for the continuation of sending missionaries, no matter the expense. Such a voice is that of Elton Trueblood, who says:

We dare not limit God's power. It is undoubtedly true that Christ has been able to reach them, even when they have never heard his name. . . . It is not the missionary's task to pronounce all other religions and philosophies totally false, for they are not. . . . In humility, the Christian must accept truth wherever it is to be found. What the Christian maintains, however, is the conviction that whatever is true in all religions is genuinely consummated in Christ. . . . The case for foreign missions, as against work at home, is simply the observation that geographical limitations do not count at all. Differences of geography and differences of culture are not for failure to spread what men and women everywhere desperately need. Herein lies the cogency of the Great Commission.[12]

Advocates of continued missionary activity live under the mandate of their Lord "as they are going" to make disciples. The basic need is for God's commissioned people to work with deep appreciation for the previous experiences of those whom they encounter in mission service. This is because there can be renewed awareness that a missionary is one who works on the basis of knowing that he is loved in Christ and, therefore, would never do anything to exploit, manipulate, or control another person. When this is done, the missionary can expect to hear the highest possible praise, "He has loved us," from the people with whom he works.

When the missionary loves and is loved, he can admit past mistakes freely. He is not tied to a system but to the people. This even allows the active missionary to hear and heed the aforementioned criticisms of those who have called for a mission moratorium. With love as the key, the mere idea of militarism, triumphalism, and spreading mainly Western ideologies seems to vanish. This is especially true when the missionary, working out of a reservoir of love, is aware of the inherent dangers of an over-under or parent-to-child mind-set. This love posture can avoid the other extreme as well—cultural masochism. That is the stance that all within the sending culture is bad and all within the receiving culture is inherently good.

The modern missionary operates with the full knowledge that the image of a missionary in a current novel is that of an incredibly narrow-minded person who has not the slightest understanding of the people and culture to which he has been sent. Into that context, the modern missionary comes with the "intolerance of truth." When one serves Christ, he does so on the basis of following the Lord of the universe at whose feet the world and its peoples will one day bow. The only question is whether they do it now or later. Therefore, missions becomes the task of taking persons to Christ and allowing him to do his work with the aid of the convicting power of the Holy Spirit. This leaves little time for imperialism. The situation is changed when the missionary speaks and works for the God who is real and in love with the human family.

Certain issues emerge as the churches proceed on the basis of the task of Christian missions being a legitmate one.

Liberation Theology

The movement called Liberation Theology burst on the missiological and academic scene in 1971 with the publication of *A Theology of Liberation* by Gustavo Gutierrez. At that time, Father Gutierrez was a Roman Catholic priest serving in Latin America and exposed daily to the sights, sounds, and smells of poverty.

Liberation theology is based on the validity of orthopraxis, straight practice. This is in distinction from orthodoxy, straight thinking. It is based on the assumption that it is the responsibility of the Christian to better the world, not become absorbed in defending obsolete creeds. Liberation theologians are calling missionaries and the churches away from a theological anthropology to an anthropological theology. That is, for Guiterrez and others in his school, it is most important to begin with persons when thinking about and serving our Maker.

The key question in missions for Guiterrez is the relationship between salvation and the liberation of oppressed peoples. This latter responsibility will be assumed only when the churches divorce themselves from their identification with the established order. Then the churches can begin the struggle for the poor peoples of the world enslaved by injustice.

Guiterrez defines salvation as something that embraces all human reality, transforms it, and leads it to its fullness in Christ. Liberation theology is Christocentric because it focuses on the work of Christ and what he said he came to do—to set at liberty the captives. For further biblical support, Gutierrez points to Moses and the Exodus event, pointing out that God is seen there as the God of political and economic deliverance.

Sin, for the Liberation theologians, is not defined as escape into fleshless spiritual-sin. It is evident in oppressive structures. It is seen in the exploitation of humans by other humans. That is why the Christian life, as in Exodus, is a position, a transition from sin to grace first, from death to life second, from injustice to justice third, and from subhuman existence to human finally. Anything less is less than total biblical salvation, according to Gutierrez. In this system, to know God is to do justice.

Liberation theology is particularly applicable to missions, according to Gutierrez, because the poor of the world are no longer just the "marginated" ones, that is on the edge of Christian realization. Rather, the poor in the Third- and Fourth-World nations are becoming aware of their poverty and feeling less willing to continue in it. The poor are seeing the universal solidarity of their condition and are becoming unwilling to settle for a "spiritual" salvation which ignores their economic and political plight.

For Liberation theologians, the poor of today's world deserve to be treated as more then victimized ploys in the hands of the rich. Rather, the Christian missionary should approach the poor as if they could contribute to the doing of theology. It is possible that the poor may know more of salvation in Christ than the rich Christian missionary. The point of missions, for Gutierrez, is to liberate human beings from all that oppresses them, particularly whatever keeps them from doing the will of the Father completely.

Critics of Liberation theology abound. There are three major charges against the movement. First, it is seen as having Marxist tendencies. One of these is seen in the emphasis on the people and their inherent right to decide their own destiny. Marx's ideas are spotted in the movement also in the terminology itself. *Proletariat, bourgeois,* and *political liberation* are words used frequently by the Liberation thinkers. This rings of socialism to some observers. Second, the Liberation theologians are accused often of not being biblically centered. This is probably because the evangelical themes are not resounded often enough in pietistic terms. This charge is especially ironic because the Liberation voices seek to maintain a balance between Old and New Testament themes. The third charge against Liberation theology is that it is so involved in political liberation that it has little time for building up the churches. The retort given by Gutierrez and others is that the church must begin to find itself by giving itself away.

All in all, Liberation theology is a major issue that will continue to be a source of controversy for mission strategists and practitioners. The questions raised are central ones to modern missionary: to what degree should theology be human-centered? What portion of the church's time should be given to social action in relation to the time demanded for social ministry? Does the church find itself by giving itself away? Should the poor be treated as valid but untrained theologians once they experience salvation and liberation? Do the poor have anything to teach the rich about church? The answers will be found only by struggling for them in the midst of mission service.

Church Growth

The movement in missions known as Church Growth owes its inception to Donald A. McGavran. In 1955, he wrote *How Churches Grow*. It started a revolution in the way the churches were to do their work. In the preface, Dr. McGavran wrote: "We have Jesus Christ our Lord. We have no one else. We have the Bible. We have nothing else. In the light of revelation we can go fearlessly forward."[12]

Based on that evangelical theology, McGavran wrote that missions must be concerned primarily with the numerical growth of local churches. The author predicted that there were some areas in the world where the quadrupling of the number of Christians and congregations would be possible by 1965.

This optimistic talk caught the imagination of disciples, especially Evangelicals, who were looking for encouragement. They soon understood that the doing of missions was not in the mere carrying on of mission work but to church the responsive unchurched in as great numbers and as rapidly as possible.

McGavran boldly stated that the numerical increase of Christians is the first task of the church. Related to this is the assumption that a fantastic increase in the number of Christians is essential to the achievement of total Christianity.

McGavran argued against the retention in mission causes of what he calls "cultural overhang." It was his idea that this evil is most evident in theological training. Instead, we should discover and include in the curricula of the younger seminaries subjects that will help students to multiply the churches they serve.

Critics of the Church Growth movement are manifold. They wonder about McGavran's premises, including:

1. The idea that it is always God's will that local churches show numerical growth;

2. The idea that groups like to gather in homogeneous units to worship the Lord;
3. The idea that missionaries are wasting time and effort if numerical growth is not occuring.

Conflicts emerge on the mission field when disciples of Church Growth insist that McGavran's premises are universally valid standards of Christian disciples. Those not exposed to or inclined toward Church Growth methods may wonder about whether the New Testament gospel transcends barriers to build local church units composed of various types of individuals from multiple social, educational, and economic levels. Those inclined toward Christian social ministries will ask such legitimate questions, How does ministry beyond church membership to the "widows and orphans" of society relates to numerical growth? Veteran missionaries who have spent entire careers in Muslim-dominated areas without seeing numerous converts may ask, Where does the "planting and watering" principle of making new converts enter into evangelism? Pastors and other church staff members may ask, Is it always God's will that local church units show numerical growth? Is there never a time when the priority is deepening the spiritual life of disciples?

The Church Growth movement will continue to cause consternation on the part of evangelical missionaries who must, in local mission station situations, decide on financial and time priority situations. Church Growth advocates already have these matters decided. Those not in total agreement will find it difficult to counter McGavran's proposals without being understood as being against evangelism and numerical growth. Both sides will need to display the fruit of the Spirit as surely as they do argue their points in mission strategy.

The Role of Women

Women and missions have been synonymous in evangelical circles since the mission societies emerged a century and a half ago. Too often the works of prayer and gathering financial support were seen as women's work. Further, single women have been encouraged to work on foreign mission fields doing the same work they are denied the right to do on their home base. Women serve as pastors and superintendents in situations thousands of miles away from home. They find a style of fulfillment there which they must forget or ignore while back home on furlough. This inconsistency is difficult to explain in light of the gospel's propulsion toward freedom.

Women in the church will be an issue in the future as more matriarchical peoples come to the Master. A masculine-dominated concept of ministry will be severely challenged by women demanding at least the same status they enjoyed in their tribes. If the gospel is heard as a step backward in social standing, it may not be heeded at all.

A current issue certain to be a source of controversy in future mission effort will be that of the role of women. This is especially true in light of the increasing enrollment in seminaries in the West of female students. Furthermore, the role of married women who go to mission fields with their husbands needs clarification. Are they to be described only as "church and home workers" when they use other skills on the field? Evangelical seminary students now show a one to three ratio in number of female students, and the number is growing. Many of these young women will seek appointment by mission boards. Mission strategists will decide their fate.

Ecumenism

Some in evangelical mission circles are extremely negative about ecumenical discussion and cooperation in missions. They maintain that the truth is that the ecumenical movement of the twentieth century has failed to mobilize Christians for world evangelism. They argue that denominations will never go away and it is they who maintain the thrust in agressive mission service. These critics also argue that ecumenics by definition gravitates toward theological compromise and sloppiness.

Proponents argue that the ecumenical dialogue process makes potential witnesses more sensitive to the integrity of evangelism. Dialogue, it is argued, produces an evangelism conformed to the spirit of the gospel. This, in turn, causes the witness to be slow to do anything that would compromise the progress of interfaith cooperation and action. This compromise could possibly come in the form of physical coersion, intellectual dishonesty, the subtle buying of new converts by offering bribes on status in exchange for conversions. This lively interchange has caused more than one observer to note that there is a widening gulf in the last generation between the ecumenical and the conservative evangelical definitions of world mission.

The roots of the ecumenical movement lie in the hopes of bringing unity, not discord, to believers. For example, at a meeting of the Student Volunteer Movement Congress held almost twenty years ago, the affirmation was made:

> As an evangelical ecumenical gathering of Christian disciples and workers, we cordially invite all believers in Christ to unite the common task of bringing the Word of Salvation to mankind in spiritual and moral chaos. Our goal is nothing short of the evangelization of the human race in this generation by every means God has given to the minds and will of of men.

In spite of these frequent disclaimers and even affirmations of evangelistic intent by ecumenical groups, such as the World Council of Churches, a sizeable number of Evangelicals remain critical of ecumenicalism and its potential for mission. Four areas of concern are usually registered. First, some ecumenical leaders speak of "Christian presence" as a workable definition of mission responsibility. That is, some ecumenists insist that a missionary's primary role is to live among non-Christian peoples with a life style that will eventually earn him a right to be heard.

Conservative Evangelicals usually object to this definition of missions because it is too slow in producing measurable results.

Second, some conservative Evangelicals object to doing missions ecumenically because that process hardly ever creates and releases fresh missions enthusiasm or commitment. It is maintained that so much effort goes toward expressing unity that little is left over to make new converts.

Third, Evangelicals have a high fear level that ecumenically minded missionaries may gradually lose theological certainty by searching for the lowest common denominators in doctrinal matters. It is charged that the most likely area of this occurence will be in a gradual move toward universalism; that is the idea that all persons will be redeemed someday. Anti-ecumenical Evangelicals often contend that theological convictions gradually give way to the lowest common denominators in dialogue.

Finally, conservative Evangelicals accuse ecumenical mission strategists of being headed toward syncretism, that is, of including so many religious expressions and revelations that the uniqueness and finality of the gospel are denied. Conservative Evangelicals fear that once the door is opened to the idea that persons can be rightly related to God in non-Christian world religions, the urgency of the gospel may be diluted if not destroyed.

In spite of all the controversy that ecumenism brings about, ecumenism and its attendant spin-offs will continue to be a major factor in missions during the last sixth of the century. There are at least two reasons for this: Jesus prayed that all his followers might be "one" (John 17:21), and there is the anthropological truth that the doing of missions in an isolated cultured setting tends to draw believers and missionaries closer together, highlighting sameness rather than distinctions along denominational lines. It is a fact that, on foreign mission fields, denominations tend to lose their sense of urgency and even the reasons for denominationalism lose their cogency. The controversy will continue.

Indigenization

Allusion has been made earlier in this chapter to the increasing problem of the indigenization of the mission task. As 1984 passes, it is noteworthy that native Christians are taking over more and more of mission action and strategy. Some predict that the next century may well see an African or Asian pope. There may be more Christians in the southern half of the earth's surface than in the northern half by the year 2000.

Evangelicals especially are discovering the truth in the statement, "We have no right to send missionaries to any group from whom we are not ready to invite missionaries." This will necessitate more doing with and less doing for. The future Christian missionary will have to be one who is a joyous and welcomed participant in the history of others. The realization of this increasing indigenous participation and leadership in missions will force changes in the future.

The twenty-first century missionary will have to be invited and welcomed into foreign cultures to be effective. Only the Christians who are self-consciously constructive in the life and thought of others will be welcomed by those natives previously abused by paternalistic and triumphalistic missionaries. This constructive attitude will have to be watched with a sound knowledge of the cultures in which they serve, including their previous religious practices.

There are capable and willing Third- and Fourth-World Christian converts who are ready to take positions of leadership either by direction or invitation of the missionaries or by beginning their own indigenous churches. These capable leaders will lead one way or another. There is daily more of a call for modern missionaries to be equippers than to be doers. The choice is a necessary one—now!

World Hunger

If the world were a global village of just one hundred people:

Seventy could not read;

One would have a college education;

Fifty would suffer from malnutrition;

Eighty would live in substandard housing;

Six would be American's and have over half the village's entire income.

It is a further truth that two-thirds of the human family will go to bed hungry tonight. It is also true that fifteen thousand will starve to death today.

The world hunger problem is being tackled from several perspectives by active missionaries today. One approach is to set up a system of agriculture in which fish and rice are grown alternately in flooded fields. Another approach is to dispense information on nutrition so as to affect dietary changes. A valid approach is to change political actions and attitudes. This is often done by sending letters and telegrams to legislators on specific bills which will affect the poor and malnourished. "Bread for the World" is just such an organization. Members of that group want to know why Americans store or destroy millions of tons of grain annually while non-Americans starve. Further, some mission agencies have set up specific collecting offices for monies that go only to world hunger relief. An example is the World Hunger Relief office within the Foreign Mission Board of the Southern Baptist Convention headquarters in Richmond, Virgina. A method now being used by some is the open challenging of multinational corporations and their profit-oriented policies which exploit so-called "underdeveloped" nations. Some Christian leaders are concerned, for example, about the fact that Americans currently feed more Peruvian anchovy to their pets than is consumed by by humans in the three largest Latin American nations combined.

Evangelical Christians concerned about social action are now convinced that feeding the hungry by distributing foodstuffs is not enough to alleviate most world hunger situations. World Vision, International, for example, is aiding in well digging, lake building, and seed development. Other Christian groups are working on the problem of preventing massive soil erosion.

Whatever the approach taken, it is apparent even to the most conservative that people who die cannot hear the gospel. It is a good idea to keep people alive if only to preach to them. There are also higher and more biblically based reasons. One is the command of Jesus to feed the hungry and this gentle but powerful reminder that the sheep and goats will be divided on that basis in the Final Judgement.

World hunger and its accompanying problems, such as permanent brain damage due to malnutrition in infants, must become a priority for future mission endeavor. It is even more the case with every passing day. There are no nations in the world where this is more true than in the two discussed in the following section.

China and India

In 1984, China has 1.1 billion people, more than the entire combined populations of North and South America and all of Africa. India has almost two-thirds of a billion people, more people than Africa and South America combined. The combined population of these two Asian nations is 40 percent of the earth's total and should be half by the year 2000. The population increase in India is currently more than a million per month. The yearly population increase in India is greater than the total number of Christians there.

India remains an enigma to most Evangelicals, especially Baptists. There are more Baptists in India than any other nation in the world except the US. (The number three nation is the USSR) Yet, India remains virtually closed to

Southern Baptists. There are now less than a dozen SBC career missionaries in India, most of them are medical personnel. None of them are involved directly in field evangelism or church growth. However, in 1983 it was announced that a new cooperative agreement had been reached between Southern Baptists and indigenous Baptists in India. Under this plan, specialists in church growth and church planting from the US serve as consultants with temporary visas for brief visits. Early indications are that these cooperative efforts are paying dividends. Hundreds of new converts are being baptized and dozens of churches are being started.

China remains closed to active and open missionary activity. Unless there is a major break-through there in the next few years, most of the people in the world may be unreachable by the dawn of the twenty-first century. It can be seen coming. At least dedicated Christians can pray.

The Gray Revolution

As life expectancy increases around the world, the contribution of the elderly to missions can be tapped as a splendid source of labor. In 1984, the number of persons in the US over sixty-five years of age is more than 24 million, or about 10 percent of the population. By 2001, that number is expected to total more than 33 million, or about 14 percent of the US population. Most of them are expected to be in good health physically, mentally, and spiritually. They will need to minister more than to be ministered to. Thus, they will constitute a vast reservoir of mission personnel.

There is a holdover attitude present in some churches that sees ministry to senior adults much as they see ministry involving children. The elderly are entertained. They desire to be used.

Life expectancy is also increasing in Third- and Fourth-World nations. The age range in Asian and African nations is placing many more persons into their fifties and the median age is climbing. When the two groups meet Americans and others, the encounter can be productive. Increased age can bring wisdom. It can be redemptive when coupled with the love of Christ.

Computers and Communication

Futurists of every sort are predicting that computer technology will revolutionize the human family as it is known today. Data banks and analytical powers are storehouses of old and newly discovered knowledge. Massive amounts of information can now be stored and processed with speed and accuracy.

Life-styles will be altered radically as the home computer revolution digs in on the American scene. More work will be done at home. Children will be capable of thinking in universal categories. The call is to transfer that capability into human concern. Creative church and mission leaders can aid in that effort by reminding committed Christians that bits of data involved humans' as God's highest creation. The positive use of computers in mission strategy can include the finding of more "hidden peoples" within huge segments of society, the tracing of population trends, and the analysis of church growth patterns in heretofore unreached areas.

The whole communication explosion will continue to boom as the twenty-first century approaches. Churches in the US are expanding their ministries through video tapes, minicams, and cable television. In 1984, the average American adult spends six hours a day watching television. The average American youth who is graduated from high school will have spent 140 percent as much time watching television as in the classroom. He has more than 16 hundred commercial messages beamed at him daily. Of these, he is consciously aware of only 70 and responds in a positive manner to only 10. This means that much communication is taking place subliminally. Therefore, the churches in a media-conscious age must be aware of their image. Just as important, it is evident that the churches face stubborn and well-financed competition for a clear hearing of the gospel. Experts in visionary techniques will be a must for mission effort in the future, especially in the Third World.

The use of satellite channels with the capacity to reach most persons in the world is a reality for use in missions in 1984. Excitement runs high among First-World church leaders as the potential evident that virtually the whole world can now be reached with the gospel.

However, a note of caution must be sounded. There are not as many electronic receivers in Asia, Africa, and South America as most North Americans imagine. In the populous nation of Nigeria, for example, there is fewer than one television set for every twenty thousand persons. While the excitement of electronic parapharnelia runs high, mission leaders must caution their personnel that there is no substitute for the personal touch. Walking missionaries with audio cassette players are still more effective than impersonal images on a screen. There is no substitute for the three-dimensional witness. The communication explosion must be tempered with the sweat of hands outstretched in love.

Leisure

The leisure revolution is a major factor in American life styles in 1984. Major changes have occurred this century in the American working place. In 1900, the workweek in the US averaged sixty hours. In 1984, it is thirty-four. It is expected to average less than thirty by the year 2000. Another way of viewing this is to say that an American worker in 2000 will have twenty-three more hours of leisure time per week than his great-grandfather had. In the US currently, 75 percent of all free time is spent at home. Free time plus affluence has enabled many families to invest in boats, lake houses, and second homes. The continuing leisure revolution confronts mission-minded individuals with two challenges: channeling the vast energy available through persons with vast amounts of discretionary time and creating ministries to those in resort areas.

Among the possibilities for mission strategists is the encouraging of family vacations spent during mission service in exotic places. Group tours with emphasis on music in evangelism is another possibility.

Mobility

Mobility, even on an international scale, is a major area of challenge to missions in 1984. Today almost one in three Americans lives outside the state of his birth. More than half of the American people moved between 1980 and 1984. In 1984, the average American moves fourteen times in his lifetime, compared with eight by Britons and five by Japanese. Each of these moves requires a certain amount of adjustment, especially those moves to a foreign land. (There will be an increasing number of Americans living on foreign soil with the search for energy sources in full swing along with assignments by nonenergy related multinational corporations.) Creative mission strategists can see American mobility not as a problem but as a dual opportunity: ministering to those in the US who have just moved and using overseas residents for evangelistic purposes. The latter can be especially true in Muslim-dominated nations where "official" missionaries are not allowed to propagate the gospel.

Urbanization

The move to the cities is on around the world. The move is creating severe identity crises in the lives of persons in the Third World. This is true because traditional tribal customs are either challenged or forsaken. Unemployment and housing become major problems, especially for young men who come to Lagos or Mexico City in search of a career.

The world's largest city in 1984 is Mexico City, with a population of more than seventeen million. That figure will be about thirty-two million by the year 2000. As in the case of most large world cities, an increasing percentage of the population is composed of "squatters" who come uninvited to live in temporary quarters on land near the edge of the city which does not belong to them. These persons live in squalor and are open to almost all types of ministry in the name of Christ.

Today extremely effective missionaries are at work in cities with neighborhood programs featuring weekly street services and medical clinics. All these efforts are coupled with evangelism. The missionaries of the future who wish to reach urbanites must continue personal evangelism, social action and social ministry.

Communism

The system now widely known as Communism is a religion. As such, it has the following components:

1. A founder, Karl Marx;
2. A holy book, *Das Kapital;*
3. An eschatology, leading toward an utopian classless society;
4. A priestly class, the Communist elite at the top;
5. A view of not-God, with clear theological statements about his nonexistence; and
6. A view of man, very optimistic with humans able to build their own perfect society without God's help.

If viewed as an alternate religion, Communists can be approachable through the gospel wherever political boundaries permit. In Western Europe, Communist-Christian dialogue has been going on for almost forty years. Among the by-products of those conversations is the Christian realization that the gospel is this-worldly and not exclusively other-worldly. Communist participants have been stricken with the realization that there may be a case for the existence of God after all.

The major problem with Communism in relation to missions, however, continues to be the Communist dream of world domination and the accompanying denial of freedom to Christian emisaries. Prayer, political negotiation, and winsome tourists and business people in contacts with Communists are partial answers to the dilemma. The total answer to openness can only come through God's power.

Conclusion

The future of missions is not totally dependent on human effort alone. As in the days of the apostolic era, missions is a partnership between God's commissioned people and the God who commissions. This is because Christianity is more a relationship than a religion. The Christian faith, more than any other, is dependent on a relationship with its founder. When political and military oppression are at their worst, Christians have relied on a personal submissive relationship to Jesus of Nazareth. His emissaries who face the unfinished task with that personal faith will be most successful. There is no substitute. Only then can being commissioned result in being channels for the desired kingdom of God be "on earth as it is in heaven."

Therefore, the future of missions is dependent on the combination of submission to God and servanthood within the human family. To be sure, there will be unforeseen social unpheaval and politcal intrigue that will rock this globe. It is also certain that new theological trends will result. God's commissioned people, however, are accustomed to maintaining a dynamic and consistent witness within the missionary movement while other social movements come and go. This is because the promise of Jesus, "Lo, I am with you alway" is a reality amid toppled empires and vanishing dreams of political despots.

The future awaiting those commissioned to do God's will among his people is a bright one. That is because it is illumined by the Light of the world. That Light shines on, even within the gritty task of being his rays in steaming jungles and urban traffic. God's commissioned people work on in the knowledge that the God of the past and present is the God of the future.

Case Study: Osad Imasogie of Nigeria

Osad Imasogie was born in Bendel state in Nigeria. He was educated, first in Nigeria, then received his Doctor of Philosophy degree from The Southern Baptist Theological Seminary, Louisville, Kentucky.

In 1979, Dr. Imasogie was installed as President of the Nigerian Baptist Theological Seminary. He is now serving with distinction in that position. That seminary is the largest of any denomination in West Africa.

Dr. Osad Imasogie is a sign of indigenous leadership in key positions in mission areas.

Questions

1. How long should American missionaries hold leadership positions in a school overseas before natives are given that positon?
2. What criteria should be used choosing appropriate indigenous leadership?
3. What advantages can you imagine for having native Christians train other church leaders in their nation?
4. Is there a legitimate place for American missionaries in the role of catalysts and consultant to the indigenous churches?
5. Should a missionary work himself out of a job as soon as possible?

Notes

1. Alec Vidler, *Christian Belief* (London: SCM Press, 1950), p. 10.

2. *Church Times,* July 31, 1953, p. 1.

3. Delacroix, *Historic Universelle,* 2, pp. 284-285.

4. See Catherine B. Allen, *The New Lottie Moon Story* (Nashville: Broadman Press, 1980).

5. Helmut Thielicke quoted on the dust cover of Charles Ray, *The Shadow of the Broad Brim* (Philadelphia: Jusdon Press, 1934).

6. Henry P. Van Dusen, *They Found the Church There* (New York: Charles Scribner's Sons, 1945), p. 94.

7. See Jesse C. Fletcher, *Bill Wallace of China* (Nashville: Broadman Press, 1963).

8. Ikeda quoted in Noah Brannen, *Sokagakkai* (Richmond, VA: John Knox Press, 1968), p. 106.

9. M. Thomas Starkes, *No Man Goes Alone* (Atlanta: Home Mission Board of the Southern Baptist Convention, 1972), p. 19.

10. "Onward Mormon Soldiers," *Newsweek,* April 17, 1981, p. 87.

11. See Jesse C. Fletcher, *Wimpy Harper of Africa* (Nashville: Broadman Press, 1967).

12. Elton Trueblood, *The Validity of the Christian Mission* (New York: Harper and Row, 1972), pp. 66-67.

Bibliography

Missions: General

Coxwell, H. Wakelin and Grubb, Kenneth, eds. *World Christian Handbook,* 1968. Nashville: Abingdon Press, 1968.

Goddard, Burton L., ed. *The Encyclopedia of Modern Christian Missions.* Canada, New Jersey: Nelson, 1968.

Neill, Stephen; Anderson, Gerald H.; and Goodwin, John, eds. *Concise Dictionary of the Christian World Mission.* London: Lutterworth, 1970.

Starkes, M. Thomas. *Mission 2000.* New Orleans: Insight Press, 1979.

Missions: History

Foster, John. *To All Nations: Christian Expansion from 1700 to Today.* London: Lutterworth, 1961.

Glover, Robert J. and Kane, J. Herbert. *The Progress of Worldwide Missions.* New York: Harper and Row, 1960.

Kane, J. Herbert. *A Global View of Christian Missions.* Grand Rapids: Baker Book House, 1971.

Latourette, Kenneth Scott. *Christianity Through the Ages.* New York: Harper and Row, 1965.

Mathews, Basil. *Forward Through the Ages.* New York: Friendship Press, 1960.

Neill, Stephen. *A History of Christian Missions.* Baltimore: Penguin Books, 1964.

Missions: Issues

Anderson, Gerald H., ed. *Sermons to Men of Other Faiths and Traditions.* Nashville: Abingdon Press, 1968.

Bradshaw, M. R. *Church Growth Through Evangelism in Depth.* South Pasadena: William Carey Library, 1969.

Brown, Robert McAfee. *Theology in a New Key: Responding to Liberation Themes.* Philadelphia: Westminster Press, 1978.

Gutierrez, Gustavo. *A Theology of Liberation.* Maryknoll, New York: Orbis Books, 1973.

Starkes, M. Thomas. *Confronting Popular Cults.* Nashville: Broadman Press, 1972.

_____. *Today's World Religions.* New Orleans: Insight Press, 1975.

Swearer, Donald K. *Dialogue: The Key to Understanding Other Religions.* Philadelphia: Westminster Press, 1977.

Missions: Theology

Jones, Tracey K., Jr. *Our Mission Today: The Beginning of a New Age.* New York: World Outlook Press, 1963.

Starkes, M. Thomas. *Foundation for Missions.* Nashville: Broadman Press, 1981.

Tillich, Paul. *Dynamics of Faith.* New York: Harper and Row, 1957.

Trueblood, Elton. *The Validity of the Christian Mission.* New York: Harper and Row, 1972.

Index

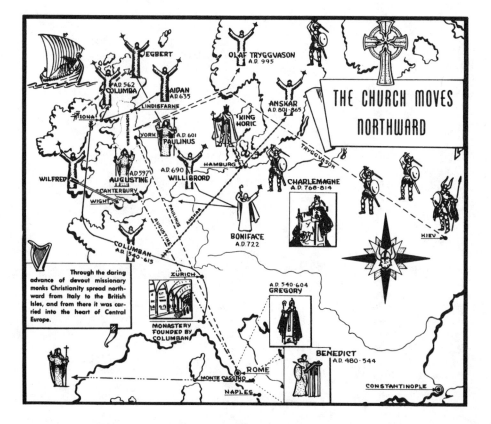

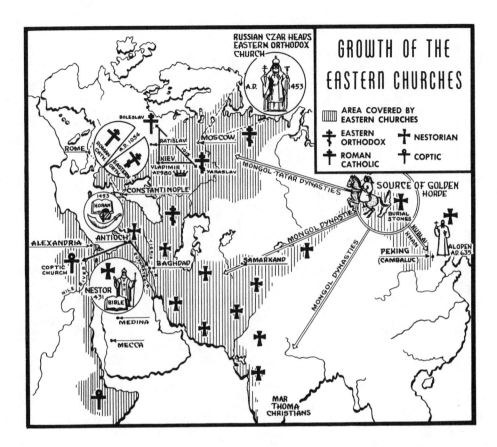

GROWTH OF THE EASTERN CHURCHES

RUSSIAN CZAR HEADS
EASTERN ORTHODOX
CHURCH
A.D. 453

AREA COVERED BY
EASTERN CHURCHES

✚ EASTERN
ORTHODOX

✚ ROMAN
CATHOLIC

✚ NESTORIAN

✝ COPTIC

BOLESLAV

ROME

ROMAN EASTERN
ORTH A.D. 1054

RATISLAV

MOSCOW

VLADIMIR
AD 980

KIEV
1015

YARASLAV

MONGOL-TATAR DYNASTIES

CONSTANTINOPLE

SOURCE OF GOLDEN
HORDE

BURIAL
STONES

1453
KORAN

ALEXANDRIA

ANTIOCH

MONGOL DYNASTIES

KUBLAI
KHAN

PEKING
(CAMBALUC)

ALOPEN
AD 635

COPTIC
CHURCH

NILE RIVER

TIGRIS R.

EUPHRATES R.

NESTOR
431
BIBLE

BAGHDAD

SAMARKAND

MONGOL DYNASTIES

MEDINA

MECCA

MAR
THOMA
CHRISTIANS

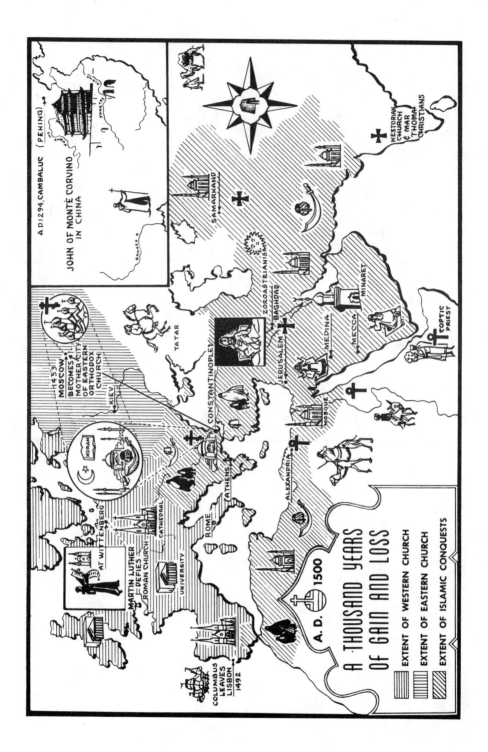

A THOUSAND YEARS OF GAIN AND LOSS

- ||||| EXTENT OF WESTERN CHURCH
- ||||| EXTENT OF EASTERN CHURCH
- ///// EXTENT OF ISLAMIC CONQUESTS

A.D. 1500

COLUMBUS LEAVES LISBON 1492

MARTIN LUTHER DEFIES ROMAN CHURCH — AT WITTENBERG

UNIVERSITY

CATHEDRAL

ROME

ATHENS

ALEXANDRIA

1453 MOSCOW BECOMES MOTHER CITY OF EASTERN ORTHODOX CHURCH

KIEV

TATAR

CONSTANTINOPLE

JERUSALEM

MOSQUE

MEDINA

MECCA

MINARET

BAGHDAD

ZOROASTRIANISM

SAMARKAND

KORAN

COPTIC PRIEST

NESTORIAN CHURCH & MAR THOMA CHRISTIANS

A.D.1294, CAMBALUC (PEKING)

JOHN OF MONTÉ CORVINO IN CHINA

YANGTSE

HOANG-HO

GANGES

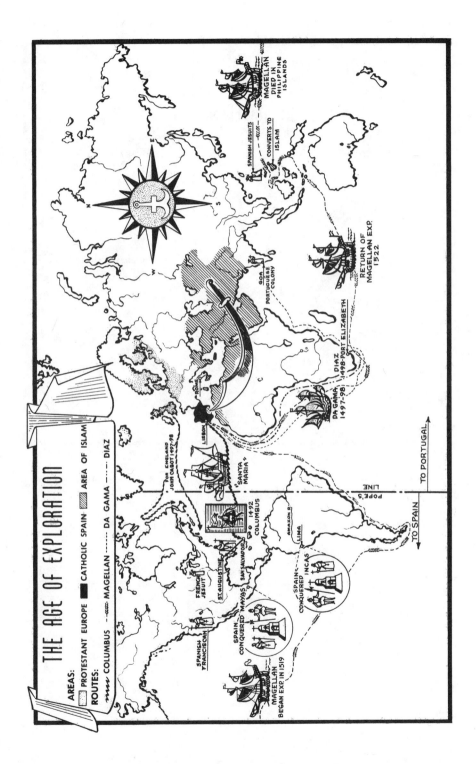

THE AGE OF EXPLORATION

AREAS:
☐ PROTESTANT EUROPE ■ CATHOLIC SPAIN ▨ AREA OF ISLAM

ROUTES:
〜〜 COLUMBUS ––⟨⟨⟨ MAGELLAN –––– DA GAMA ––– DIAZ

TO ENGLAND
JOHN CABOT 1497-98

LISBON

ROME

SANTA MARIA

1492
COLUMBUS

POPE'S LINE

TO SPAIN

TO PORTUGAL

AMAZON R.

LIMA

SPAIN–
CONQUERED INCAS

SPAIN–
CONQUERED MAYAS

SAN SALVADOR

ST. AUGUSTINE

FRENCH
JESUIT

SPANISH
FRANCISCAN

MAGELLAN
BEGAN EXP. IN 1519

DA GAMA
1497-98

DIAZ
1498–PORT ELIZABETH

GOA
PORTUGUESE
COLONY

RETURN OF
MAGELLAN EXP.
1522

MAGELLAN
DIED IN
PHILIPPINE
ISLANDS

SPANISH JESUITS
CONVERTS TO
ISLAM

Maps are from *Forward Through the Ages* by Basil Mathews, Friendship Press, 1951. Used by Permission.